Jimmy Bowen

AND

Jim Jerome

SIMON & SCHUSTER

ROUGH
MIX

AN UNAPOLOGETIC LOOK AT
THE MUSIC BUSINESS AND
HOW IT GOT THAT WAY—
A LIFETIME IN THE WORLD
OF ROCK, POP, AND COUNTRY
AS TOLD BY ONE OF
THE INDUSTRY'S
MOST POWERFUL PLAYERS

 SIMON & SCHUSTER
Rockefeller Center
1230 Avenue of the Americas
New York, NY 10020

10 9 8 7 6 5 4 3 2 1

Library of Congress Cataloging-in-Publication Data

Bowen, Jimmy.
    Rough mix: an unapologetic look at the music business and how it got that way: a
lifetime in the world of rock, pop, and country, as told by one of the industry's most
powerful players / Jimmy Bowen and Jim Jerome.
        p. cm.
    Includes index.
    1. Bowen, Jimmy. 2. Sound recording executives and producers—United States—
Biography. I. Jerome, Jim.
ML429.B68A3   1997
781.64'092—dc21
[B]   96-51007   CIP   MN
ISBN 0-684-80764-5

ACKNOWLEDGMENTS

I WOULD LIKE TO thank several people whose contributions greatly enriched this project. First of all, my father, Asa Bowen, and stepmother, Frances, provided rich detail on my ancestry and New Mexico roots. Donnie "Dirt" Lanier, my lifelong buddy, generously shared his vivid memories going back to our early-fifties West Texas football wars and our wild, if short-lived, ride to the top as teenage rockabilly idols with the Rhythm Orchids. Dirt also helped me recall stories from the Sinatra years at Reprise in L.A. and, having been my matchless "song man" in our glory days at MCA in the late eighties, added plenty of details from our years together on Music Row.

Thanks also to MCA Records/Nashville president Tony Brown and chairman Bruce Hinton for offering their reflections on the work we did together. Other Nashville insiders made important—if discreet—contributions, preferring to make their comments without credit. They know who they are and I owe them a debt of gratitude.

I would like to thank Otto Kitsinger for compiling my comprehensive producer's discography and John Lomax III for the extensive interviews he conducted during my MCA years with many people closely involved in my life and work. Both documents proved invaluable. The Country Music Association provided useful data on the industry, and my friends Mike Post and Red Steagall added amusing tales from the late sixties and seventies.

I thank my wife, Ginger, for helping to straighten out some of the book's events and time frames, but, most important, for being the wind beneath my dreams even when they clashed with her own.

Several books proved interesting for their versions of certain events in which I was involved. Others, such as the *Billboard* chart compilations, were indispensable for their data and anecdotes about pop and country music since the fifties:

Joel Whitburn's Top Country Singles, 1944–1993 (Menomonee Falls, Wisc.: Record Research Inc., 1994); *Joel Whitburn's Top Pop Singles, 1955–1990* (Menomonee Falls, Wisc.: Record Research Inc., 1991); *Sinatra! The Song Is You: A Singer's Art,* by Will Friedwald (New York: Scribner, 1995); *The New Country Music Encyclopedia,* by Tad Richards and Melvin B. Shestack (New York: Fireside, 1993); *Get Hot or Go Home: Trisha Yearwood, the Making of a Nashville Star,* by Lisa Rebecca Gubernick (New York: William Morrow, 1993); *The* Billboard *Book of Number One Country Hits,* by Tom Roland (New York: Billboard Books, 1991); *Garth Brooks: Platinum Cowboy,* by Edward Morris (New York: St. Martin's Press, 1993); *Reba: My Story,* by Reba McEntire with Tom Carter (New York: Bantam, 1994). The detailed discography that accompanies the 1995 MCA Records/Nashville four-CD box set by George Strait, *Out of the Box,* was also useful. It was compiled by Dee Henry Jenkins, and features liner notes by Paul Kingsbury and interviews with George by Kay West, and it included many of the studio albums George and I did together.

Thanks, too, to the folks behind the scenes who truly held the project together from day one: Jim's literary agent, Amanda Urban of International Creative Management, and my agent, Jan Miller of Dupree/Miller & Associates in Dallas; my ever-efficient, always cheerful longtime assistant Debbie Tidwell, for keeping track of, and tracking down, research documents, personal records, and old photos from way, way back; publicist Cathy Gurley, who helped Debbie assemble photos and press materials; Jean Brown in New York, who transcribed thousands of pages of interviews in record time; Herky Williams, my golfing buddy and talent scout (John Berry, Deana Carter); and our editor, Chuck Adams, whose commitment to the story gave it life and kept us going, and whose light but knowing editor's touch was akin to having a fine sound engineer by my side in the studio to sweeten and enhance the rough mix.

Finally, a special thanks to my collaborator, Jim "One Million Questions" Jerome, for being a truly interested and positive force behind this book. I always felt Jim believed this book was worth writing, and that gave me invaluable support during an especially trying time in my life. With Garth, cancer surgery, retirement, and this book all happening at the same time, without him there would have been no book. Thanks, Jim!

P.S.: You're a damn good writer, too.

PROLOGUE

THERE ARE all kinds of promises a record label president likes to hear from his franchise superstar. This one is not among them: "I'm not delivering any new music as long as Bowen's running Liberty Records."

It was the middle of 1994, and after nearly forty years in the music business, I could easily have ignored an ego trip like that—had it come from any other act on my roster. But this ultimatum came from Garth Brooks, not only the top-selling artist in the history of country music but an act whose tonnage had at times accounted for more than 80 percent of Liberty's sales. Garth was using that leverage now for a him-or-me power play.

The message was delivered to Charles Koppelman, president of EMI–North America, which included Capitol Records and Liberty, its country cousin, and which was part of EMI's Worldwide system. It was all owned by Thorn Industries, a British conglomerate associated with furniture rentals, light bulbs, and now Nashville's heavyweight "hat act," Garth Brooks.

I had taken over EMI's Capitol-Nashville division at the end of 1989. I renamed it Liberty two years later to reflect my insistence from day one that we operate with the autonomy of a label rather than as a mere division. Traditionally record companies like CBS (Sony), RCA, MCA, and Warners ran Nashville divisions. I wanted my own marketing, legal, and finance people, budgets, and decision-making independence from EMI–North America—and I had gotten it.

What I *didn't* have was autonomy from Garth Brooks.

●

The problem was that Garth's sales had been slumping by about half, and he was blaming me. Of course Garth's idea of a slump was relative: his fall 1993 album, *In Pieces*, had sold in the 4-million-copy range, a career milestone for any other artist. But his first album had sold 5 million and the next two a phenomenal 10 million *each*. Then *The Chase* had slipped to 5 million before *In Pieces*. That a *quadruple-platinum* CD felt like a failure not only said a lot about Nashville in the nineties, it suggested Garth was getting a little big for his britches.

Garth was also angry over some changes I made involving people he felt had been key players behind his rise; he believed Liberty wasn't committing the same marketing and advertising resources it had in the past. And like almost every other label head in town, I had passed on Garth (I'd been working for a different label) when he was just another kid looking for a deal.

During several long meetings Garth seemed unwilling to hear that his music might be part of the problem. Garth was turning into a control freak, wrapped up in details his people should have been handling. His explosive success and new fame—he externalized it as "the GB thing"—had distracted him. I felt his recent music wasn't up to his earlier work; the critics and the public seemed to agree. He needed to delegate, go into the studio with his producer, Allen Reynolds, and focus on making great music again. None of this went down real well with Garth.

I also sensed a dark, almost self-destructive aura swirling around him. His recent comments in the media had damaged a once-pure, heroic persona. He acknowledged cheating on (and patching up with) his wife, Sandy, in a national magazine. He talked of retiring. His eyes teared up when he told *Dateline*'s Jane Pauley that while sitting with his baby daughter he realized "how unhappy I'd become with all the crap. So that's why hanging it up is so near to me right now." In a *Life* magazine piece he said he had briefly imagined suicide as a "way out" of his high-pressure business interests. In a Barbara Walters interview he talked cavalierly about his wealth and even "outed" his own sister, who played bass in his band.

I sensed the tide turning against Garth within the industry. Having once walked off with armloads of awards, Garth had been giving up ground to less tormented talents like Vince Gill and Alan Jackson. The halo above him had cracked. And, bottom-line, his sales *had* fallen off 50 percent.

Moreover, by "going to war with the label," as he put it, he was taking on all Nashville labels and their CEOs. Our showdown could set an ugly precedent—and Music Row was watching. In our talks Garth was his courteous, polite, brooding self. But he resisted what I told him. Instead he bought the view—and, I felt, the manipulation—of his handlers: he needed a scapegoat, and its name was Bowen.

"The GB thing" brought turmoil and tension to Liberty. It was getting harder for us to nurture acts like Tanya Tucker, Billy Dean, John Berry, Chris Ledoux, and Suzy Bogguss. Having put in eighteen-hour days for eighteen years in Nashville, I began to wear down, get short with people, feel the heat from corporate. My wife, Ginger, was noticing the changes. I just wasn't myself. Even my early-morning golf game, a daily ritual that had helped keep me sane through the years, was showing the effects.

Liberty had come to expect a new Garth CD by late summer, one that would produce a couple of giant radio hits and sales of 4 or 5 million through the holidays. That enabled me to send up a substantial profit to corporate—some $80 million over four or five years. Without a new Garth we'd maybe break even for the year, *if* a couple other projects sold 200,000 each. So we began lobbying Garth for at least a greatest-hits package by year's end to boost his five-CD catalog through Christmas. That way we'd have some profit for corporate by the end of the fiscal year on March 31, 1995. The scenario was getting tense.

And bruising. With an eight-hundred-pound hillbilly gorilla on my back, I was vulnerable. At the core of my problem with Garth was corporate politics. When I refused to give Garth a new contract barely one year after renegotiating his original deal, he shook his cage. He went around me and won himself a rich, precedent-setting "joint venture" package from EMI–North America in New York.

I warned anyone who'd listen that the deal had the potential to destroy the label. It would cut deeply into our funding for new artists because we'd be sending corporate a big chunk of our profit so that they could pay Garth's giant back end.

Garth was holding a gun to Koppelman's head, hoping to nail my ass and have me replaced with one of the loyal, trusted people in his camp who he felt had been there for him all along.

When Garth shut down the music pipeline, pressure mounted.

I was no stranger to shaking things up. I'd been at it my whole life. When I left the bleak Texas Panhandle as a teenager, I was determined never to look back. I was thrown into the heady mid-fifties rock-and-roll scene with Buddy Knox and the Rhythm Orchids when our first record, "Party Doll," hit No. 1. Suddenly we were barnstorming across America with rock pioneers like Buddy Holly, Bo Diddley, Chuck Berry, Fats Domino, the Everly Brothers, and Little Richard.

I then spent fifteen years in the L.A. music scene, half of them as in-house producer and head of Artists and Repertoire (A&R) for Reprise Records. I helped revive the careers of Frank Sinatra and Dean Martin by producing No. 1 records for them—at the height of mid-sixties Beatlemania.

Having been present at the creation of rock and having bucked the British Invasion to make hits for the Rat Pack, it was inevitable that I'd fall in with Nashville's "Outlaw" faction when I arrived there in 1976.

Music Row, the fabled, laid-back patch of Nashville where most studios and record and publishing companies were located, was an insular, incestuous world—somewhere between close-knit and closed-shop, depending on if you were an insider or, like me, on the outside looking in.

I wasn't greeted warmly by the Old Guard clique of publishers, producers, and label executives. For decades they had a lock on the music and artists of country—and got rich, by pennies and nickels, without selling many albums. Nashville seemed at least a decade behind pop in every way—and I saw plenty of opportunity for change. But when the Establishment kept its distance, I found another way in.

Fortunately, I had my own network of West Coast pop-music power brokers—Elektra's Joe Smith, Mike Maitland, and then Irving Azoff at MCA, Mo Ostin at Warners—who would turn to me to run their Nashville divisions. Working on the inside gave me a power base to change the way hillbillies made and sold records.

I pursued my vision for country. I pushed artists to seize control of their own music by taking it away from the old-boy publisher-producer system. I spent more money than anyone else to produce better-sounding albums. I urged studios to go digital.

Naturally, I was seen as both maverick and madman. But I also produced more hits than anyone else around—more than 130 Top 5s and 67 No. 1s. And I probably made more enemies than anyone in Nashville history. I wiped out entire staffs when I took over, and then dropped dozens of acts to trim my rosters.

By the nineties my vision had become reality. One trade magazine called me the Messiah of Music Row. Nashville had gone from a $50-million-a-year business to $1 billion a year, and had taken its place in the American mainstream. The sound quality and market share of country rivaled that of rock. Country made the covers of *Time* and *Forbes*. It had finally become big business.

Capitol was my sixth Nashville division in little more than a decade. My passion for rebuilding a label matched my love of creating tracks in the studio. I've always been excited by the challenge of starting from the ground up, creating something of value that didn't exist before. The perfect mix for me was to run labels and be an in-house producer.

When I got to Capitol, the division was struggling. One bright spot was a heavy-set kid from Oklahoma with a big cowboy hat and a fierce intensity glowing in his eyes. Just as I was taking over, in December 1989, Garth Brooks had his first No. 1 record, *If Tomorrow Never Comes*.

Five years and a history-making 35 million records later, that promise had turned to enormous profit. To the extent that Garth's success epitomized the "New Nashville," I should have been, as one of the booming music center's architects, on a career high. Instead our newly crowned King of Country was asking for my head.

Garth's "Dump Bowen" campaign had gained momentum months earlier during a European tour. When Thorn's chairman, Sir Colin Southgate, visited Garth backstage in London, Garth let him know that he wouldn't turn in a new record with me in place. Garth knew this would get Jim Fifield, EMI Music's president and CEO, and Koppelman all worked up. A couple weeks later I flew to New York to close a deal for Liberty to purchase a Christian-music label to be distributed through EMI.

After that business was done, Koppelman, Fifield, and I had a lunch off Fifield's office in Carnegie Towers. The purpose was for us to get up to speed on the GB situation.

I walked into an ambush—and ended up discussing my early-morning golf game. Charles spoke up first. "You know, Bowen, we have this problem. I wouldn't be saying anything to you about it, but the auditors found this *irregularity* on your expense report. They showed me where you played golf a hundred and twenty times last year."

"Oh, is *that* all it was?" I asked back.

"No," Fifield chimed in, "that's all we *paid* for."

There wasn't anything irregular about this. I played golf almost every morning at the Legends and did most of my face-to-face business that way. Everyone knew that. I heated up. I had a suspicion where this was coming from. Likely prodded by his co-manager, Bob Doyle (Pamela Lewis was then Doyle's partner), and his business manager, a CPA named Kerry O'Neil, Garth had tried to connect his slumping numbers to my golf game by claiming I wasn't running the label. He was turning golf into a contact sport.

"The problem you have isn't golf," I said. "It's Garth."

It was clear, though, where this confrontation was headed. Koppelman could run with it and use golf as his one and only excuse to fire me. When the gorilla rattled his cage, New York listened.

The irony here was that golf was supposed to *reduce* stress. In a crazy, goofy business where I had thrived on workaholic intensity, golf was my lifeline, a mental escape. (It was also good for my back muscles, which had been permanently injured during kidney surgery thirty years earlier.) It was absurd to be on the defensive about it.

"Your *problem*," I went on, "is you've got a spoiled-brat artist sellin' four million instead of ten million and he's gotta blame somebody and that somebody's me."

They seemed unmoved. "I'm always first off the tee," I explained. "If I'm short on time, I go out as a twosome, get around in under two hours, and can make a ten A.M. meeting."

I wondered how my lousy 120 rounds of golf and $50 green fees would tally up next to all their chic Manhattan lunches and dinners. I didn't question their T&E and resented them questioning mine. "It's about perception," Koppelman said. "And the perception is that you're playing golf."

EMI was paying me a fortune in salary and bonuses on my five-year contract, and it didn't *look* good for Nashville's highest-paid CEO to be golfing every weekday. I conducted most label business from home and rarely showed up at the office—part of my "maverick" thing. I was a big target. But my numbers spoke for themselves.

"It's not about perception," I said. "It's about fabrication, twisting the facts to suggest I'm not running the company. I've got a cellular phone in my car if anybody needs me that bad. Funny, isn't it, how you didn't hear Garth bitchin' about all this when his records were at ten million."

"I don't know how you can run a label without being there," Koppelman said.

"Well, I can. I work seven days a week. My life is unique. If I change it to satisfy you, it screws the whole thing up."

We agreed on one point: That my biggest mistake was not hiring a VP-GM to run the label day-to-day after Garth took off. We agreed to find one. I also said I'd spend two weeks, not four, at my vacation home on Maui. And I vowed to make Liberty a winner. "I'm glad to hear you say that," Fifield said. "Knowing you, you could tell us to stick it up our ass and leave."

He was right. If I were forty with another twenty years ahead of me, I'd have told them to stick it, cashed out, and gone to a rival label. But I wasn't. My five-year deal would run out when I'd be sixty—a nice round number for retiring. And I had a Christian-music operation in place worth millions over the life of my contract. For now, I figured, I'd hang in, check the ego at the door, ride out the GB soap opera.

I knew something was wrong with me when my golf scores started rising. Instead of 74 or 75 I would sometimes go to 80 or above—and wonder what was wrong. My mind would drift. I'd blow short putts. By late fall I began to sense that my whole body—not just my golf game—wasn't up to par. I was exhausted, irritable, burned out. I had been producing albums for Willie Nelson and newcomer John Berry and dragging my butt. I had just turned fifty-seven, but my energy level normally wore down kids in the studio half my age. I didn't feel healthy.

I made an appointment at the Mayo Clinic for a major workup. I had had polyps removed from my sinuses three years earlier and was told they'd likely come back in four or five years. The polyps had been a wake-up call to stop smoking grass after years of smoking four or five joints a day. I went cold turkey after surgery. I also went on a low-fat diet, dropped twenty pounds, and reduced my cholesterol. *So why was I feeling so miserable?* It seemed like a good time to get everything checked out again.

Ginger and I went to Rochester, Minnesota, for the physical in the first week of December 1994. Rochester is a fascinating place that time of year. If you went up there sick, you'd die if you had to go outdoors. Much of downtown and the Mayo facilities are connected by a network of overhead and underground pedestrian tunnels to protect people from the brutal cold. It was minus 4 degrees Fahrenheit when we arrived.

My first day of tests—physical, blood, blood pressure, cholesterol, lungs, X ray, EKG, treadmill—all checked out A-plus. Weight was down to a solid 205, cholesterol was at 159, good cholesterol had doubled to 44.

There seemed to be nothing to explain why I felt so bad. I was in such great shape, I started pissin' and moanin' to Ginger about wasting valuable time in the coldest place on earth.

I'm real glad I stuck around to see the sinus guy.

Dr. David Sherris poked and prodded and told me the right-side polyps had started to come back. The left side was pretty clear. He said I should probably return in a year or two to have them removed. He walked to a table to write me out a prescription for steroids to shrink the polyps. "After the next surgery the polyps shouldn't come back anymore."

As he came over to hand me my prescription, he bent over and stared straight at the front part of my neck. As he patted around and just below my Adam's apple, he asked the question patients dread hearing the most: "What's this lump here?"

Poor Ginger. The very sound of the word struck terror. Ginger's eyes turned to saucers as she froze in her chair. I had shaved two days earlier and hadn't felt anything strange. None of the other doctors had noticed it.

But when Dr. Sherris took my finger and pressed it into the small hollow where tracheotomies go in, I could feel a hard, obvious mass where there should have been a sort of soft depression. Feeling it stunned me.

"We'd better aspirate," he said, using a cold clinical term for sticking an eight-inch needle into the lump and sucking out enough stuff for a tissue biopsy. He swabbed me with a cotton ball, and in that baby went. To put it succinctly, it was one of those deals in life where you try real hard not to shit your pants. Texas boys are supposed to be tough, right? I got tough in a hurry.

He did his best to reassure us that thyroid tumors were usually benign. I just kept repeating to myself, *Well, I'll be damned.* I doubt anything could have comforted us. I was kind of in shock. "I'll call you tomorrow," he said.

It shouldn't have surprised me. There was a history of enlarged thyroids—goiters—in my family: my father, his mother, and two sisters had all had them. And my mother had had throat cancer.

Next day Ginger and I woke up, walked through some tunnels, and had breakfast. We were nervous and edgy and couldn't avoid the subject at hand. One consolation, though—at least we weren't talking about Liberty and Garth. None of that mattered at the moment.

When we got back to our suite at the Kahler Plaza Hotel at around eleven A.M., the phone's message light was on. I took a deep breath as Ginger went to another phone where I could see her.

"Listen," Dr. Sherris said, "we got your biopsy back. Unfortunately, we found some abnormal cells that we could not distinguish as being cancerous. We should go in and take out the tumor, have a look at it, and try to preserve the thyroid."

Ginger turned white. I was still stunned. Surgery was scheduled for the next morning.

When a friend later asked me if I had the typical "Why me?" reaction, I said no. My first reaction was: *Thank goodness I'm already at the Mayo.* I wasn't asking, "Why me?" A more reasonable question might have been "Why not?"

When you've drunk booze and smoked grass over a twenty-five-year stretch, been married five times, put in more eighteen-hour days than you can even remember, and coped with the pressures of producing and moving $1 billion worth of music through Nashville alone, you'd *better believe something's* going to go wrong.

I'd simply lived too much life to wonder, "Why me?"

What I needed to answer wasn't why, but *how:* How do I come out a winner in these two battles? As I told a friend, "I'm going to get on top of this and deal with it head-on. If I don't, then if GB *doesn't* get me now, the big C will."

When I was born in the tiny mining town of Santa Rita, New Mexico, on November 30, 1937, my father, Asa Bowen, was working long, back-breaking days as a blast-hole driller and prospector for the Chino Copper Company. We lived in a small company housing unit in the mountains, where Mexican and American miners all got along peaceably. The company hospital sat barely a half-mile from the edge of the vast pits along what was called Kneeling Nun Mountain. Chino later became the Kennecot Copper Corporation.

Only a few hundred "payroll people" lived in Santa Rita, in the southwest corner of the state, so when I was three or four, we moved to Silver City, New Mexico. Asa never made more than a dollar an hour and often had to barter for necessities at the company store. But as a union activist, he also stood up for what was right and fair for the miners: he made his share of enemies fighting for safer working conditions, higher pay, better medical coverage—and against communist infiltration. Between the politics, the brutal extremes of weather, and the wages, life was a hard and humbling, yet proud, struggle.

Ours was not a warm, happy home. My parents fought and argued and never seemed to get along. They divorced when I was about seven. My mother, born Stella Ballard, stayed in Silver City to pursue her dream of being a nurse. My sister, Patti, born five years after me, lived with her. My mom stayed there a few years, marrying a physician, Dr. Raemer. After they divorced, she moved to Los Angeles when I was eleven or twelve. She married again, to a sweetheart of a man named Harold Fransen. They were together until my mother's death in the early 1990s. I never spent much time with her early on, never shared the kind of warm, hugging, loving bond most kids have with their moms. I felt time with me was more of an obligation than a pleasure for her. Whatever hurt or sadness or rejection came from that I simply blocked out.

I grew up with my father, whom I idolized for his integrity and moral clarity. When my father got run out of the Santa Rita mines because of his union activities, he made his way to the bleak Texas Panhandle town of Dumas, where he remarried and became the chief of police. He kept the peace in a town of drunken, brawling oil- and gas-field workers without once drawing his gun in the line of duty. He was a forceful, fair, no-nonsense cop. No one messed with Chief Bowen. To him a man's word was everything. A strong work ethic, a code of honor, a fascination for challenging the status quo and shaking things up—that all runs in my blood.

But so does the restless, independent spirit of a nomad. Coming from a forties broken home in the desolate Southwest, it's not surprising that it would take me four unsuccessful marriages before I could make one work. Settling down was never my main goal. Not at home and, after nearly a dozen record labels, not in music. Rather than seek security and comfort, I've lived more for the rush—and risk—of starting over, creating something where there wasn't anything before.

I spent my career in studios and at record labels turning artists' words and melodies into gold. My father blasted rock and hauled dirt out of the mines to turn it into copper. The vast pit his explosions created was an awesome sight to a young boy. The deep strip-mining cuts; towering sixty-foot-high derricks and monster shovels; deafening jackhammers and dynamite blasts rocking the earth—these are things I never will forget.

My father's own early childhood had been spent at a remote forest ranger station near Durango, Colorado. His father, Clarence Bowen, was a ranger, who married Lucy Britain, daughter of a local county official. Asa lived in fear of his father, a drinker whose fits of rage and physical abuse left him feeling trapped with nowhere to run. Clarence whipped and beat Lucy, hollered mercilessly, then turned on his four kids.

When Lucy refused to take it anymore, Clarence left for Arizona. Asa was six. Lucy moved with her children to Silver City, a busier town with a state university branch, some thirty miles west of Santa Rita.

Grandma Lucy was a proud, resilient frontier woman who washed dishes in a Chinese restaurant to feed her kids. She did crosswords with a Lucky Strike dangling from the corner of her mouth and she could shoot jackrabbits from a car going fifteen miles an hour. "Often wondered why she didn't just use that gun on Clarence," my father used to say.

Lucy married a kind but crusty local deputy sheriff named Claude Hollis. Maybe he wasn't perfect—he'd kick off his day by tilting his head back and chugging down a pint of whiskey—but he was a good stepdad.

Asa grew to be a rugged six-foot-two-inch, 230-pound natural athlete who played football and basketball in high school and at New Mexico State Teachers College in Silver City. That's where he met and fell in love with a beautiful dark-haired student named Stella Ballard, a country girl from Animas, way down in the southwestern tip of New Mexico. Animas had only a few dozen people living there.

I was their first child. Patti came along almost five years later. By then Asa had quit college and gone to work in the copper pits. It didn't take long for him to show he was tough. Shortly after becoming union president, his rig was struck by lightning, causing a light bulb in his cab to explode in his face. He snapped his head back and got a whiplash so severe he had neck pain for decades.

The hospital doctor checked him out and reached into a giant container of aspirin tablets. He scooped out a couple handfuls and put them in a sack. "Here," he said, "Take these." Outraged by the doctor's cavalier—and unclean—methods, Asa scattered the aspirin all over the floor. "This isn't the way to handle medicine," he yelled. "I'll tell you somethin.' If I ever catch you grabbin' another aspirin from that jar, I'll shut this son of a bitch [mine] down so tight you'll never see any ore come outta here the rest of your life."

The M.D. was so struck by my father's fiery spirit, he stopped by the house that night and tried to get him to join the Communist party. That was the doctor's second big mistake of the day. Asa told him no way he wanted to hear about "Commies" in his union, so he sent the guy packing.

Though my father swore off ever raising his hand to a woman, he and my mother fought all the time. As a kid I felt the tension and unhappiness. It was mostly about my mother's reluctance—she'd had me as a teenager—to stay home with two small children when she had studied at college to be a nurse. Prevailing wisdom at the time had it that women were supposed to cook, have babies, express no opinions. My mother never bought into that program, and motherhood got in the way of her life's ambition. Two or three decades later she'd have been a staunch equal-rights feminist.

I admit I never cared for her the way most kids love their moms. I remember her slapping me around a bunch of times to keep me in line and forcing castor oil down my throat every time I sneezed, sniffled, or coughed. She did this so often, the silver on the big old tablespoon was all eaten through and dulled. If it wasn't castor oil, it was a trip to a clinic to have my blood tested, swallow a pill, or get poked at for some damn thing or other.

I blocked out most of my early troubles with her—except the time she caught me playing with myself, warning that I'd go crazy if I kept doing it. I wasn't more than five or six and I was pissed: the *nerve* of her coming into my room like that—even if that's what they taught her in nursing class. I went to my father and asked if it was true. "No." He shrugged. "What'll make ya crazy is gettin' caught by her again."

A year or so later my parents split up.

They weren't saying anything, but I figured something was up. I was sent to stay with my father's parents, Claude and Lucy Hollis, just outside Silver City. My mother would visit me there once or twice a week. One day, as she took me for a ride in her car, she said, "Monday, your father and I are going before the judge, and one of you two kids is gonna live with him and the other's gonna live with me. Now, I'm not supposed to discuss this with you, but I need to know, who do you want to be with?"

"My dad." I remember it coming out just like that—and then thinking, *Holy shit.* I don't think that pleased her.

Earlier that morning I had killed a snake in Grandma Hollis's yard. When my mom took me back there and was leaving on a dirt road alongside Grandma's yard, I curled the dead snake around a stick, ran up to the fence at the edge of the roadside, and flung the snake into the open window of my mother's car. It landed right on her leg. She went berserk, damn near wrecked the car.

I guess I was mad she was leaving me. I got slapped around and punished big-time. It was like, *Screw you for making me make a choice like that at seven years old.* Small wonder I never shared much warmth or intimacy with her until much later.

•

I grew up without much of a sense of roots. The notion of set-tling down and raising a family never took hold as a younger man. I was in my mid-forties before I was able to achieve a strong, trusting, loving partnership in marriage. I spent much of my childhood feeling like a pawn, handed off between homes and relatives. Vacations were approached with more dread than eager anticipation. Holidays just meant going somewhere far away to stay with other people.

My parents' divorce was hardly ever discussed. Unlike today, there was no effort to examine or explain things so that kids can understand what's going on. Families just got on with it.

In the late sixties, as I was divorcing my second wife, the singer Keely Smith, we both went to a psychiatrist for counsel-ing. He sensed—quite reasonably—that something from my early relationship with my mother was impeding my dealings with women. He asked me to call my father for clues. I did call, and as we spoke, a very hazy memory came up. "You know," I said, "something happened that has caused me to not be able to have normal warmth and closeness with women. Can you tell me anything that might help me understand?"

He said it had to do with my mom messing around with a neighbor, a discovery that had torn my dad up at the time. With-out being specific, he said I had actually witnessed something going on with them, but had blocked it out all those years. It's a kid's best means of escape, a way of keeping his sanity when his world around him at home seems to be falling apart. I was al-ways real good at throwing up a wall—as a kid and later as a husband.

It wasn't until I had been a record executive for a number of years that I gained some serious understanding and appre-ciation of my mother's drive to be an independent, successful, career-oriented woman. That helped me let go of some of the anger I had felt since childhood. As I worked with excellent careerwomen in music, I came to see that the classic sexist at-titudes I'd been brought up with regarding women were wrong. That helped erase some of that negativity toward her.

Neither my father nor my mother was your loving, affection-ate, hands-on type of parent. But the most painful effect of the divorce was the traveling. As my father's union troubles mounted, he would spend more time off in the West Texas oil and gas fields. So I'd shuttle between both sets of grandparents, the Hollises in Silver City and the Ballards down in Animas.

That's why holidays have always brought back almost nothing but painful memories.

A holiday was when I left one parent for the other, left my school buddies behind, and had to sit in an old uncomfortable train for hours with Grandma Lucy. Thinking of my dad in Amarillo or Dumas, or my mother in Los Angeles, was like trying to imagine the far end of the earth. Those sensations stay with you all your life.

If I resented my mother's ambitions, it didn't take nearly as long to embrace my father as a role model. After the divorce the union in Santa Rita wanted to get my father out of the mines and lose him in Utah or somewhere in the Panhandle. His campaigns for mine safety and workers' rights had made him a pain in the butt for a lot of people at Chino.

One of his big successes was suing the mine and winning "portal to portal" pay. The settlement meant that miners could be paid for the hour or more spent every morning preparing their equipment and making their descent before actually punching in by seven-thirty. His own check was an enormous $300; other miners got far more. The settlement was retroactive.

Safety was an even hotter button to push for my father, whether it was for better blast warning signals so that workers in changing rooms didn't walk right into a blasting area, or better equipment to handle the electric cables that circled up and coiled behind the rigs.

He worked his way from union president to district president and international representative; but his anti-Communist position made him enemies inside the union leadership. (They never did gain control at Chino.) It was his belief that executive board members were left-wing provocateurs seeking control of the union. He was known to stand before his own local and denounce the union leadership as "a dirty rotten bunch of Commie-infested rats."

When, after ten years in Silver City, the union decided to "transfer" him to a small town in Utah, it was ominous news. There *was* no town there—just a long-abandoned mining camp. What they meant by transfer was exile—or worse. The story around the mines went that union bosses would dispatch troublemakers to Utah, where hitmen dumped them down an open-pit mine shaft.

An anti-Communist friend of my father's, a member of the

union executive board in Denver, tipped him off—and urged him to head instead for the Texas Panhandle to organize refinery workers in the gas fields around Amarillo and at the smelter in Dumas, fifty miles to the north.

My father was furious, but proud, so off he went to build himself a new life in a far-off place called Dumas.

He traveled back and forth for more than a year while he got his bearings. I spent much of that time shuttling between the Hollises' farm outside Silver City and the Ballards' in Animas. The uprooting was confusing, and I never took much to rural life.

My grandparents were quirky characters. Visiting them was never dull. The Hollises had chickens, a few cows, and a barn out back. Grandpa Claude even gave me my own little horse when I stayed there. During the war people raised a lot of their own food. I had my own pet hen, Goldie. When she quit laying eggs, Grandma Lucy and Granddad Hollis announced we were having Goldie for our Sunday dinner. It was a couple years before I could eat chicken again.

When W. A. and Edith Ballard moved to Animas, it was little more than a stretch of railroad track with two or three old buildings on one side and three or four on the other. The family owned most of it. They were out in the middle of absolutely no-place. The flat, barren desert just stretched so far that you could see a visitor on the dirt road kicking up dust miles away on the horizon.

W. A. had a barbershop first, then a grocery store with two gas pumps out front. He also delivered mail from Animas down to the Mexican border and took me on his mail routes, stopping for lunch at ranch houses with long strips of homemade beef jerky hanging down on the porch. The cowboys would all eat around a giant table, throwing a common rag around to wipe their faces.

One of my uncles, Hollis Williams, who married my mother's sister, dug wells for the whole valley. I'd go visit Uncle Hollis and hang around with cousins my age and their friends from nearby ranches. We'd ride horses, swim across the water tanks, and hunt rabbits on quarter horses. There wasn't much to this, since a quarter horse'll cut left and right real sharp and stay right on the rabbit. All you had to do was hang on and hope you didn't get thrown—or shot at by these crazy kids. They shot anything that moved—coyotes, rabbits, birds, each other. Gunplay freaked me out, but eventually I got pretty good with a .22.

I might have finally felt at home there, but I developed terrible allergies. My eyes would swell shut, and my cousins would have to lead me back home. At night the mesquite pollen swirling in the dry desert night air made me crazy. I'd have to come home and lie down with a wet rag over my face, my head pounding with a terrible headache. My mom came down once to scratch and prick my back all over, then rubbed in samples of just about every damn thing she could find to figure out what I was allergic to. It turned out that what I was allergic to was New Mexico.

If being a cowboy meant getting a kick out of watching bulls get branded and castrated, I guess I wasn't cowboy material. Now *there* was some cruel shit. I knew I'd never fit in.

Uncle Hollis was a great hunter of bobcat, mountain lion, coyote, and wildcat. He was one tough hombre. Had pieces of two fingers missing. He chopped them off himself after he reached into a rabbit hole and a rattler bit him.

I blew any chance to ever prove my manhood to Uncle Hollis and the cousins the night we went hunting rabbits. The kids would sit on the big front bumpers of the truck and hang on to the hood ornament. Then Hollis would spot a rabbit and aim the headlights at it. I shot one in the road, but didn't kill him. Left him wounded, stunned, blinded by the car lights. Of course Uncle Hollis wanted me to finish him off. "Just grab him from behind and crack his head against the fence post by the road," he hollered impatiently. I couldn't imagine anything more cruel. I knew Uncle Hollis thought I was the worst kind of sissy. I stood frozen in the lights, kind of stunned and confused myself.

I'll never forget how it felt to whack that rabbit's little head against the post until I felt him go totally limp right in my hand. It just about made me sick to kill him. Kids were expected to be proud of their blood-sport kills, but not me. With that the killing part was over for me.

Eventually my idea of a good time around the Ballards' ran more to music. Being restless, and having a short attention span, I was never much of a reader. We'd all sit around and listen to H. B. Kaltenborn's war reports on the big old radio. But mostly I liked sitting around and listening to Granddad play his fiddle while the family sang songs. One of the uncles played guitar, one of my aunts played piano. Granddad taught me piano chords and wrote out sheets with diagrams for my fingers. I could spend hours by myself, picking out chords. Then I'd sit in with the group when they played their songs.

Music turned Granddad on more than anything. Twice a week I'd ride with him on bumpy old dirt roads up to Lordsburg, where he got supplies for his store. He'd stop in at the music store in town, take out his fiddle, and try to read the sheet music for songs he'd heard on the radio.

It's a wonder I ever got music at all, considering how awful the off-pitch screech of his fiddle sounded. I hated fiddles for years. When I first got to Nashville some thirty years later, it never even occurred to me to book a fiddle for a recording session until Mel Tillis showed up one day with one.

When I was almost eight, my father decided it was time for me to move back in with him in Dumas. I was real happy to go. My grandparents drove me from Silver City to Albuquerque and put me on a train to Amarillo. My father met me there in his car. It was during the fifty-mile drive to Dumas that he told me that on one of his trips from Silver City up to Santa Fe he had met a waitress from Ohio named Frances Wilson. They chatted just a few different times when he'd pass through, but a couple weeks later he just called her out of the blue and said, "Hey, meet me in Clovis. We'll get married."

Clovis was near the eastern border of New Mexico, a few miles from Texas. It was where kids could get a "grab and run" marriage. Asa didn't do much running after Frances grabbed on: in June 1995 they celebrated their golden anniversary.

It was real strange. I was going to a new home in a new town, a new school with new kids—and a new parent. It was just like starting my life all over again.

TWO

I T TOOK A FEW rough years to adjust to Dumas, and then things picked up in high school. Texas high school in the 1950s was girls, football, music. But by then I vowed I would leave that part of the world and never look back.

From day one I hated Panhandle weather, which was even more severe than New Mexico's: frigid ice storms in winter, choking dust storms in summer, brutal winds year-round. Until I left Dumas, I thought rain, snow, and ice fell horizontally. You had to put wet handkerchiefs over your face in order to breathe during dust storms. The air got so thick with it, you couldn't see someone sitting across your living room. For a person with allergies, it was a miserable place.

At home Frances and I fought like hell because I was unaccustomed to discipline and structure. In school I had trouble keeping up even though I had skipped two half-grades in Silver City. I was still printing block letters when the other kids were writing script.

As far as family ties went, I was pretty much a loner. I didn't feel sorry for myself. The flipside of being a loner was self-reliance. As I approached my teens, I started to feel like, *The hell with 'em, just look out for yourself.* My father avoided confrontation with me; Frances and I went at it a lot. But she was a wonderful influence. She taught me what I needed to know: values, responsibility, taking care of myself. Her belief was, the younger you are when you start running your own life, the faster you'll be movin' when you hit the street.

I sensed on some level that life rolls along like a wheel, with spokes and a hub. If you're a spoke, you're dependent on the hub, you're on the bottom for part of every spin through life. I knew that I had to be a hub, be the center. It was the key to survival.

I didn't let myself regret not having a more tight-knit, nurturing hearth. Instead I came to see the uprooting as a liberation, a signal to seize more control over my life. I've always known people who'll say they need to go home to their roots, for that fix of comfort, spiritual renewal. I have never allowed myself to feel that sentimental need for attachments. Maybe that helps explain my marital track record, or the "maverick" who was unafraid to mess with the status quo. Nashville has always presented itself to the world as a close creative "family"; I wasn't invested in the "family" way of doing things, especially when I believed the so-called family was doing things all wrong.

My father was always looking to stir things up, too, which he did by battling the local union that covered oil and gas workers in Dumas. The constant battling got to him, though. He quit for a while and sold sand and gravel for construction projects. But too many people took advantage of his decent, trusting terms and burned him.

One day my father needed a new tire and drove to a garage owned by a city councilman. A local scandal was brewing at the time: people were allegedly being pistol-whipped by Dumas cops; there was political pressure to investigate for police brutality and reform the department. "I hear you're looking for a new police officer," my father said to the councilman.

"Well," he nodded, "we've got to clean up the situation. They're beating up everyone they arrest. It's no good."

"I've never been a police officer," my father answered, "but I lived with one almost all my life. Stepdad was deputy sheriff out in New Mexico." My father must have sensed an opportunity. The councilman was listening. "I'll tell you what. You give me the job and I'll clean this place up in six months—and you won't see me pistol-whippin' anybody."

The man was intrigued. He discussed this with another councilman, went over the mayor's head—he did not want a stranger on the tiny force—and offered him a job as deputy police chief. He moved up to chief awhile later.

Dumas had fewer than 10,000 people, but with all the smelters and refineries around, almost three times that many passed through daily. If I never saw evidence of segregation or racial tension, it was because Dumas was as lily-white WASP as you could get. Still, Dumas was known in those days as a sun-down town—it was posted on the outskirts of town. If you were black, you could drive through town after dark, but you kept going. You didn't want the sun setting on you in Dumas.

Once he worked his way up to chief, my father brought law and order to the department. As he liked to say, "I do a lot of things different now from the way they done 'em before."

His most common concerns were burglary, drunk driving, and drunk and disorderly conduct at the bars and pool hall. He developed a reputation for firmness mixed with compassion and restraint. He was the kind of cop who'd haul in a half-dozen drunks and keep them overnight in a cell, but awaken extra early so that they'd have their day in court and still make it to work. He felt they shouldn't lose a day's pay for one lousy bender.

I don't imagine I'd have gotten off so light. But I wasn't likely to wind up on the wrong side of the law. Once I could drive, at fourteen, I couldn't run a stop sign without it getting back to the chief. That knowledge alone tended to keep me in line.

Being police chief's son did have its advantages: my dad's police cruiser was about the hottest, fastest car in Moore County. It was a beautiful souped-up, low-to-the-ground Studebaker Golden Hawk hot rod, perfect for running down Okie bootleggers coming through our county.

If my dad didn't need the Hawk at night, there was nothing cooler than to pick up some friends and go driving my own cop car with a police radio inside. And my voice was a dead ringer's for his. Frances became the dispatcher when the Dumas PD finally got one. Until then there was just a tall post outside a drugstore with a light on top. When someone called the station to report trouble, the light went on and the cop would go to a phone booth and see what was going on. Frances kept things moving. She had worked at the phone company office and also kept all the police files in order. I occasionally filled in for her when she needed time off. Dispatching was a real kick; I had cops going all over the place, throwing around cop phrases like "That's a ten-four" and "Ten-ninety-eight."

In junior high I made a new friend—a tall, skinny, quiet kid named Donnie Lanier. We all called him Dirt, after a school janitor named Dirty McCool, who was always covered in soot. When

Donnie showed up as filthy as Dirty one day after working on his car, he became Dirt. Dirt's got his own version of how he got his nickname, but this one's good enough for me.

We quickly got to be best buddies. We did everything together, but then summer would come, and during my brief vacations, I'd go off to see my grandparents or my mom before heading back to Dumas and some awful summer job. By then she was living in Los Angeles with the new man in her life, Harold Fransen, an aerospace engineer. They eventually married. When I spent a couple weeks with them before my freshman year, they gave me a strange little present—a four-stringed ukulele. I spent hours messing around with it, figuring out chords, singing songs, strumming away.

Coincidentally, Dirt won an acoustic guitar at a grand opening for Dumas's new music store. Naturally he and I started hanging out together with our new instruments, mostly in his room at the back of his house on the north side of town. We tried putting together songs by the current pop stars—Eddie Fisher, Dean Martin, Kitty Kallen, Julius LaRosa, and Teresa Brewer. Dirt liked guitar pickers like Chet Atkins and Les Paul and was more into country music. Bob Wills and the Texas Playboys had played at barbecues on Dirt's family porch. Our tastes were a little different: my favorite was Al Jolson. Mother had all his records, and I'd sit for hours and play "Mammy" over and over. Different tastes aside, this music thing was definitely something we could get into.

Football, on the other hand, was something I dreaded. Dirt and I had played in junior high, but hated the win-or-die attitude of Texas sports. I hated the coach and didn't get off on banging into kids and trying to hurt them. *I* was getting hurt, and had barely survived junior high. My dad and I clashed on this all the time. In his book boys had to be macho. It was bad enough you couldn't kill small animals, but if you didn't play Dumas football, you were a sissy, or worse, flat-out "queer." I was always in conflict with that macho thing. With barely sixty kids in a grade, it wasn't as if no one would notice if you weren't on the team—unless you were the class genius, which for me was *not* an option.

Nor were Dirt and I wild about summer jobs. Once I had gotten into junior high, I wanted to work for my pocket money. After school I sacked groceries, which was fun for a while—until my first paycheck netted me all of $27 for a week's work after taxes.

One summer my dad got me a job to work the cotton fields north of town. Someone handed me a hoe and told me to work a row that seemed to stretch clear to Canada. I was only supposed to chop weeds, but kept chopping cotton instead, so they got on me every time I did.

I made it all the way up the row and back down by eleven-thirty A.M. My back was killing me. I saw a horse tank about a stone's throw from where I stopped working. I threw down my hoe, nodded to the foreman, and jumped into the horse tank. It wasn't exactly lake water in there. But I didn't care. I stayed there for thirty minutes. When the flatbed truck that had brought me and a bunch of other kids out arrived with lunch, I quit, got on the truck, and rode back in to Dumas. My cotton-pickin' days were done.

Dirt and I got hired together once to lay curbs—and lasted three days. We spent most of that time near the water bucket, it was so damn dry out there. We got a job pouring concrete to build tall grain silos—and I was scared of heights. I was always afraid our wooden platform would slide off the wet concrete and we'd drop 120 feet. Hated that job.

Picking up roadside litter and painting road signs for the county weren't a whole lot better. *Any* manual labor in that heat—football practice included—was awful.

I did discover a far more pleasurable kind of summer heat in the town of Animas after my sophomore year. As the last two years of high school approached, I dreaded staying in Dumas. I went down to the Ballards' to think things over, and decided to not go back to Dumas. One big factor: Animas was so small the school didn't even field a football team. Instead I could play basketball, a perfect solution. Another factor: my first girlfriend.

She was a half sister of my cousin and she was a knockout. It was a good thing she picked me. I didn't have enough good sense to know how to go *about* picking up girls. It was my first real physical contact with the opposite sex. I didn't even know what sex was. Sex ed in Dumas didn't exist, and fifties movies didn't show you what to do. There weren't even any hellfire and brimstone Bible thumpers in my family to tell me what *not* to do.

Aside from being told of the one main anatomical distinction between the sexes, you were pretty much expected to get your ass up the dirt road a good mile by the railroad track, or head for the irrigation fields and start messin' around to figure that shit out on your own. She and I mostly just got all sweaty and worked up.

When I broke the news to Granddad Ballard about staying in Animas, he told my dad, who told him, "You put my boy on that train to Amarillo and I'll pick him up. Tell him that if he comes back here for a couple of weeks and still wants to leave, he can. And, well, that'll be fine. But not before he comes back here, faces me, and does it the right way."

When I got back to Dumas, my father made it clear he wanted me back home with him. He had two surprises waiting: a late-forties bubble Ford, and permission to not play football.

Of course once my dad and I had this breakthrough, I decided to suit up with the Demons anyway. The point was to avoid being called "queer" and to impress girls. The gridiron was a more likely place for me to do that than the classroom.

I never liked school. Most of it meant absolutely nothing to me. I hated having some guy tell you if you poured H_2O into some other stuff and then fired it up and mixed it over there in that jar, that it'll blow up or turn red. I did once send a Bunsen burner clear up to the ceiling. Self-reliant as I was *I* was the best judge of what I needed to know—and that didn't include tearing up frogs in science or dissecting Longfellow in English. I had absolutely no attention span, no retention. Today I'd be diagnosed with attention deficit disorder.

Not that I wasn't competitive. I managed to figure out how to pull about a B-plus average, which got me to the low end of the National Honor Society. I was also president of my senior class. Hell, with three or four kids on the ballot and a graduating class of sixty or so, campaigning was easy. There wasn't any. I was also in Glee Club and Library Club and Dance Band, because clubs got you out of class.

I got through a little better than Dirt, only because I learned better how to play the game and beat the system—which is what most of the real world's all about anyway.

The only game Dirt and I played together was football—and we both got beat up awfully bad. Friday-night Texas life revolves around school football. It was like they built the stadium first, put up the lights, and the hospital came later. There were parades, parties, pep rallies, dances, all kinds of betting going on. Half the townspeople would drive two-hundred miles to fill a stadium. Games were serious business, with Panhandle bragging rights on the line.

I never could run fast enough to carry the ball, so Dirt became our stick-thin fullback. When I finally started at quarterback, I couldn't throw more than twenty yards, and wasn't real accurate at twenty. I called about forty running plays for Dirt, whether we ran a single-wing, split T, or whatever. Didn't matter. By third quarter the defense had it all figured out anyway.

That pissed Dirt off. We played both offense and defense, so the only rest he ever got was if he limped off the field and faked an injury. With no bench depth, we played hurt. We hated our son-of-a-bitch coach. Dirt once complained to Coach that the referee was lining up behind the line of scrimmage, blocking the flow of our plays. "Knock'm on his ass," Coach said. Dirt ran over him and broke the ref's leg.

I must have got knocked cold a half-dozen times. I'd come to just enough to call plays and take the snap, groggy from that point on. For all the heroics, we could still lose big, like 66–6, to Phillips—and that was with home-field advantage.

If you got injured, they taped you up and sent you back in. Dirt had groin and hamstring pulls all senior season, bone chips, and bursitis in both elbows his whole life from getting slammed to the ground forty times every week for three seasons.

By senior year I was so banged up, I needed an extra hour before games to work on a screwed-up shoulder, tape both ankles, put steel braces around my knees, and rig a pad to protect my hip pointers, which have bothered me into midlife.

I recall one play that established a lifelong pattern in my friendship with Dirt. As linebacker I intercepted a pass and started chugging up the sideline with nobody between me and the goal line sixty yards ahead. Still, running hard as I could, it wasn't long before the herd closed in on me.

Dirt was hustling up behind me, trying to get out in front and block someone. I was running so hard I dropped the ball. This startled Dirt, who threw his bony 160-pound body on the fumble—and just got smothered. He had the wind knocked out. He got up real slow and shot me a look. "You son of a bitch." Oh, was he pissed. It wouldn't be the last time.

We did have our glory days. Senior year we destroyed Shamrock, Dalhart, and Hereford by combined scores of 127–0. And Phillips, state champs that year, edged us in a relative cliffhanger, 20–0.

When it came to dating girls, Dirt and I found ourselves on a more level playing field. Football gave us an edge over the competition, even if there wasn't much of a litter to pick from.

Dumas's "culture" was a pool hall, a youth center with Ping-

Pong, Carwell's Carhop, malt liquor, and a drive-in movie or two. There were sock-hops, proms, and parties, but dealings with girls were on an everything-but basis. Not many of us were going all the way. The trouble with Panhandle drive-ins was that it got so cold at night, you had to keep the motor running with the heater and defroster on and the windows rolled up, cracked just enough to hang the sound boxes. Forget *watching* the movie, since the windshield steamed up from all the grunting, grinding, groping, button popping, and heavy breathing.

Only about two or three girls really "put out" and went all the way. The "nice girls" were hard-core Bible belters "saving it" for their wedding night. Marriage was about the only way any of us could get laid.

I did have a few girlfriends back then. One was a beautiful girl named Caroline. Talk about romance getting nipped in the bud. She was the daughter of a druggist who made the mistake of selling a prescription drug without a prescription. When Asa learned of this, he had no choice but to arrest him and throw him in jail. Made me just a bit uncomfortable picking up the daughter at her home!

Then there was Sue. She had a birthday coming up and I needed to buy her a gift. Frances came up with the bright idea to buy her a friendship ring. I took Sue to a movie. As we parked and got a little hot and heavy, I thought it a good time to present her with the friendship ring. She opened up the little box and when she saw the ring, her eyes widened with a gasp.

"Oh, yes," she said, "of course I will."

I was like, *Oh, shit. Will* what? *Wait a minute here.*

Trying to explain to poor Sue that a friendship ring was not the same as an engagement ring turned into a major disaster.

Because Dirt's acoustic guitar kept drowning out my little ukulele, I bought a guitar to match his so that we could continue working up songs together.

When Dirt got himself an electric guitar, I got myself one to keep up and play rhythm. Soon we were joined by our school friend Ernie Munkres, who could sing much better than we could. Now the three of us could put together hit songs by popular artists of the day, like Eddie Fisher and Julius La Rosa.

By the end of junior year our trio debuted in school at an assembly. It was amazing to see the effect playing onstage had on the girls. We were the closest thing to stars Dumas had. We were getting calls to do dances, cotillions, and barbecues.

I was increasingly drawn to the music *business*. I knew the man who owned Dumas's radio station, KDDD, or "K-Triple D," because they broadcast our football games. I got a summer job there as a disc jockey before senior year. It was about the only creative thing you could do in all of Dumas. Triple-D was a 250-watt daytimer with block programming, which meant some guy could buy a block every day and preach for thirty minutes; I picked the songs for my hour-long country-and-western *Tumblin' Tumbleweeds*. That was great fun—old Sons of the Pioneers (the show's name came from their big hit), early Marty Robbins, Leroy "The Auctioneer" Van Dyke, Frankie Laine ("High Noon," "Rawhide").

Pop music through the first half of the fifties was just so boring to teenagers. It was old-people's music. And I had little feel for country. So little in fact that more than once I stayed out late, overslept, and never made it to the studio for my show. Anyone hoping to hear *Tumblin' Tumbleweeds* heard nothing but static until I tumbled out of bed and made it into the studio.

The station was in a tiny cinderblock building with the transmitting tower beside it. There was one little studio for the deejay and a slightly larger room off to the side. That's where Dirt, Munkres, and I would go at night to practice. Sometimes I would rig up a tape machine and record us so that we could listen to the playback.

In our senior year the trio played a dozen gigs. I was now behind Ernie and Dirt with a stand-up bass. We did a supermarket opening, played off a flatbed truck going through town and played a ladies' club that couldn't pay us because it would end our status as sports "amateurs"—as if we were on our way to the Olympics. Instead they gave us all wild orchid-colored shirts. We decided to call ourselves the Orchids.

We were only playing for the hell of it, and if I had any career ahead of me in music, it would have been in radio. Performing just gave us an edge in getting girls. If I'd stayed in Dumas, the career track ahead was to be on the police force.

At that time my ticket out of town was basketball. I was slow and could barely get off the floor for jump shots and rebounds. But I was deadly from the line (125 foul shots in a row once), and deadly from downtown before they counted for three points. My family had no money, so Eastern New Mexico University, in Portales, offered me a full basketball scholarship. But when I got there, the coach took one look at my unorthodox set shot and tried to change me to a jump-shooter.

"That won't work up here," he said. I agreed and packed up my bubble Ford and headed back to Dumas. Then I wangled a football scholarship at West Texas State University in Canyon, Texas.

At WT I moved into the athletic dorm. I didn't have a prayer. I would have needed growth hormones to make it. In my first scrimmage I got knocked out cold and woke up in the infirmary. That was scary. I switched back to a basketball scholarship, just to finish out the year. It became clear, though, that basketball wasn't going to be my ticket anywhere. Music was looking better all the time.

I became popular on campus for writing and singing parodies of current hit songs at assemblies and pep rallies. I'd adapt the song and come up with lyrics that satirized an opposing team or some aspect of life at WT. I was beginning to hang out with a new crowd of students that was more serious about doing music.

I witnessed two performances during that year at Canyon that changed my feelings about a career as a rock-and-roll performer. The first was Bill Haley and His Comets doing "Rock Around the Clock," one of the earliest radio hits of the rock-and-roll era, in the movie *Blackboard Jungle*. It was the top hit record for two months during the spring and summer after we graduated from Dumas in 1955. After all the mellow pop stars of the early fifties, it was obvious a new sound was emerging. Watching Haley bounce around with his smirk, his spit-curl hanging down across his forehead, and that big old electric guitar, my reaction was "Ho-ly shit."

The year 1955 was a transition between two eras. The big radio hits ranged from "Cherry Pink and Apple Blossom White" by Perez Prado (No. 1 for ten weeks) to the McGuire Sisters, the Four Lads ("Moments to Remember"), Pat Boone's lily-white cover of Fats Domino's "Ain't That a Shame," and Tennessee Ernie Ford's "Sixteen Tons." Perry Como, Nat King Cole, and Frank Sinatra were still holding on—barely—as the kings of pop. But all that was about to change.

A brash, sneering kid named Elvis Presley headlined a show at the civic auditorium in Amarillo that first year I was at State. He had been barnstorming all through the South and appearing on radio's *Louisiana Hayride*. Elvis's first records for Sun had gotten regional airplay. Girls became hysterical when he came onstage, grabbed hold of the microphone, and started to sing and gyrate. I could barely hear any of it above the shrieking and wailing, but what I heard—a mix of country, gospel, and rhythm and blues—was unlike anything else around.

Hearing "That's Alright (Mama)," "Good Rockin' Tonight," and "Mystery Train," you knew it was only a matter of time. This was the calm before the storm in 1956, when "Heartbreak Hotel," "I Want You, I Need You, I Love You," "Hound Dog," and "Don't Be Cruel" chased an aging generation of fifties vocalists into oblivion, transformed Elvis into "the King of Rock and Roll," and changed American culture forever.

But at that moment I wasn't thinking about a social, cultural revolution; all I knew was that I was amazed, and turned on by music like never before. Elvis was already a fabulous, electrifying showman with enormous power over his audience. His connection to his fans was immediate and passionate. He was a *star*—and he was our generation. At the end of the performance, girls scratched their names into the side of his Caddie, smeared love messages across it with lipstick, and pulled off any souvenirs they could.

This wasn't just about music—this was about rebellion, hysteria, worship. And clearly it was also about sex. This was a rhythmic music that got bodies moving and turned kids on. Girls weren't just listening, they were swooning.

And I was up there in the balcony, thinking, *Now* here's *a way to get the girls. And make a living. Wow!*

THREE

M Y BASKETBALL SCHOLARSHIP required me to work in a small recording studio in the speech department. By second semester Donnie Lanier and I were hanging out again, using the studio equipment to make demos. After brief visits to Texas Tech in Lubbock and Southern Methodist in Dallas, Dirt transferred to West Texas.

We soon met Buddy Knox, a folk-singing student who played at parties. Buddy came from Happy, Texas, and was more than four years older than I was, but he seemed determined never to graduate. He had a good voice and a clear twang, but so far he hadn't done much more with it than serenade coeds at the girls' dorms in a campus group called the Serenaders. He also wrote folk-style songs with long, rambling verses.

By early 1956 Buddy, Dirt, and I were fooling around with two guitars and my bass, using the studio after dark to rehearse on a small stage and make acetate demos of Buddy's songs. These demos—like vinyl records—were recorded by a machine that carved narrow grooves into vinyl disks. One of my jobs was to brush off the curling vinyl shavings and pull them loose so that they didn't clog up the needle. Shavings in the grooves caused surface static on the records. I just threw them all into a trash can.

We had no intention of performing, but we got a kick taping songs, listening to the playback, and improving our "sound." Buddy and I sang, I played stand-up bass, Dirt played lead electric riffs, and Buddy strummed acoustic rhythm guitar.

We were just a bunch of flat-bellied Texas kids with lots of hair on our heads, looking to have some fun. Buddy was about five-feet-nine inches tall, on the stocky side, with light brown hair. He was shy and easygoing, but he'd get nervous and seemed to have trouble remembering his own lyrics. I was five-foot-eleven-and-three-quarters with long, wavy black hair—the gorgeous one slapping the big ol' bass. We got along fine and, probably because he was a better singer, Buddy and I were never competitive. He had no problem with having another vocalist in the group. As close friendships went, it was more Dirt and Buddy and Dirt and me than Buddy and me. But there wasn't any rivalry between us that would keep us from playing music together.

Campus notoriety was far easier to attain through mischief than through music. Knox once thoughtlessly tossed his lit cigarette into the trash can full of flammable vinyl shavings and very nearly burned down the Speech Department. We managed to snuff out the smoldering shavings while choking on caustic smoke.

Then Dirt and Knox damn near got busted by the cops for their role in a panty raid at the girls' dorms. I ran back to my room and, before the cops came looking for me, stuffed a bunch of panties into the f-hole cut-out of the front of my hollow bass. I slipped my robe on, rolled up my britches, cracked open a book, and seemed to be deep in study when the cops burst in.

"Is there a problem, officer?" I asked, trying to look bewildered by all the commotion. "I'm tryin' to study here."

He had a look at the bass in the corner and took off.

We tried for months to fish the panties out with hangers. Finally I gave up and just played the damn bass, although it sounded dead and muffled.

As rock and roll's impact began to spread, the Orchids started playing beer parties on campus. RCA had bought Elvis's Sun contract for about $30,000, and by the spring of 1956 he was a national sensation with "Heartbreak Hotel," his first gold record. In the summer "Hound Dog" and its B-side, "Don't Be Cruel," both stayed at No. 1 for three months, still the most successful rock single of all time. Elvis would wind up having five No. 1s in 1956, selling an estimated *10 million* records.

This new raw, throbbing music appealed almost exclusively to hormone-crazy teenagers and college kids, driving a wedge between them and their parents. Radio stations were jumping on new acts such as the Teenagers with Frankie Lymon, the Platters, the Chordettes, Little Richard, Gale Storm, Fats Domino, and Gene Vincent and His Blue Caps. Rock was more than a musical fad: it was fast becoming the sound track of an emerging youth culture.

In the spring I saw a young singer out of the tiny West Texas town of Wink fronting a rockabilly band called the Teen Kings. He had been at North Texas University, but, boy, this kid could sing. Roy Orbison's voice was like none I'd ever heard. His first record was "Ooby Dooby," on the obscure Je-Wel label, and it had gotten some regional play.

After the show I went backstage and, knowing Roy was a West Texan, asked one of his Teen Kings people where they had recorded "Ooby Dooby." Norman Petty's place, out in Clovis, I learned. From my deejay days I knew Petty was a piano player and record producer who had had a 1954 hit, "Mood Indigo" as the Norman Petty Trio, with his wife, Vi, and Jack Vaughn. He had converted a small building he owned at 1313 West Seventh Street from a rehearsal room into a recording studio. There, he would make a name for himself recording rockabilly acts.

I called Petty, thinking the time was right for the Orchids to take their shot. I had no illusions about becoming rich or turning into the next Elvis—not with a fifty-pound stand-up bass to haul out onstage. It was a lark and, frankly, still all about getting girls. Now the gettin' had gotten much better.

A couple of weekends later we drove to Clovis to work on our demos. Petty's setup was a tiny one-room studio and control room at the end of his apartment complex. The studio was across from the garage where his father worked on cars. Petty's echo chamber was above the garage, and we were also just off a highway and near a train track. It was a funky deal. Anytime a big truck or train rumbled by, we'd blow the take. Or Norman's dad would start banging on cars and we'd have to stop. Still, there was a warm, tight sound inside the studio.

We decided to cut an up-tempo song of Buddy's called "Party Doll." But it was way too long to be a single. We cut out a bridge in the middle and worked those lyrics into a second song called, "I'm Stickin' with You." Which was just as well, since we didn't even have a B-side to go with "Party Doll." Then, as an acoustic trio, we cut both demos and returned to Canyon.

Petty had us come back for a second session to record the masters, working with his own drummer, Dave Alldred. Dave was tired of playing air-force-base dances around the state and itchin' to hit the road. Petty also put us in touch with the owner of Je-Wel Records. He was Chester Oliver, a very pleasant middle-aged Panhandle oilman who worked for Phillips Petroleum. Having brought Orbison to Petty, he then helped finance our next trip to Clovis and set up our label, Triple-D Records, after KDDD in Dumas. It was a fifty-fifty deal between him and the three of us. If he or any of us had any idea what we were doing, he'd probably have ended up a very wealthy man.

We were so young and nervous in these strange surroundings that we sort of choked. Dirt was jittery on guitar and made mistakes. When I sang "I'm Stickin' with You," I kept popping the microphone whenever I got to the line "Be-BOP! I love you baby, be-BOP! I don't mean maybe." My *p* would slam the recording-level needle. I was too shaky and inexperienced to figure out I could just turn my head away. Instead I changed it to "be-BAH!"

This kind of music was in its infancy; no one knew what the rules were in capturing it live in the studio. There were no rock magazines to read about being a rock star; none of us knew what that lifestyle was even like—or if it *was* a lifestyle.

That second session was more elaborate, with six or seven mikes. Though recording in mono, Norman was excited because he had gotten a second mono machine. "What's it for?" I asked.

"I'll Ping-Pong back and forth," he said. That made no sense to me.

When we *really* got down to business, Alldred, who was maybe ten years older that we were, was on drums. Except that we ended up using two drummers. Petty decided to rig up a large cardboard box to sound like drums. He buried one of the mikes inside a towel, then stuffed the towel inside the box. But it was no easy trick for Dave to beat on the box, hold it between his knees, *and* tap down on the foot pedal for the high-hat, or sock, cymbal. No problem: a girl Dirt was dating happened to play drums, too, so he had hauled over another set of drums for her. As he recalls, *she* actually played sock cymbal on our first two records. It was amazing, but once Alldred got into an R&B-style double backbeat on that box with one half-shut drum brush and a stick, the sound just *worked*. That muffled percussive sound of Petty's became a true fifties rockabilly signature.

The "Party Doll" session took eight hours. We blew lots of takes and had to start over every time. If it wasn't a truck or train, it was Buddy's terrible sense of meter. He had real trouble coming into a song.

Halfway through the session it was decided we needed girl backup singers. Fortunately, Buddy's sister, Verdie, had two friends along and they could all sing pretty well. This was a truly makeshift operation, but Norman seemed to know what he was doing.

In order to dub background voices for "Party Doll," Petty started "Ping-Ponging" his two mono machines—a clunky but then-inventive means to overdub in the one-track era. Once he had the basic band track and lead vocal on the first machine, he'd run that through to the second machine while the singers added their harmonies to machine two (listening to a playback in their headphones). If they messed up, all he did was run machine one back from the top through machine two and start the harmonies over again. Everything—the band, lead, and backing vocals—then wound up on machine two.

It took a day or so and we were done. I handed Norman $300 cash for studio time and for his extraordinary patience as engineer and producer. He had needed eight hours to get a two minute-and-two-second A-side out of four half-assed musicians. And then we walked out of there with our master tapes—probably the last group ever to leave Clovis with their masters. After us Norman got smart: he signed people to publishing and recording contracts. When Buddy Holly and the Crickets later recorded there, Petty owned the records and their publishing rights.

Our business partner sent the masters to a pressing plant in St. Louis. It cost $1000 to get a thousand records pressed. We pooled all our money to come up with our half and he came up with the rest. "Party Doll" was the A-side, "I'm Stickin' with You" the B-side. That was all the recording we ever figured on doing.

We took a bunch of our singles to the Dumas music store where Dirt had won his first guitar and told the owner, "Here, see if you can sell these." They sold out like hotcakes.

We took some more singles to KDDD in Dumas, and dropped some off at KZIP and at record stores in Amarillo. When they played it at both stations, records flew out of the stores. It was amazing to see the connection so clearly. We did damn good business, considering that our main distribution system was us selling our singles out of the trunks of our cars. We basically sold out.

But the most important Triple-D record we sent out was the one Dirt got to his sister, Teddie, who lived in New York. She knew the big-time show business operator named Morris Levy.

Levy, a onetime promoter, was an owner of the legendary Bird-land and Roundtable jazz clubs as well as the Gee, Rama, and Tico record labels. He had Latin bands like Tito Puente and rock and roller Frankie Lymon and the Teenagers, whose big hit was "Why Do Fools Fall in Love?" Morris was tied in to New York City concessions and music publishing, and was also thought to have some unsavory connections to the underworld.

I got a call one day from Levy himself at KDDD while I was back home working a shift. He said he was wiring me $1000 and wanted to fly us to New York to discuss buying our masters for a new label named Roulette. I was stunned. It took all day to get the thousand-dollar money order cashed in Dumas because it was probably the biggest one they'd ever had there. Then, the three of us flew TWA to Kansas City and on to New York.

Levy wanted to build up a new rock-and-roll label. We went to his offices in the Brill Building on Broadway and Forty-ninth Street and negotiated for an hour. At about four-thirty on a Friday afternoon he gave us an advance—ten crisp hundred-dollar bills. He told us he had a meeting to go to, said have a nice week-end, we'll finish this negotiation on Monday.

It was a brilliant move: by Monday we didn't have but about forty bucks left and had to accept whatever offer he made. We had stayed in a big hotel, gone to fancy restaurants—tipping generously the whole time of course—and craned our heads up at the skyline, amazed at everything going on around us just like the bunch of hillbilly kids we were.

We closed the deal with Morris and got to work. In all, Morris would pay us $3000 for the Triple-D masters and another $5000 for publishing rights. Our man in the Panhandle got his half, which left us a little something.

Toward the end of 1956 Morris decided to break our single into two records. He put us in the studio with a producer and record-label associate named George Goldner at Bell Sound Studios to cut two B-sides to go with the A-sides. George had good ears and was a respected fifties New York producer. We had a couple of songs we'd been fooling with, so we were ready to go down to Bell Sound with Goldner.

To say we had trouble finding our groove puts it mildly. Whether it was the big-city pressure or his bad syncopation, Buddy froze up behind the mike and could not get it right. You could count it out for Buddy all day long—a-one, anna-two, anna-three, anna-four—but he couldn't find a-one and never came in right. Another problem: the studio was directly over the subway. Every time a train rumbled by, you could hear it on the tape, so a bunch of good takes had to be redone. This just made Buddy more nervous.

I had to step in and sing both B-sides—"My Baby's Gone" for "Party Doll" and "Ever-Lovin' Fingers" for "I'm Stickin' with You." Goldner pumped the echo to it so high on my voice that you could hardly tell it wasn't Buddy, though my voice was deeper and less twangy. When the session was over, Morris realized he hated the group's name—Buddy Knox, Jimmy Bowen, and the Orchids—and told us it would have to change. "You kids go on back to Texas," Morris said, "and we'll take care of that."

When they mailed us our records, I couldn't believe it. "I'm Stickin' with You," was now by Jimmy Bowen with the Rhythm Orchids. The shock wore off, though, and it was a real kick to be on a New York label with our records going out all over the country. "Stickin'" was Roulette 4001, the label's debut release. "Party Doll" was Roulette 4002, by Buddy Knox with the Rhythm Orchids.

In January 1957, Morris flew us in to promote our records. The orchid shirts were history. Morris set up a photo session with the celebrity photographer Bruno of Hollywood. We did our eight-by-ten glossies in black tuxes and red bow ties. (We fought him on the Stetsons and boots.) We were rock-and-roll westerners—not cowboys or rockabillies. While Bruno was shooting at his studio, someone said, "Hey, Bowen, we got Earl Wilson on the phone for you."

"I don't know who Earl Wilson is," I answered to the amazement of everyone at the session. They said Earl Wilson was one of the country's most influential nightlife columnists and that people paid tons of money to get in his "Talk of the Town" column. I'd had no idea. Earl Wilson was never the talk of *our* town in the Panhandle.

Morris hired Hugo & Luigi, who wrote and produced rock songs, to handle A&R (artists and repertoire) for Roulette. Their full names were Hugo Peretti and Luigi Creatore, and they released a few minor singles of their own. They figured they'd cut us just like normal artists, so they optimistically booked us for a three-hour session, imagining we'd lay down three or four finished songs. Having required back-to-back eight-hour marathon sessions in a Clovis garage to cut two sides, we weren't ready for a rushed, three-hour session in a fancy midtown studio.

Hugo and Luigi were truly partners. Their desks faced each other, which helped them made some awful partner decisions together. They weren't the best match for our sound, not to mention our unschooled, instinctive way of doing things. They took us into the vast Columbia Studios, which were big enough to reenact battle scenes from World War II. The control booth was way up in the back behind some glass where you could hardly see it. It felt all disjointed.

We were out of our league. As we arrived, Rosemary Clooney and her world-class orchestra musicians were leaving the studio, making way so that we could use up most of our expensive three hours just tuning our instruments.

We were convinced this wasn't going to work. When we cut "Rock Your Little Baby to Sleep," Buddy got so jammed up, I had to stand next to him and point out the beats so that he could come in right. He had a wonderful in-tune voice and played neat rhythm guitar, but then he'd do a vocal fifty times right and come in too early the fifty-first. You could never take your eye off him for a second—either in the studio or onstage. Now he was coming in before Dirt finished his guitar break, or forgetting to come in at all. I had the solution: "We've got to miss it *with* him."

We got Dirt's break on tape, and Hugo and Luigi simply spliced it in between Buddy's vocals.

It would eventually take us three months before we could find, rehearse, and record enough songs to do an album by Buddy and one by me.

Despite the know-how, fancy equipment, and big-city egos, Hugo & Luigi failed to draw out of us the raw magic that Petty had captured in Clovis. We should have insisted on going back to re-create whatever it was that excited Morris in the first place.

"I'm Stickin' with You" came out at the end of February 1957, and "Party Doll" a week later. That song's lyrics were on the suggestive side for 1957, and had people thinking it was about a whore. *"Well, all I want is a party doll; to come along with me when I'm feelin' wild."* It had lots of echo and a crisp thump from Alldred's makeshift drum kit. Dirt had two electric guitar solos, and Buddy's rockabilly voice broke just right on "be my pa-harty doll" and "run her-her fi-ingers through-hoo his hair." A lot of hooks for two minutes of music.

To our great astonishment "Party Doll" exploded. Many people assumed we were black, which is maybe why Steve Lawrence covered us. Then came covers by Wingy Manone, a one-armed trumpeter, and blues singer Roy Brown.

But only one version would achieve rock-and-roll immortality: "Party Doll" reached No. 1 on *Billboard's* pop chart, on its way to becoming a gold record based on sales of a million units. It was an incredible week: "I'm Stickin' with You" got to No. 14. Incredibly, three decades later, in the mid-eighties, "Party Doll" reached the rare and prestigious "Million Performance" milestone, according to BMI, which tracks radio plays.

There was no turning back. Dirt and I had dropped out of college, Buddy had graduated. We were ready to take the Rhythm Orchids on the road. I was only nineteen, but there was no time to waste: my six-month career as a teenage idol was about to begin.

FOUR

THE RHYTHM ORCHIDS started performing at the top—the legendary Alan Freed shows at the Paramount Theater in Times Square—and worked our way down.

Freed was rock's first famous deejay, the man reputed to have coined the phrase *rock and roll*. Over Easter holiday in 1957, as "Party Doll" and "I'm Stickin' with You" were taking off, we were part of his extravaganza at the Paramount, joining many future giants of rock.

Part of the intense excitement about the Times Square gig was walking there from the President Hotel on Broadway. As we headed toward Forty-second Street, all we saw was cops, a few of them sticking up on horseback, and thousands of kids jamming the sidewalks and spilling into the streets. The streets had been blocked off because of the mob scene. We barely fought our way to our dressing-room entrance.

The Platters were headlining a show that included Frankie Lymon and the Teenagers, the Cadillacs, Joanne Campbell, and many other great names. We came out just before the Platters' finale. It was an unbelievable moment for us—kids grabbing at our legs in the front rows and a packed hall of deafening hysteria. We were so scared, we could hardly start the first song. I sang "I'm Stickin'" and then Buddy sang "Party Doll" and off we went. (For our road gigs, Dave Alldred finally left Clovis and Norman Petty to be our drummer.)

As the crowd screamed for an encore, we were backstage

with Freed going, *"What* encore? We don't *have* an encore." We almost got into a fistfight. But the crowd wouldn't shut up until we came out. We did "Rock Around the Clock."

I could spin my bass, lift it, throw it between my legs, up over my shoulder. But in the frenzy of the encore the rubber tip at the bottom of the metal stand that steadied my bass slid off. Dirt had strayed out in front of me onstage, which he never did. As he backed up, I was doing some hot-dog move with the bass and the spike raked the side of Dirt's leg and nearly nailed his foot to the stage. Blood was coming through Dirt's pant leg—and again I heard Dirt muttering, "You son of a bitch, Bowen, I'm gonna *kill* you."

At the Paramount, we did six or seven shows a day from late morning on. After our first gig we tried to go out and get some lunch and got slammed against the building. Girls were flashing razor blades and scissors to slice off some hair, a piece of ear, clothing, whatever souvenir they could rip off you. We fought our way back in and didn't get back out until nighttime.

Impressed by all the fancy footwork by the Teenagers, Cadillacs, and other doo-wop groups, we had to start jumping around ourselves. But I had a fifty-pound unamplified bass that no one could hear past the first row in that pandemonium. There was no way I could play it for real while spinning and kicking it. So at one point I got the bass player in the pit orchestra to cover my bass parts so that I could do my choreography. When my wife, Ginger, heard this story, she called me the first Milli Vanilli.

We never did get our moves down real well. We once spent weeks working up three-part harmonies for some new song. We rehearsed night after night in motel rooms. Onstage, with only one mike, we had to scoot in real tight for the vocals. The first time we tried it, just as I came roarin' up to the mike for the harmonies, one of the four giant tuning pegs at the top of my bass clocked Dirt right upside the head. He never knew what hit him. He staggered back, sat on his amp, and once again wanted to kill me. "James, you son of a *bitch.*"

Dirt then made me get one of the early Fender electric basses. It not only felt wrong, you could hear everything I played. Big mistake. I always said, "If they quit screaming, we're in trouble." After three days the band just hired a bass player.

By the time Freed staged another show at the Brooklyn Paramount later in 1957, we were headlining above Bo Diddley,

Buddy Holly and the Crickets, the Del Vikings, Little Richard, and Charlie Gracie, whose No. 1 that year was "Butterfly."

Freed wanted us as the finale behind Bo because "Party Doll" was No. 1 and "I'm Stickin'" was a big East Coast hit. I suggested to Freed that he seriously reconsider. "This is my show," he said bluntly. "I know how to schedule these things." I nodded obediently.

Diddley then came out with his raw, electric rhythm guitar and a powerful band that included a maracas player who could shake three or four in each hand. He kept that *chunk-a-chunk-a-chunk-a-CHUNK-CHUNK* groove building until he had whipped the kids into a frenzy and was shaking the Paramount to its foundations. Kids were ripping seats apart and throwing the stuffing all over. They were just going berserk. No way we could follow that.

When Freed announced us, I don't imagine anyone even heard or cared, given the chants of "We want Bo! We Want Bo!"

For the second show Freed tried using Charlie Gracie for the finale, and that didn't go much better. Finally he came around—and let Bo follow *us* for the finale.

We stayed out on the road for weeks at a stretch, traveling mostly by station wagon with a U-Haul trailer. If we had a home base at all, it was the President Hotel on Broadway and Forty-seventh Street in Manhattan, home to dozens of rock and rollers passing through town. The President was located near the studios, across from Mama Leone's and down a block or two from the Brill Building at Forty-ninth, home of the fabled Tin Pan Alley crowd. Great location.

It was a funky old residence hotel. One day you'd come across a kid with a strange name like Ersel Hickey, whose one and only hit would be "Bluebirds Over the Mountain" the next year. Or you'd run into, as I did one night, a short teenage kid who grabbed my arm and asked me for an autograph. "My name is Paul Anka, I'm a songwriter from Canada, and I don't have any place to stay."

Paul was barely sixteen, but he had already been performing in Canada for a few years. He was in town pitching some songs and looking for a record deal. I let him sleep in my bathtub for a couple of nights and agreed to give a brief radio interview with a deejay friend of his back in Toronto, which probably made him seem like a big shot back home. I also took Anka over to Hugo & Luigi, Roulette's A&R wizards. They heard Paul sing a few songs, including something called "Diana"—and passed. "That'll never work, no thank you," they assured him.

We were in a rehearsal studio near Times Square when a young kid breaking into publishing came in and needed a favor. He was Don Kirschner, and, he said, "A buddy and I are cutting a demo around the corner. We need to borrow an acoustic guitar."

Knox loaned Donnie one of his guitars and he invited us stop by the session. Donnie's friend was a good-looking kid named Bobby Darin. He had cut some songs the year before on Decca as the lead for the Jaybirds. Donnie was trying to get Bobby's songs recorded. After getting to know Bobby, I brought him to Hugo & Luigi for an audition. They clearly had no feel for this new young music. They thought Bobby sounded too much like Eddie Fisher. Not long afterward Bobby recorded "Splish Splash," the giant hit that launched his career. When I played Hugo & Luigi some Buddy Holly masters a while later, they complained his sound was "too country." Not many A&R people can boast of passing on Paul Anka, Bobby Darin, *and* Buddy Holly.

Bobby Darin was a supertalent—but also one intense, serious, driven guy. He had more confidence than all four Rhythm Orchids *combined*. He believed he was the greatest thing walkin' and wasn't a damn bit afraid to show it.

A few years later I got to hang out more with Bobby in L.A. He'd come by for what they call "guitar pulls" in Nashville—informal jams where everyone shared guitars, swapped tunes, took turns singing, banged on pots or tabletops with spoons, and rattled maracas. Bobby was a real neat, likable guy, but he always predicted he wasn't destined to live long. "I'm gonna be bigger'n Sinatra before I'm thirty," he'd say. Sadly, though, Bobby died at thirty-six from heart disease dating back to his childhood.

When we went home to Dumas during a break from the road, we were local heroes. We had been on Steve Allen's television show and Ed Sullivan's Sunday night *Toast of the Town*. My stepmother, Frances, was our biggest booster. She answered fan letters and sent out glossies, gave away records to radio stations, and cut off locks of our hair for fan-club members. There were Rhythm Orchids outfits: black tops and orchid skirts for girls, black pants and orchid shirts for boys. Frances hung an Orchids poster on my dad's Golden Hawk when she visited record stores or radio stations.

The highlights of the homecoming were the parade and the

concert at the local theater. Our opening act was Buddy Holly. He was from Lubbock, and was just beginning to make a name for himself all around West Texas. He had been with Decca for a year or so and been to Nashville to record as a trio called the Three Tunes.

Buddy performed some terrific songs that day that perfectly fit our rockabilly sound. Norman Petty then sent us some acetates in New York and, between Knox and myself, figured on cutting "That'll Be the Day," "Maybe Baby," and "Every Day."

Even after Buddy formed another backing trio called the Crickets and began recording in Clovis, we had a loose agreement with him: if nothing happened at Decca, we'd cut his songs with his blessings. But then Petty called sometime later to announce he had been asked to play his Holly masters for Roulette and other labels.

One day Dirt got a call out of the blue from Holly. "Hey, do me a favor," he said. "Please don't do those songs we talked about. I think I've got a deal on Brunswick." We were disappointed, but the right thing was to back off and let Buddy cut them himself. The rest, you could say, is history.

We spent most of the rest of 1957 and almost all of 1958 on the road, playing close to two hundred gigs. At one point, we even lip-synched a couple of songs on a New York City soundstage so we could appear in a feature film called *Jamboree*. On the road, we would share the stage with the likes of Little Richard, Gene Vincent and His Blue Caps, Anka, Connie Francis, Eddie Cochran, Ruth Brown, the Spaniels, the Drifters, Clyde McPhatter, Bobby Rydell, Don and Phil Everly, LaVern Baker, Fats Domino, and, of course, Buddy and the Crickets.

A number of our shows were part of Irving Feld's "The Biggest Show of Stars" tours, grueling, three-month, cross-country campaigns of one-nighters. For the Feld tours a bunch of us were packed inside Greyhound buses. The white kids usually sat in the back. Artists like LaVern Baker were so damn good, if they wanted the front of the bus, that was good enough for me. Altogether we must have had eight or nine acts on these buses. And these seats didn't have dividers. It was more crammed than a schoolbus. We used to hoist Anka up and let him stretch out and sleep in the overhead luggage rack.

Having grown up in a virtually all-white town, I didn't see outright segregation until we got down south on the Feld tour. It never occurred to me *not* to like black people or want to hang out with them. Racial awareness had never soaked in. Being in New York, I was for the first time becoming aware of black people, as well as other ethnic groups and nationalities.

We stayed in cheap motels and hotels. Chuck Berry and Fats Domino were older and wiser and had their own cars. The joke with Chuck was that he had to have his own wheels because he couldn't take underage girls across state lines in a crowded bus.

When we played the East and Northeast, there was no segregation, and all the members of our racially mixed troupe stayed in the same places. It wasn't until we played the Deep South that I saw segregation at work: places where blacks had to eat and sleep in separate facilities.

The first time it happened, I was stunned. We got to some southern city, pulled up to a hotel, and one of the black artists told us, "You guys get off here. We can't stay here." That seemed so weird. So a couple of us said, "Well, fuck it, we'll just go stay with you guys." And they said, "No, you can't do that either. You really better get off here."

Now when we got to San Francisco, we all said, "Screw it, we'll stay where you stay" and we did all get rooms in a hotel in a black neighborhood. But no one was going to get shot there.

My very first trip to Nashville in 1957 proved rather prophetic. The Rhythm Orchids were booked at the Grand Ole Opry when it was still at historic Ryman Auditorium just off Broadway. Right away I was introduced to the difference between the worlds of country and rock. When we arrived at the artists' entrance, a guard saw our drummer with all his gear and said, "Whoa, we don't *have* drums in the Grand Ole Opry." They refused to let him in the door. I argued, saying, "Well, now, wait a minute here. See, the solo in my big hit single, 'I'm Stickin' with You,' is a drum solo." That at least got us in the door; as a compromise they put a blind up all around him so that the audience couldn't see him—or hear him. And they only let him play a snare. The same uptight approach to making hillbilly music was still in place two decades later when I came to town to produce records.

Most of us white acts were show business novices with little sense of showmanship. The great, great black acts were almost all older, veteran performers who had played their hearts out for years in relative obscurity on the R&B "chitlin' circuit." And that music sounded great with a big orchestra to drive it.

There were some exceptions. Buddy Holly could hold a crowd with just his voice, those songs, and his guitar, bass, and drums. He was exceptional. The Everlys could capture a hall just with beautiful harmonies and their big Gibson acoustics. Eddie Cochran was a real good showman—a cocky kid with his big twangy guitar sound on hits like "Summertime Blues," "Sittin' in the Balcony," and "C'mon Everybody."

We liked hanging out with Eddie. We thought *we* drank a lot back in Dumas because we drank every weekend. Then we saw Eddie drink every *day*. That amazed us. We could barely remember our songs *sober*, and not at all if we were drunk. Plus I might have maimed or killed Dirt with my bass if I was drinking.

Eddie, though, could swig straight from the bottle in the wings as they were announcing his name, toss the bottle away, and stride on out there, playing the hell out of that guitar. Like Bobby Darin, Eddie had a brooding, fatalistic, destructive streak. He was always muttering how he wasn't going to live long. That seemed so weird to me, but he seemed to *know*. I asked him once why he drank so much and he snarled, "Why not? It's all one big party. I'm not makin' it past thirty anyway." (Eddie never even made it to twenty-five: he was killed in a car crash that also injured Gene Vincent in England in 1960.)

Most of us white acts, frankly, weren't that good. But virtually every black act that broke through was wonderful. Lloyd Price had his own band and just set the place on fire. Chuck Berry was mesmerizing when he started singing and duckwalking his guitar all over the place. You never wanted to follow Chuck on-stage—or get too close to him offstage. He was extremely aloof. If we played twenty shows with him, I don't imagine we exchanged four words. But he was smart. He collected his cash, he opened, he got off, he split.

LaVern Baker, Clyde McPhatter, James Brown, and Ruth Brown were blues greats who could blow you away with tight big-band arrangements. These artists had been around for years, unable to break into mainstream radio because they performed "race music." So they paid their dues in chitlin'-circuit clubs.

When rock and roll put them before big, racially mixed audiences they already knew how to work a crowd. They were electrifying. We were along on these tours because we had hit records, but these artists had never drawn crowds based on record sales or airplay. Instead, they were sensational, seasoned, talented performers whose gifts were only now being showcased as rock and roll.

To hear the difference, all you had to do was listen to the covers white artists did of some of this great black music. Was there any comparison between "Tutti Frutti" and "Long Tall Sally" by Pat Boone versus Little Richard's originals? Pat's "Ain't That a Shame" and Fats Domino's original of the same song? The black artists would cut a great song, and the white acts would have the big hit. But onstage the black artists blew everyone away. It was like a glass of milk versus a shot of whiskey.

Who wanted to follow a string of wonderful doo-wop showmen in pastel-colored tuxes like the Cadillacs, the Teenagers, Silhouettes, and so on? They'd come out dancing, doing splits, spins, jumps, and steps to hits like "Speedoo" or "Why Do Fools Fall in Love?" Then we'd walk on out there and barely shake our scrawny white butts. As showmen we were uniformly mediocre to awful.

There was no more spellbinding artist than Little Richard. I admit I was scared to death of him from the time we heard he was gay. They didn't teach you much in West Texas about that, except that a "queer" was something you must not be. A queer was someone who didn't wear a football uniform. Little Richard may have worn shoulder pads, but they sure weren't part of any football uniform.

The idea of his being black *and* gay was too much. We didn't know how to walk by him backstage, didn't know how to say hello. Richard of course never forced himself on us, but we didn't know for sure that he *wouldn't*. In our naïveté and ignorance we were keeping a certain distance.

But we were in awe of him the second he stepped into the lights. Richard was a master showman, one of the great innovators, and a key link between the roots of R&B and rock and roll. He came out dressed in padded, sequined red or chartreuse suits with jewelry hanging off him, his face all painted up pretty, hair piled high and glistening, his eyes glaring out from under all that eye shadow. He was just so cool and outrageous. He could pound that piano and shriek like nobody else, plus he was backed by a sensational hot R&B band called the Upsetters. They worked his crowd into a frenzy with a brief set before he even came out. We just stood off in the dark and watched.

Richard was apparently no less a crowd-pleaser offstage. Indeed he flaunted his eccentricity. He often had a gorgeous blond mulatto girl with him. Seemed Richard liked nothing more than to have somebody else screw her so that he could watch and jerk off. Right there that was about three or four things goin' on we hadn't even known *existed* back home.

And yet the boys who hipped us to what Richard was up to were West Texans themselves—Buddy and the Crickets. Richard made no secret of watching other men with Angel. In fact, in his memoir, Richard told of the time Buddy was still in the act backstage at the Paramount when his name was announced to come out. He barely had enough time to zip up his pants before hitting the spotlights, or so Richard claimed.

Fats Domino was on the other end of the spectrum of excitability. If James Brown's show climaxed with him throwing himself off the stage into the crowd, the excitement with Fats was whether he'd ever get himself *onstage*. We did one tour with Fats, and half the time he just wouldn't come out of his backstage room. His band would have to go out first and heat up the crowd because he was never on time. Someone would go knocking on his door, calling out, "Fats, Fats? You ready? You're on."

Fats was one of the most reclusive people we ever came across. Didn't talk to anybody. His songwriting partner, Dave Bartholomew, talked to us instead. One time the promoter gave the Fat Man a new record player as a sweetener just to make sure he'd come out. They would beg him, coax him, pound on the door, tell him the crowd's going crazy. And Fats would be in there fooling with his new record player or new watch, doing his thing. Was it all just showbiz? A way to whip up a crowd? Bad blood with the promoter? Was he bored after being on the road so long? It was all so mysterious. We had seen so little of the world before being thrown into this exotic new wonderland of rock. This sort of stuff amazed us. Hell, we were just glad to be there.

But Fats's show was worth the wait. He'd amble out with his trademark flattop hair and diamond rings, sit at the piano, and kick into "Blueberry Hill" or "Blue Monday" and it was all over. Once Fats got into his bluesy New Orleans groove, he could bring the house down as well as anyone.

Our main booking agent, who never saw us work, must have thought we were black. Why else book us a number of times into all-black venues? If closing a show behind Bo or Richard was ludicrous before midtown or midwestern crowds, it was absurd in the heart of the black part of town.

We once drove through Detroit's "ghetto" until we found the marquee with Buddy Knox, Jimmy Bowen, and the Rhythm Orchids on top—and Little Richard's name just below. I knew right there we were in a bad spot. I went straight to the black promoter: "I know we're headliners here, but we cannot close this show after Little Richard. There's been some mistake."

The guy looked us over and, being a reasonable man who did not want to see his hall destroyed any more than we did, nodded. "I see what you mean."

"Maybe we should just go out there first and open." Not a bad idea, he agreed.

Before the curtain went up, I peeked out and saw that we were the only whites around and had to face an audience primed for serious R&B. The moment they saw a quartet of white kids and their rockabilly gear, the energy of the place sagged with a collective gasp of disbelief. I decided to be straight with them and cut everyone's losses. "I'm sure you're as surprised as we are. There's no way we're following Little Richard. Trust me. He's just too great." There were shouts of approval. "So we'll do our records and get outta here so you can have a great evening."

It had to be the most rushed set in rock history. I sang my hit—to polite applause. Buddy did his hit—to polite applause. And I figured, quit while you're ahead. "Thank you very much," I said, and we hauled ass. Then I watched Richard's set. I was convinced, after hearing him rip through "Long Tall Sally" and "Lucille," they'd have not stuck around for "Hula Love" and "Rock Your Little Baby to Sleep."

We got booked into all kinds of strange places—from the odd college campus jazz festival to the dilapidated "polka palace" ballrooms of the Midwest. We often seemed to come in right after Gene Vincent. These ballroom owners couldn't believe what their quaint Old World way of life was coming to when the rock kids showed up. They hated our music and couldn't stand how loud it was. They usually liked us, though, particularly after Vincent and His Blue Caps. We were choirboys next to them. They were like a gang of grunge hoodlums who hadn't bathed for days on end and smelled it. Taking one whiff of a dressing room, we always knew when the Blue Caps had come through town right before us. And they were rowdy. We showed up at one ballroom and parts of the stage were boarded up and under repair. As we heard it, Vincent's drummer stood up to pound his drums and kept jumping so hard, he went clear through the stage into the basement.

We did one tour in rural western Canada in a place called Dawson Creek, which was three-quarters mean-looking, hard-drinking lumberjacks. Buddy had decided to get himself some .38s to practice quick-draw out there on the frontier. The show was a nightmare—a fight broke out every five minutes, and they kept asking for songs like "Tennessee Waltz." Those boys were seriously out of the loop. We'd fake the lyrics and finesse the rest because we had a general feeling they'd kill us if we didn't honor their requests.

They paid us in silver dollars, and as we were fixin' to leave, some of the lumberjacks lined up to watch us. We thought maybe they'd like the coins back—a couple grand in silver. So Buddy strapped on his gun—as if that would intimidate anyone. But it worked. They snarled at us but let us go with our loot.

With constant touring and promotion, we kept "Party Doll" on the charts for almost half a year. "Rock Your Little Baby to Sleep" made Top 20. We got lucky again when Buddy's "Hula Love" was a long-running Top 10 hit—though it wasn't near the record "Party Doll" had been.

After that kind of takeoff, it seemed we were already peaking. My follow-up singles to "I'm Stickin' with You" were the B-side, "Ever-Lovin' Fingers," and "Warm Up to Me Baby," which Kirschner cowrote with a friend of mine named Lou Stallman. Neither of them even cracked the Top 50. A year later I tried to get a hit with the old standard, "By the Light of the Silvery Moon," which I had played on Dick Clark's *American Bandstand*. It was the last record I charted, and it didn't get any higher than No. 50.

Then Buddy's luck on radio waned too. His single, "Swingin' Daddy," didn't push past No. 80 in February 1958. The best either of us did was when his song "Somebody Touched Me" almost made it into *Billboard*'s Top 20 in August. That was the final time a member of the Rhythm Orchids would appear on the pop charts.

It had been one big year-and-a-half-long party. What had begun with my ukulele and Dirt's music-store guitar had lifted us out of the Panhandle and carried us into the Paramount, into the eye of the rock-and-roll hurricane sweeping America.

It had been an incredible ride since cutting those first tracks with Norman Petty in Clovis. Now, with our record sales and airplay starting to fade, it was a good time to take a look at our royalties situation—and discover how the record industry *really* worked.

FIVE

MORRIS LEVY could be one charming charac-
ter—when he was on your side and using his influence and connections for you. But he was also someone you didn't want
turning *against* you.

Morris was in our corner at the start. This became apparent
when I was in Boston on a promotion tour to work our singles.
Before Roulette's promo guy called on a radio station he handed
me a brown bag: "Take Bob's lunch in to him."

"Bob" was a local deejay. I had done this a couple of other
times, but it didn't hit me until then: *This is the lightest damn
sandwich I ever carried in a paper bag.* Bob took the bag and nodded with an awkward, "Uhhh, yeah, thanks." He couldn't have
been too hungry because he never opened the bag or looked inside.

What makes one record a killer and another a stiff remains
one of the great mysteries in music. But back in the mid-fifties it
definitely had something to do with how much "lunch" deejays
were getting from their friendly promo men. There have been
record people whose "golden ears" can hear a new track or an
unknown voice and break a monster hit. But long before computerized SoundScan, before labels spent millions on focus
groups and market research, one factor in the mix never failed:
payola.

The late-fifties' payola scandal ruined the career of Alan
Freed, among others, and made it more difficult—but hardly impossible—for promotion, marketing, and other executives to buy

the airwaves and record charts. The scandal made it illegal to offer cash for airplay. Until then it had been wide open.

If you "bought" one power jock in, say, Detroit, that was all
you might need, because his rivals would jump on the record
just to keep up. A small-label guy could get a hit record then for
between $5,000 and $7,500. Sometimes you'd only need to go to
four guys at key stations who could "break" records. Freed, king-
pin of radio in America's top market, was the main man for anyone looking to break a record. Morris was Freed's manager.

Roulette's promo guys told all sorts of tales out of school on
Morris, or Moishe, as he was also known with a mixture of rev-
erence and fear. Moishe made no secret of the fact that he paid
to get our first two records played. This was not long before the
congressional hearings. It took a while for such unseemly facts
of life to sink in.

But sink in they did. It wasn't only cash. Levy got at least one
key deejay in his pocket by building him a swimming pool. But
when Morris told him, "Play this record," the jock wouldn't go
along. He still considered himself free to decide his playlist—and
flaunted his independence to Morris. Big mistake.

"What're ya gonna do—take back my pool?" he asked defi-
antly. Morris didn't drain or pave over the pool. But as we heard
it, in hushed terms, he did persuade the jock that the song was in
fact worth some airplay. Became a Top 20 hit in fact. Morris simply must have told him it was time to sink or swim.

Through the years, influence peddling in music has taken on
less obvious forms, particularly in pop and rock, where the
stakes (and costs) are so much higher than in country and where
there is so much more money floating around: lavish gifts,
drugs, travel, women. All the usual suspects. Congress, the Federal Communications Commission, and the FBI have long
sought to keep things clean and on a level playing field. But that's
an elusive goal in an industry where the line—often a white pow-
dery one—between business and pleasure is notoriously difficult
to define.

(Bob came through the fifties unscathed. He was a great guy
with an easygoing sense of humor—and a huge future ahead of
him in the business as one of pop's movers and shakers. Our
"lunch" began a long personal and professional relationship that
has lasted through the years.)

If the Rhythm Orchids got to the top, in part, with payola, it was going to take a lot more than a few funny lunch bags and backyard pools to keep us there. Worse, when the time came to count up our royalties, we discovered the hard way that Morris Levy wasn't our biggest ally anymore.

Our deal with Morris was for 2 percent of 85 percent of gross sales. Despite considering Morris a friend and mentor, he had this irritating aversion to paying royalties. "You want royalties?" he was fond of saying. "Then go to England!" All anyone sold then was singles, not albums. One hundred thousand albums was huge—so there was never much profit anyhow. But like any artist who hits No. 1, we became a valuable commodity.

That's when other managers and agents come out of the woodwork, warning you that "your people" are screwing you and you'd be better off with *them*. We had had such incredible beginners' luck, our feeling was, Why fix it if it ain't broke?

But we were more broke than we knew. We were counting on very big royalty checks, even with 45s selling for 98 cents. I knew "Party Doll" had sold 1.2 million singles, and "Stickin'" was up to 900,000. But the royalty statement reflected payments on only 600,000 copies of "Party Doll" and 300,000 copies of "Stickin'." Even we knew that the difference between royalties on 2 million records and royalties on less than 1 million was a good chunk of change.

That's when we started listening to the "they're screwin' you" types. We were also advised that it was against the law for the same individual to sign you to publishing, recording, management, and agency contracts. Being surrounded in such "personal services" situations was illegal in New York.

By this time Roulette was hot. Hugo and Luigi came through for Morris by signing Jimmie Rodgers, whose huge hits were "Honeycomb" and "Kisses Sweeter Than Wine." I visited Morris at the label's new offices in Hell's Kitchen.

"So, kid, what can I do for you?" he asked. Morris gave off an aura of supreme confidence and power. He was a record mogul riding a hot streak, he had two hot nightspots, and he had real power. Besides, he had two very large, very silent men with him.

I got my nerve up. "Well, Morris, our royalty statements weren't that big. But the main thing is, as I understand it, it's against the law for you to have us signed to record, publishing, management, and agency all at one time."

Morris, a rather stout, imposing presence even though he was probably only in his early thirties, could look and dress like an underworld boss from Central Casting. When he saw I was done, I exhaled and waited. "Is that all that's botherin' ya, kid?"

I shrugged. With that he opened a desk drawer and pulled out a thick stack of papers. "*This* here is your management contract," he announced, and ripped that sucker in his large thick hands, tossing the ripped deal in the trash. Then he looked back to me and asked calmly, "Now, anything else I can do for you?"

I was half-scared, half-amazed by what had just gone down. And very impressed by his strength. I didn't *get* what was going on, but it occurred to me that our "discussion" of the royalty situation was over and that I was about to wear out my welcome. I figured: *Don't get greedy. You're out of the management deal, you've achieved that much. Now get lost!*

"I think that'll actually do it for today," I muttered. Then I stood, turned, and got the hell out, nodding nervously to the two big boys as I made for the door.

I was then told by music insiders that our Roulette deal had not been sanctioned by the American Federation of Musicians because our back end was low even by the harsh standards of early rock. We were advised to leave Roulette and sign elsewhere for more money. We were hot.

Dirt and I visited the A.F. of M. and learned that my sources' hunch was dead-on: "We absolutely do not condone this deal," a union guy told us. "We consider it invalid because your piece is simply too low. We will back you up completely."

We walked out feeling light-headed, optimistic, ready to break free of Morris and clean up big-time. Our elation was short-lived. The union guy called me a day or so later. "I got bad news. We can't go into civil court on this and interfere with this contract. You are in fact under contract to Roulette."

We were crushed—and still didn't get what was going on. Acting on another piece of advice, I hired a lawyer and showed him all the relevant papers. An hour later he concluded, "Open-and-shut case. For one thing you and Lanier were minors when the contracts were signed. And they're not fair. You have not been accounted for properly. Don't sweat it. This is easy."

Again I walked out elated, only to be brought down a day later. "Please come by and pick up your papers," the lawyer said. "I'm sorry, I'll be unable to represent you in this matter."

In my naïveté I figured: Just a scheduling conflict. I picked up the papers, found a second lawyer, then a third, and both times was told, "Open-and-shut." Then *they* bailed out.

When the last one called a few days later to summon me to his office, I blew up. "This is the third damned time this has happened. What the hell's goin' on here?"

"Listen, kid, I got a house, a good career, family to support, you know what I mean? Just please get your papers and get outta my office. Can't help ya."

As it dawned on my dumb hillbilly head, I started shaking so hard, I could barely push the elevator button.

A short while later I ran into a music-industry guy named Tommy V., who managed Jackie Wilson and ran Dahl Records. Tommy had heard about our efforts to get off Roulette and assured me: No problem. I'd heard that before, and all I had now was problems. Tommy figured he was going to take us to MGM, a major label that paid legit, and get us $50,000 to sign and 7 or so percent—a much bigger deal than we had.

"I can handle Levy," he said. "I'm not scared of Moishe." Tommy set up a meeting at a lawyer's office on Fifth Avenue.

I showed up alone, because Buddy Knox had gone into the army to serve his six-month ROTC stint at Fort Knox—a nice touch, I always thought—and Dirt had the flu. As I waited outside the office, off the elevator came Morris Levy flanked by two immense guys with overcoats. They went right into the lawyer's office. Next Tommy bolted from the elevator, flanked by two more immense guys. With a cocky shrug and a wave of the hand he indicated to me that there was absolutely nothing to worry about. Open-and-shut case. And they went into the office.

I was still waiting to be called inside when yet another trio came out of the elevator—a short, stocky Italian fellow whose name turned out to be Sonny, and a third pair of immense guys who didn't say nothin' to nobody. They just walked in.

Finally I was summoned. I took a quick look around. It hit me: I was on trial. Sonny was the judge behind the desk with his guys; Morris's team was over here, Tommy's boys over there. Everybody talked rough just like Moishe.

Sonny laid out the basics of the situation as he saw it; then Morris and Tommy talked, and I answered a few questions. I sensed some heat between Tommy and Morris as they argued the case before Sonny, the Don Corleone role in this courtroom drama.

Sonny sat back, looking side to side at the two teams, nodding silently, taking it all in, the scales of justice beginning to tip back and forth in his brooding head. I sat there amazed, soaking it all up, finding it hard to believe that only a year or so ago my idea of getting into trouble was stuffing coeds' panties into my bass at W.T. What was unsettling was that I had started out in this gangster movie as the plaintiff against Morris Levy but had somewhere along the way been recast as the defendant. The script was pretty much what you'd expect.

Morris: "This is my act, see, the Rhythm Orchids. I signed these kids, spent thousands on 'em, we got a contract."

Tommy: "Yeah, but Moishe ain't payin' 'em proper, ya see, he ain't takin' good care of these kids."

After closing arguments Judge Sonny eased back, looked at me, and waved me away: "Kid, you can leave. You'll hear from us."

I was gone. I hit the street runnin' and went back to the President Hotel and just sat there on the edge of the bed trying to figure out what the hell had gone on.

When the verdict was handed down, Tommy lost, I lost, Moishe won, and we stayed with Roulette. I didn't see Tommy again for eight or nine years. When I ran into him at a party in Los Angeles, even a brief, superficial chat made him uncomfortable. My assumption is that he had been warned to "never go near these kids again"—and he took it literally.

Levy must have gotten a kick out of all this, seeing us as dumb Texas kids. It probably irritated him some that we wanted out of Roulette and bitched about the royalties, so he beat us at hardball. He knew we didn't know what the hell we were doing.

I thought I had one more card to play against Morris—the chief of police down in Dumas, Texas. Levy took the trouble, my father likes to recall, of calling him and inviting him up to New York to discuss our situation. His hope was that my dad would talk some sense into us and get us off Morris's back.

My dad arrived in the city wearing his on-duty brown sheriff's pants, big Stetson hat, and cowboy boots. He didn't bring his piece. My dad did not love New York with all those tall buildings. He felt smothered by the congestion, the noise, the attitude, and the towering skyline all around him. As he observed, "Damn sun never does come up here, does it? It's always covered or blocked."

He went straight to Morris's office for a tense showdown with the slick mogul who was giving his son a hard time. As soon as my father walked in, he noticed a checkerboard. It so happened that my dad, being a checkers fiend, got to talking checkers with Morris, and before anyone could say "royalty" or "contract" or "two percent," they threw themselves into an intense marathon game of checkers behind closed doors that went on for three hours.

At one point, after telling my father how the music business worked and how much money the label had invested to break us, Morris offered a bet: Roulette Records for Dumas, Texas. This was seductive, high-rolling Morris at his best. What an image: my dad running a rock-and-roll label, Morris running Dumas. They just had themselves the *best* time. Then Morris sprang for lunch at one of his regular midtown joints. Schmoozed the hell outta Asa.

"I think you're gonna have to stay with this guy," my dad said when he came back. He was no help to me, but that was Morris. A charmer who never lost in a New York City court of law.

Morris had all our original publishing rights for twenty-six years before they reverted back to us. For the longest time I didn't get any publishing royalties. But in the late sixties I started to get checks for $250 to $400 two or three times a year. Usually, a detailed royalty statement comes with a check, with a break-down showing how X or Y amounts were generated by such and such a song or source. It was Morris's own quirky way of doing things that our checks never bore any such documentation. He seemed to get a kick out of sending us only the check, or a check wrapped in a blank piece of paper. That was just his way of com-municating with us.

I once found two checks inside. The top one was for $1,250. I noticed that the signature in the lower right corner had been torn off. Behind the first check was another, signed, intact, for $250. I knew exactly what happened: Morris probably had a new, overworked accountant who had mistakenly written the first check for $1,250. While signing, Morris noticed the error and tore his name off. He signed the correct check and included both, just for laughs, so that I'd see how he almost screwed him-self out of $1,000.

Morris got our masters and publishing for a total of $8,000. "Party Doll" was probably worth $400,000 in publishing alone. If we'd have been more experienced we would have kept the pub-lishing and made a lease deal for the masters. But we didn't have a strong negotiating position: No one else had wanted our mas-ters. All the majors had passed on us or not responded. Dot Records even sent a letter saying "Party Doll" was obscene.

What was obscene was the amount of money Morris Levy made off us. Yet without Morris, his lunch bags, swimming pools, and connections, we'd have likely never had our No. 1 hit record.

•

In the end I hired an aggressive music-industry lawyer named Marty Machat, who had worked for James Brown and knew his way around the business. He managed to negotiate a little more money and avoid a costly lawsuit we would never have won.

It was time for us to move beyond the madness with Morris, get on with our lives, and make some more music.

SIX

ONE OF THE MAIN REASONS we got into the music business was to get girls. Once we were teen idols and could get them anytime we wanted, we had to figure out ways of *avoiding* them. One of the more effective ways, it turned out, was getting married.

On the road we often had to come and go through underground tunnels or side and back entrances to hide from the insane crush of hysterical fans. That madness came with the territory.

Once free of Dumas, the rest of the world was so much *looser*. According to the twisted values where we grew up, it was cool to get laid on a one-night stand with a stranger; but if you loved someone, you couldn't have sex until you got married. The road was a whole other world.

We had all the gorgeous, willing young girls we could ever dream of—a new name and face in every city. These girls were all so much more knowledgeable—and direct—than any we'd seen back home. We were kids in the candy store—and back then we didn't even worry about cavities.

Our worst fear wasn't AIDS but a paternity suit. We all managed to dodge that bullet. I had a close call. I got a knock at the door of my room at the Forest Hotel in New York a couple weeks after a gig in the Northeast. Standing there was a stunning young girl I'd partied with after that gig. She had come a long way and she seemed distraught. I asked her in.

"I'm pregnant with your baby," she announced tearfully. Now, she'd also told me she had been sleeping her way through the Top 20 artists as they came through town. I convinced her that she'd be better off telling her story to one pop star in particular- whose hits she really liked. "Listen, my career's probably a one- hit thing," I said. "I may not be around that long and don't have that much money. He's a *great* singer with a *tremendous* night- club act. You'd be much better off going after him than me."

It took me about an hour, but she finally agreed. When she left my room, I fainted.

Our real concern wasn't even fathering a groupie's baby, but being old enough to be a groupie's father. Our drummer, Dave Alldred, had a thing for younger girls. Dave messed up big-time when we went home to Dumas for a gig. He hooked up with a very sexy, precocious teenager who happened to be a family neighbor. She looked quite a few years older. Not a smart move, considering my dad was chief of police. Her father was in an up- roar and wanted to nail Dave's ass. Fortunately, that never hap- pened. Soon after, Dave left the band and formed Dicky Doo and the Don'ts.

We attracted all different kinds. Dirt, being an electric-guitar player standing a little farther back, could pick 'em out better. Dirt always got the sultry, oversexed, goofy ones, who were sometimes as *married* as they were sultry.

Dirt once hooked up with a groupie in New York who roughed him up worse than any Texas high-school linebacker. She came backstage after a New York show and grabbed on to Dirt and didn't let him go for days. She was a tall, Irish, womanly model. And someone else's model wife. Dirt and I had two little beds in our room at the President, and Knox and the drummer had a room next door. After losing track of Dirt, I was sitting up in bed one night and heard the key nervously scraping around the lock. I realized it was Dirt fumbling to get in. He burst in, huffin' and puffin', shut the door, leaned his back against it, and said, "If a woman shows up here and if you let her in, I'll kill you."

Dirt staggered to his bed and gingerly lifted off his shirt. His back looked like he'd been mauled by a tiger at the damn zoo. She was a wild one.

Knox, being the blond-haired lead vocalist, and I seemed to attract the wholesome, slightly older girl-next-door types. And for some reason I was the Rhythm Orchid who also attracted the gay-next-door type.

After one of our shows at the Brooklyn Paramount, Dirt handed me a fan letter left for me backstage. I read it aloud standing next to him. It was from a fan with a mad crush on me. Then I got to the bottom, where it was signed, "I love you, Bruce." "Aaagghhhh!" I screamed, dropping the note. I was shocked.

When Dirt, Buddy, and I left the theater to go to our hotel nearby, we got a few blocks before I sensed someone following us. I turned quickly and saw a man a few years older than us and knew right away it was Bruce. We all kept walking and didn't know what to do. Then I wheeled around and tore after him, chasing him up the street like a mad dog, with Dirt workin' him over verbally right behind me. Bruce disappeared into the night. It was a dumb way to handle that situation, but as with Little Richard, we just didn't understand gays, and I didn't know any better.

After three consecutive one-nighters around Washington State, we had a fourth show in a large armory. While I was singing my hit song, I looked over and saw Dirt, Knox, and the drummer grinning and cracking up. They almost had to quit playing, they were coming so unglued.

Dirt nodded down toward the front rows, and when I fixed my eyes there, I saw what they found so damn amusing: against odds I'd conservatively put at 10 million to one, each of the girls who had partied with me the three previous nights in three towns were all standing in front of the stage. They couldn't have known each other, but had followed us all over the state, winding up shoulder-to-shoulder, bouncing, clapping, singing along to "I'm Stickin' with You"—and these three apparently were.

I broke into a sweat. My anxiety got worse backstage. Those sons of bitches in my band didn't help me either. They wanted to see me squirm and lie to finesse my way out of this jam. As the girls approached me backstage, the guys locked me out of the dressing room. It didn't take long for each girl to figure out I knew the two others. I felt awful, but managed to double-talk my way out of the mess. That was one night I was happy to spend alone.

Talking our way out of tight spots with groupies was one thing; getting Uncle Sam off our backs was another. Toward the end of 1958, Knox, who had spent enough years in ROTC at West Texas to come out of there a damn *general*, spent six months at Fort Knox. He learned to shoot guns, march, spit-shine his shoes, drive tanks. Then Dirt was called up for six months' active duty with the National Guard at Fort Chaffee, Arkansas. The idea behind ROTC and the Guard was to stay out of Korea.

There were some other major changes that brought our life in the fifties' fast lane to a crawl: first I got married, and then Knox married his girlfriend, Glenda.

My first bride was Darlene Enlow and she was one beautiful girl. I met her at Petty's studio in Clovis, where I had gone to cut some tracks on my own after we dumped Hugo and Luigi. Petty was also recording a Dallas band called the Big Beats, whose lead singer was a young Trinidadian named Trini Lopez. The Big Beats had been talking about getting rid of Trini because of his accent. They were also my backing band for these sessions. When an instrumental of theirs became a theme for *American Bandstand*, they voted Trini out because they were going to make it as an instrumental group. Having also asked me to record some vocals with them, they then decided not to use me either.

I suddenly had too much time on my hands. Norman had added a little apartment to the back of the studio with a couch, TV, kitchen, and bed for musicians camped out in Clovis. Darlene came from around Kansas City, but we met at Petty's because she was dating the Big Beats' sax player. She had nothing to do while they were in the studio, and for that matter neither did I. So we got to hanging out and getting to know each other.

Darlene was the ultimate fifties girl. A gorgeous, shapely blond baton twirler from the heartland—part Marilyn Monroe pinup bombshell, part wholesome beauty-pageant angel. Oh, God, was she perfect. Darlene had the perfect face, perfect hair, perfect body, a woman about my age. The works. And she was no groupie. I was hooked—and ready.

After Clovis I sensed the sax player's days with Darlene were numbered. I split for the road and she went home, but I was soon rerouting myself all across America to see her. I only needed three or four visits before deciding we should elope to Oklahoma or Arkansas, where you didn't need a blood test and a week's wait. It never occurred to us that age mattered.

Darlene said yes. I was ecstatic. We headed south for what my dad might have called a "grab and run" marriage.

I couldn't get there fast enough—but I was actually a few weeks early. When I got into Oklahoma, I woke up the guy who was supposed to put it together for us. That's when he broke it to me that eloping was illegal unless the man was twenty-one. I was just short of my twenty-first birthday. Darlene was eighteen. So we drove across the border into Arkansas and woke up the justice of the peace of some small town. He told us the same thing. Feeling dejected, we drove back to Kansas City, where I bit the bullet and went along with a big church wedding, just what her mother wanted.

Darlene's mom, one of those fifties mothers who lived her whole life through her beautiful daughter, didn't care for me at all. I wasn't settled down, I was an itinerant musician, a far cry from what she had in mind for her girl, and she was hung up on what her neighbors would think. But there wasn't a whole lot she could do. Agreeing to a big church wedding was the least *I* could do to make things a little easier for her to accept.

The day came and, so help me God, one whole side of that church was filled with her people and the only one I had on my side was my best man, Dirt.

I was too dumb to notice, but God always sent me a sign when I was about to marry the wrong woman. Dirt and I were off in an anteroom as the organ played. Just before heading down the aisle, I bent down to tie my shoes and the back seam ripped down the middle of my britches. We hustled around and found a couple of safety pins to keep it mostly closed. It was a bit breezy back there, but those old tux tails kept everything nice and covered.

Darlene and I drove off, tin cans dragging behind, for a week's honeymoon in Lake of the Ozarks. Nomad that I was, I had made no reservations. We must have stopped at fifteen motels before we got a cabin around the crack of dawn. We were both so exhausted, we stumbled in and crashed. Not exactly your dream wedding night.

Looking back on it, I think all young couples should be given a step-by-step instructional brochure when taking vows—information on how to make a marriage work. Hell, they give you one with VCRs and lawnmowers. Neither of us had the slightest idea of what to do *with* each other, *to* each other, *for* each other. For both of us the honeymoon was a letdown, a far cry from the incredible fantasy we projected. Before we could figure anything out, it was time to hit the road again.

After Dirt began his National Guard stint, Buddy left Fort Knox and married his girlfriend, Glenda. It was our impression that Glenda put the idea in Buddy's head that he was good enough to go solo. Anyway, a short time later the Orchids' partnership started to weaken. Then Buddy and Glenda flew into New York, where they visited our accountant, Allen Klein (of future Beatles fame), and cleaned out our joint bank account of some ten thousand dollars. Buddy must have felt entitled to it, since he was the best singer. Then they had their honeymoon.

Things never really got back on track for us. Dirt got done with the National Guard and he and Buddy resumed working together on the road for a couple of tours. Knox continued to record for Roulette as a solo.

Meanwhile I had to eat, had to try to make a go of it with my new wife. A promoter out of Minneapolis named T. B. Scarning, who had done some early bookings for us, got me into some of the midwestern ballrooms we'd played. Through the end of 1958 and early 1959, he put me on the road with the Big Beats, whose sax player had moved on after Darlene to a new girlfriend. They'd open the show and back me as the headliner. It was no big deal having him around us, and we all got along okay. It's amazing what you can cope with when you're hungry.

T.B. was a great character. He looked like Peter Falk's Columbo, with a long brown trenchcoat over a funky old pin-striped blue suit, an old dirty shirt, and a tie hanging out. One mystery I never solved was how he conned me into copromoting a series of shows by "The Man in Black," Johnny Cash.

It was the first part of 1959 and I was based out of Minneapolis. T.B. got me to put up twenty grand of my own money, which was about all I had, and he put up twenty grand. He booked Cash, Johnny Horton, and a couple other acts for a half-dozen shows, kicking off in Fargo, North Dakota.

"This man is a star, he'll be a sellout," ol' T.B. said. How could he not? Cash had been on a hot streak since "I Walk the Line," his 1956 Sun Records rockabilly classic, stayed at No. 1 for six weeks. In 1958, Cash's "Ballad of a Teenage Queen" was No. 1 for ten weeks, and "Guess Things Happen That Way" for eight. The Orchids had done a couple of shows with Cash and Carl Perkins on the early rock circuit, but Johnny was real shy and aloof and hard to hang out with. But he did a killer show.

Johnny had just left Sun for Columbia and hit big with "Don't Take Your Guns to Town," which was No. 1 for six weeks. So it was a strong bill, especially since Horton's "The Battle of New Orleans" would stay at No. 1 for *ten weeks* in the spring. We couldn't miss.

There was just one problem. The son of a bitch in black never showed. I was off being a rock star in Quincy, Illinois, when I came off the stage and phoned T.B. to see how we did in Fargo. "Cash didn't show," he said, "and we had to refund all the money. You lose your deposit on the hall and the advertising money."

Talk about being Cashed-out: Johnny didn't make any of the six gigs, and I lost all $20,000. T.B. told me he'd get the deposit back, but if he ever got it back from Cash, I never saw any of it.

I wasn't done with Johnny. In the mid-sixties, I lived in L.A. and often flew to New York and Nashville to hunt songs for Dean Martin, whose albums I was then producing. I once sat next to Johnny on a flight to New York. He was a towering presence with his long black coat, solemn, craggy face, and dark aura. He looked like Abe Lincoln. Well, Abe Lincoln on *pills*. Johnny seemed to be into uppers and couldn't sit still. He'd tug at his ears, tweak his nose, go into the lavatory and come out even more squirrelly. He was a wreck. It was like trying to talk to two or three people at once.

When I told him that Dean Martin loved country, he offered to come to my hotel and play me some of his songs. I said fine. He came by the next day—actually for him it was still the *same* day, since I don't imagine he had been to bed. He jerked out his guitar and played me eight, ten bars of maybe fifty songs. He couldn't finish one of them. A couple started off pretty good, but he'd stop, and go, "Aw, I can't remember that one, but here's another one I got." And he'd pull out a piece of paper, squirm around, start another. I was drinking Jack Daniel's just to try to get someplace where I could deal with him. He was so out of control that *I* was a nervous wreck when he finally left.

Next time we crossed paths was in the mid-eighties. Johnny had just been unceremoniously dropped from Columbia after thirty years, having become a folk hero in popular culture. I was running MCA Records in Nashville when he called me about signing a deal. I was open, but I told him I'd need to get a feel for the songs he was into, to see if I could work him properly.

The following week he showed up and—again—he'd play me eight, ten, twelve bars and just quit. After the third or fourth song the poor man said, "Y'know, I have never been this nervous in my whole life." And I said, "Me neither. My God, to have Johnny Cash *audition* for me."

I didn't give Johnny a deal, but Mercury Records did.

Almost as quickly as they began, my days as promoter were over. Likewise, my days as a performer were numbered. The idea of closing for Bo Diddley or Little Richard was a distant memory. If I was setting any attendance records, they were for new lows. Darlene and I were living out of the red Plymouth her mom had cosigned for so that I could buy it. Some of the more obscure gigs frankly scared me to death. Just like playing bass, I knew the minute the girls stopped screaming and heard my slightly flat voice, it would be time to find something else. Well, by now the screaming had all but stopped.

I pulled into Wichita for one gig in front of eight hundred or nine hundred kids, and up onstage was an old, *old* woman playing the organ. Had to be in her seventies. With her was a man just as old playing on a snare drum, a couple of cymbals, and a high hat—and a guy past retirement age on sax. They were my opening act. The promoter had promised to put together my backup band.

I figured, *Well, the kids will be so bored after these geezers come off that I'll light 'em up real good.* I went to the promoter and said, "What would be great is to get with my backup band now so that we can go over the set and get our keys and stuff."

He looked over at the stage, then back at me. "No problem. They should be off real soon, and then y'all will have a thirty-minute break before going on. You can work it all out then."

For a few seconds I was so stunned I couldn't speak. Then, nodding toward the stage, I asked, "You mean—that's my band?"

Those were the gigs I was getting—one horror show after another all over the damn map. I'd show up, meet the local band, and lay out the song list. They'd check off the ones they knew, then tell me what key they knew to play them in. So my show became doing the songs they knew in the keys they played. It was a nightmare. That went on through the first part of 1959.

Knox wasn't doing much better. In January two of his singles snuck onto the bottom end of the charts for two weeks but never made it past the mid-eighties of the Top 100. In April, he hit the mid-fifties with a song called "I Think I'm Gonna Kill Myself."

It hadn't gotten that bad for me—yet. But things were going to get worse before they got any better. I was in Wyoming doing a set with an awful backup band when I noticed there were almost as many people onstage as in the audience. I was smart enough to figure, *Game over.* My gut told me the time had come.

I called a radio executive named Ken Palmer at KYSN in Colorado Springs. I'd met Ken while doing some radio shows for him for KIMN in Denver with the Orchids. I told him I was in the area, that the Rhythm Orchids were over, I was sick of the road, and wondering if he had anything for me in radio. Ken was a part-owner of the Rocky Mountain Network of radio stations, and we'd always liked each other. Ken told me exactly what I wanted to hear. "I have a ten-to-one slot over in Colorado Springs."

I drove straight down from Wyoming to work for Ken at KYSN.

I was a bit rusty for morning deejay work. I talked too fast and mumbled. Sponsors got pissed off when I read their commercials, so other jocks had to come in and read them for me. Or I carefully prerecorded them. I also had a helluva time just getting to work before my show started. I never worked before eight at night as a rock and roller and never had to be *anywhere* at ten in the morning. When they gave me a theme song—Ray Charles's "What'd I Say?"—the producer just doubled the five-minute version to almost ten minutes. That way, as they segued in from the show before, if I was still flyin' down the street to get to the studio, they could simply keep it playing until I arrived. I sure ended up hating that song.

Ken and I would hang out a lot at night—drink, eat, and play liar's poker. I spent six months there and knew all along it wasn't my future or my lifestyle. Ken got a bank to give me a house trailer to live in, a place I came to hate because I was always banging my knees and head on corners and cabinets.

Darlene hated the trailer too, but it still beat living out of a car and hotels. Post-rock life was a little slow. To entertain ourselves, we once went to an auction, which I thought was cool. I'd never been to one before. I got into the spirit of bidding and went after an old handmade sailboat about six feet long and four feet wide. I was just playing along, driving the price up against a woman across the aisle. I never went above what I had in my pocket, which was $600. Trouble was, neither did she—and I went home $600 lighter and one boat heavier.

We barely got that boat into the trailer. It took up the whole living room. I sold it for $300, so to make up for that fiasco, I gave guitar lessons. I didn't play real well, so I had to go buy myself a book first. Local mommies would bring their kids over with their little guitars, and I taught them, making sure to stay two or three pages ahead of my students. At the end of that first book I had to shut the school down because the kids had all caught up with me and I couldn't go any farther.

•

Colorado Springs was the perfect layover—a change of pace, new job, a place to recharge and adjust from my teen-idol phase. It seemed now that this was how my life was probably meant to go—things would just flow and fall into place according to gut instinct more than calculation. Six months of trailer-park life was just enough time to bid farewell to the Rhythm Orchids, to the fifties, to my youth—and move on.

This time I was heading west. I pulled the house trailer up in front of the bank on a Sunday, wedged some rocks under the wheels to keep it from rolling, left a note thanking my banker for use of the rig, and drove off to California.

SEVEN

MY FIRST JOB in California was writing songs for $75 a week with a tall, blond singer-guitarist named Glen Campbell. Glen and I worked at American Music Publishing Company. I got there through Jerry Capehart, whom I'd known since the days when he managed Eddie Cochran. Capehart also had a record label that made demos for American's songwriters. He had known and worked with American's owner, Sylvester Cross, and always said, "Kid, if you're ever in L.A., come see me."

Glen had come to town just a month before I had, and we hit it off right away. He was born in Arkansas, but he had been playing a small club in Albuquerque. Glen had a smooth, rich voice and he was getting lots of work as a sessions picker.

Glen soon had a chance to be a friend in need. While visiting my mom at her home in Playa del Rey near the beach, I began passing blood in my urine. My mom, being a nurse, was scared to death. She rushed me to a kidney specialist, who did an excruciating cystoscopy (I recommend anesthesia) and discovered that a vein had swelled up across a duct in the kidney, blocking its drainage and causing the vein and kidney to swell.

The cure nearly killed me. I was sliced open from the front halfway around the back. The surgeon cut the kidney in half to remove the swollen vein, put the kidney back together, and repaired the cut muscles. A tube was inserted into the kidney to drain my waste into an external bag.

I was hospitalized for two or three weeks and then had to keep the bag for months as the kidney healed. Darlene and I spent most of six months at my mother's. It was the only time in my relationship with my mom that I ever felt any warmth and closeness with her. She was wonderfully attentive and caring and looked after everything for me. Maybe she was just a better nurse than mother.

Everyone seemed to come through for me. Darlene and I had had our rocky moments, but she hung in there. Cross, a neat, eccentric old man whose three shaggy dogs shed all over the office and wreaked havoc on my allergies, was real decent. He paid me my $75 a week throughout my convalescence.

And Glen and I, who never made much money for anybody writing songs, struck it rich in our friendship. He'd come over, we'd write a couple songs, and I'd get up and move around a bit with my little bag pinned to my robe. Glen always checked in by phone and was a dependable pal when I really needed one.

I couldn't get around much strapped to a tube, so I sold aluminum siding. Actually, I cold-called prospective customers, and got $5 for every time I convinced someone to make an appointment and check out the company's siding. In a good week I doubled my $75 from American.

When the doctor removed the tube, he slapped me on the back and said, "Well, that kidney should last you twenty, thirty years at least." And he warned me to stay away from booze. This was just as I was developing a taste for Jack Daniel's.

By the late fall of 1960, John Kennedy had been elected president, my kidney had healed, and I had my own New Frontier: Las Vegas. A sexy dance craze had been sweeping the nation and, as JFK himself might have put it, Ask not what you can do for the Twist; ask what the Twist can do for you. What the Twist could do for me was eighty grand for two months' work in a tux.

Every tacky lounge in Vegas was scrambling to ride the Chubby Checker trend. I got a call on a Wednesday from an agent connected to the Dunes. "I'm coming into town at five P.M. on Friday," he told me. "Do you know a twist band? Can you help me put a twist show together by then?"

It was a two-part question, but when he offered ten grand a week for eight weeks, I answered that I didn't but I would. "Great," he said. "Gold Star Studios at five on Friday."

I got some L.A. musicians together, hired my own sexy wife and another knockout to be my Twist girls, put them in short tight dresses with tassles, showed up at the Gold Star with four songs down, and got the gig. Even after expenses, $80,000 for a couple of months' work was amazing bread.

I didn't mind the two shows a night; it was that the Vegas-never-sleeps thing gets to you after eight weeks. But the strangest twist to this gig was that by the early part of 1961, Darlene and I had decided to go our separate ways. We had grown apart and were stagnating. We had hooked up before we ever had a chance to know each other and now seemed to have less in common than before. We lived on the road and never made a home anywhere. We were young and emotionally inexperienced. As for true intimacy, neither of us frankly knew much about it. And we weren't taking the time to work on it together. It wasn't her fault or mine; our marriage was just a lie.

Darlene was a good person who wouldn't bail out while I was sick; she was a trouper in Vegas. But somewhere along the way we had evolved from lovers more into friends. It was becoming more uncomfortable to appear married to the world. It was the wrong time, the wrong way to live, and I vowed never to do it again.

Back in L.A., I returned to American Music. When Darlene left for good, she was making some inroads in modeling and commercials. She went on to join *The Jackie Gleason Show* as one of the sexpot "Gleason Girls."

In mid-1961, Glen Campbell cut a record for Crest called "Turn Around, Look at Me," which Jerry Capehart wrote. It was a killer song and a great vocal for Glen. I got picked to go out on the road to promote it on radio. That's one tough, tough racket—especially when working an obscure small label. And I couldn't bring anybody any lunchbags anymore.

I went out on a four-week tour and came back after two. "That's it, not doing this anymore," I announced. No one had heard of Glen or the label, so getting him airplay at all was a coup. In fact we got Glen somewhere in the sixties on *Billboard,* but promotion is a terrible way to make a living, with intense highs and even more intense lows. I've had great empathy for promo guys ever since.

Glen and I did team up on something we both liked: we recorded and produced the demo tapes and records that American's songwriters pitched to artists. Glen was one of the most naturally gifted talents I ever came across. He could hear a song once, get the melody and harmony down, then figure out some neat little guitar lick and vocal harmony. This gave our demos a much fuller sound. He could sing a harmony with a damn car horn.

Before his big late-sixties hits with Capitol, Glen was one of the busiest, best sessions pickers and backup vocalists in L.A. He even played with the Beach Boys in 1965. Glen was so respected that he could just walk in on a friend's session—whether he was booked or not—and start pickin'. I later hired Glen for a lot of Sinatra and Dean Martin sessions a couple of years later. But mostly I remember Glen saving my butt when I was producing Buddy Greco, a onetime vocalist with Benny Goodman, when Buddy was doing an album of Beatles songs.

For one cut I needed to overdub an acoustic guitar part, an electric guitar part, and three-part harmonies. This was one of two or three songs I'd hired Glen for. I was in the control booth and Glen was out in the recording room tuning his acoustic when Buddy walked in behind me.

Buddy was a nice enough guy, but he could be a nervous twit who could drive everybody nuts. He was watching Glen from behind the glass, nervously checking his watch and pacing around. He was past his glory days and had become insecure—which he covered up with bravado and bullshit. This was the mid-sixties, and like many older artists, he was barely holding on to a career.

I asked Buddy what the hell was buggin' him. "Where are the electric-guitar player and the three background singers?"

I laughed. "They're right here, Buddy." He listened and watched intently as Glen effortlessly put down a beautiful acoustic lick, plugged in his electric, and put down another tasty hook. "Damn talented, isn't he?" he said, nodding. I nodded back. "But where the hell're the background singers?"

"They're here too." Buddy's jaw just dropped.

Buddy had written all the harmony parts and given them to Glen—except Glen couldn't read music. I was off doing something different while they rehearsed. Buddy came busting back into the booth. "Bowen, dammit, this kid doesn't even read music. How the hell can he do harmony parts?"

"Buddy, you're gettin' to be irritating. You go back out there and do your part. Trust me, Glen'll be on you like stink on shit, don't worry about it." Buddy sputtered off nervously.

I cued up and started rolling. Everything that came from Buddy's mouth Glen covered beautifully. There wasn't a melody line from the Beatles to Beethoven that Glen couldn't add harmony to. Glen easily nailed all three vocal parts, and though it took all damn day because of Buddy's fidgeting, we got the tracks done. For Buddy it had definitely been a hard day's night.

Most of my socializing with Glen took place on the golf course or in the studio. I've stayed good friends with him through thirty-plus years, but not without him going through a wild streak on cocaine that marked a six- or seven-year period we were out of touch. We were both better off that way. Glen is and has always been one of the sweetest, gentlest people I've known. But I was lucky enough, frankly, not to be around him then. For one thing the drugs we were on were too opposite. I'd gone on to Nashville to do my thing and smoke a bunch of pot; he got hung up on coke. There was no way we could communicate.

I couldn't imagine Glen being strung out on cocaine because I knew from our early days together that Glen's perfect pitch wavered even on two scotch and waters. The minute he messed with that fine instrument of his, it went to hell.

Glen would call me every once in a while to read to me from the Bible, wired out of his gourd on toot. I'd just lay the phone down and walk off awhile, then come back and he'd still be runnin' Scripture on the other end. If I had opportunities to be around Glen, I mostly avoided him.

I hated cocaine and what it did to people. It would never have been my drug of choice, not with my energies—and allergies. Glen, though, was one who got through it and came out the other side all right. He first had to get past his turbulent, gossipy love affair and marriage to Mac Davis's ex-wife, Sara, and then his turbulent, gossipy love affair with Tanya Tucker a few years later.

Then he returned to Phoenix, went cold turkey, married a beautiful gal named Kim, started a family, and found religion for real. All that helped straighten him out.

After he found God, Glen helped me find golf again. I had had back-muscle problems so bad, I couldn't bend over to putt and hadn't swung a club for nine or ten years. The muscles were misaligned and of unequal strength due to the kidney surgery. In the mid-eighties Glen was in Nashville and showed up one day with four extra-tall-style putters Orville Moody had used on the pro tour. "Here, Bowen," he said, "pick one of these. You're gonna start playin' golf again. This is ridiculous."

Golf was my born-again salvation. It gave me exercise, allowed me to relax, and helped me de-stress from the long days and nights running labels and producing. It was a lifesaver. Glen and I were now at least hooked on the same drug—golf. It was also a healthy high that got us back on track as friends.

For several years after Darlene, I lived in a succession of "bachelor pads" with one or two roommates. By splitting the rent I could afford to live in a nicer house. And I almost never had to leave home to find a party. The house I shared way up on Coldwater Canyon with Lindsay Crosby, Bing's youngest son, became ground zero for a wild "young Hollywood" party scene that never let up. The Crosby brothers were all screwed up one way or another, it seemed, because of the way "Daddy Dearest" raised them. Lindsay coped by drinking hard and partying harder. It was a wild, booze-fueled open house.

It never ceased to amaze me how many gorgeous party girls cruised L.A.—and how many of them kept showing up at our house. It was happy hour around the clock. Lindsay would go out for a drink and come home with a half dozen or more great-looking girls for a party. For me it was as if the candy store had reopened. Only this wasn't crazy groupies and jailbait, but eager starlets determined to see, be seen, get discovered. I discovered a bunch of them—and none of them ever made it in the movies.

Small wonder the testosterone got a little heavy up on Coldwater when the entourage gathered for the booze and the action. (If there were any other drugs going on, I was too dumb to know it.) One new friend was Johnny Rivers. He was only about twenty then and was trying to break a solo career. Johnny rolled up every few months to tell us he was broke, had no place to go, and needed to crash for a day or so—and then he'd stay a month. And there were the colorful Burnette brothers, Dorsey and Johnny.

While at American, I wound up managing their fading careers. Dorsey had had a couple of hits like "(There Was a) Tall Oak Tree" and "Hey Little One," and Johnny had had big hits with "Dreamin'" and "You're Sixteen"—all in 1960. I produced some tracks for Johnny in Nashville as well. By now they were starting down the other side. Why else come to me for management? I'd never managed anyone.

Just managing to keep them from killing each other was a job in itself. Dorsey had trained with heavyweight boxer Sonny Liston and loved to brawl. One night Dorsey and Johnny were going at it over something and Dorsey pinned Johnny up against a wall with his right arm. He was about to pound him with his left fist when I ran up, drink in hand, and got in between. Without letting go of Johnny, Dorsey threw me like a housecat clear back across the living room and right into a plate-glass window. I bounced off, slid to the floor, and slurred, "Well, then *kill* the son of a bitch, damned if I care. I'll just have another drink and watch."

That cracked them both up. They hugged and loved each other again and got over whatever the hassle was.

One night Dorsey took me to the Palomino Club and swaggered in ahead of me. My eyes were almost adjusted to the dark when I saw lights: a big rough-looking guy slugged me right in the mouth. Knocked my staggering ass all the way out across the sidewalk and into a parked car. Just *seeing* Dorsey made him take a swing, but Dorsey, skilled boxer that he was, dodged the jab and I got KO'd instead.

Another party boy at our place was a handsome divorced film star who had fallen in love with a Catholic girl. But he was depressed because her father wouldn't let her marry him. When he showed up looking glum, I turned in early.

I had a beautiful bedroom with a stark white bathroom. The bathroom had two doors—one to my room, the other to the living room. As I was drifting off to sleep—the bedroom-side door was still open—I could see the drunken actor go in from the living room. I couldn't believe it when I saw him reach into his pocket, pull out a razor blade and—*rrrip!*—slash his wrist. Blood gushed all over my gorgeous white bathroom. Oh, was I pissed.

I jumped out of bed, threw on a robe, and tossed him out into the front yard. "You bastard," I yelled, "if you're gonna kill yourself, that's your business, but don't ruin my white bathroom. Bleed out here, you ridiculous son of a bitch." I stormed inside and slammed the door. Lindsay called an emergency line, and medics arrived in time to save him and cart him away.

I stayed on at American through the early part of 1962. Having done lots of demos with Glen, I was becoming more interested in producing than in the publishing side. Phil Spector often worked in the big studio at Gold Star when Glen and I had the small room. I spent a lot of time watching him work on his famous "wall of sound," and he was a real inspiration.

But then I ran into Frankie Avalon, whom I had known from the rock circuit of the fifties. Frankie was always a straight-shooting, warm, likable, genuine guy. He reintroduced me to his manager, Bob Marcucci, and Marcucci told me he was looking for someone to run Chancellor Records' West Coast office. I told him he could stop looking.

Chancellor was home to heartthrobs Avalon and Fabian in the late fifties, but both of their recording careers had sharply declined. It was obvious this was not a major label if I was running its West Coast office. But it gave me a chance to see how a record company worked. Though there wasn't much music business in L.A., you sensed it would be the new pop frontier. Capitol was just about ready to release the Beach Boys' first hits; Columbia and RCA still only had small West Coast outposts, Warner/Reprise was just getting going, and there were small labels like Chancellor. It was a good job for me.

Marcucci had made me an offer I'd have been awfully dumb to refuse: $150 a week plus room and board. Which meant moving into and working out of Avalon's spectacular Frank Lloyd Wright house just off Sunset Boulevard. Frankie's Uncle Joe was the live-in chef, and he cooked my meals. Frankie was a super guy, but he was always gone, making movies and touring.

The only big hit Chancellor had on my watch was "Party Lights," a Top 5 record by Claudine Clark in the summer of 1962.

It was a fitting title for my life then. Girls would be calling the house around the clock for Frankie: Where's Frankie? When's Frankie comin' back into town? How long's he gonna be away? I told them all the same thing: "No, no, no. Frankie just went downtown. He should be back any minute. Come on over."

Any night we wanted, my buddies and I found ourselves surrounded by California beauties, hanging out, hoping to party with Frankie in a house Frank Lloyd Wright had built for Errol Flynn. When Frankie failed to show, I'd have to shuffle a bit and explain that I didn't honestly know *where* he could be, or, simply lie and say he'd be back any minute. It didn't matter. Partying then was like buying a suit: you tried on six or seven and walked out with the one that looked and fit best.

Errol Flynn had Wright create some features designed to help the dashing film legend swash and buckle in private. There was a two-way mirror between one bedroom and an adjoining bathroom. In the master bedroom pin spotlights were aimed from the ceiling to the bed. The whole place looked like a movie set. At $150 a week, Marcucci was overpaying me to live there, given the food, girls, and optical effects. The party lights never went out there.

My job at Chancellor involved meeting music-publishing reps who'd pitch their writers' new material. Murray Wolf was Bourne Music's West Coast rep. Murray was a neat guy who took me to Dodgers games. I didn't know it, but I was about the only one to see him, and he didn't know it, but he was one of the few who called on me. Chancellor wasn't exactly in the loop.

But one of Murray's best friends wasn't just a major artist in the loop, he *was* a loop all by himself. Murray called me out of the blue with amazing news: His friend, Frank Sinatra, was looking for a "young guy" to take over and revamp his tired roster and A&R department at Reprise Records. The label needed a shot in the arm by tapping the youth market.

Sinatra had angrily left Capitol in 1960 after a long and storied association, and had founded Reprise Records. He was furious that rock and roll had knocked him off the pop charts and become the dominant force on radio and at the major labels.

Reprise's first release was his own "The Second Time Around" in March 1961. It vanished from radio and barely dented the charts. Over the next two years Sinatra's half-dozen singles all stiffed way down in the Top 100. He hit Top 50 with the movie theme to "Pocketful of Miracles" in late 1961. He even tried a single called "Ev'rybody's Twistin'"—but it left him twisting in the wind, peaking at No. 75.

He stubbornly wanted to do it his way: he ruled out rock and roll at Reprise and packed his well-paid roster with aging, fading sidekicks, who were making almost no impact commercially. Sinatra was losing millions his way.

But he was "rethinking" his game plan, Murray said, looking to bring a younger, hipper edge to Reprise. Murray wanted to recommend me for the job. I was amazed and said, "Sure, go for it."

It was the end of 1963 and the timing was perfect. After partying it up for a couple of years, I was partied out. I had turned twenty-five and was getting restless. I'd dabbled in radio, music publishing, songwriting, producing, concert promotion, record promotion, management, and running a label—and still hadn't found a home in the music industry. I needed to focus, to settle in, start from the ground up again. That seemed to bring out the best in me. What I needed was to grow up, get down to business.

I had had my rock-and-roll career out of New York and I had come to L.A. to make my mark in pop music. Working for Sinatra was a once-in-a-lifetime opportunity.

A couple of weekends later, Murray phoned from Palm Springs, speaking in a whisper. It was the first time it hit me that people around Sinatra always whispered. "Bowen," he whispered, "I got you the job."

"No shit, that's great," I said.

"Now, hang on, Frank wants to talk with you," Murray said.

This was all happening so fast. It hadn't even begun to sink in when I heard that unmistakable golden voice. "James," he said. "Glad to have you aboard."

Click. He hung up on me before I could say thanks. I put the phone down, and all I kept thinking was, *I'm twenty-five, I'm going to work for Sinatra. That's cool. I can deal with this.*

I'd soon find other ways to properly thank the Chairman of the Board.

EIGHT

I JOINED REPRISE in the fall of 1963 and found myself on a steep learning curve. Mo Ostin, the future chairman of Warner Bros. Records and one of the most influential shapers of pop music from the sixties through the nineties, was running Reprise.

Mo offered me $150 a week, but I talked him down to $100 a week plus a 1 percent royalty deal on anything I produced for the label. No producer had ever had an in-house royalty deal there. Mo figured that with no track record as a producer he was giving up 1 percent of nothing—and was already fifty bucks a week ahead. For me it was a front-end gamble on the back end, but we both got what we wanted. He cut his overhead, I had a profit incentive, and we shook hands on the deal.

On my first day at work Capitol Records' president, Alan Livingston, called to steal me away—even though we'd never even met. It was his way of getting back at Sinatra. Sinatra had been reportedly tangling with Capitol—unsuccessfully—over Capitol's release of his fifties catalog at steep discounts. That was not only disrespectful to Sinatra, it probably hurt Reprise's market share. Livingston offered to double my base salary and back-end percentage. "Problem is, I'm already here," I said.

"You got a contract?"

"No, not yet."

"Then we can still deal."

"Not really. I have a handshake and I gave my word—and that's as good as a contract for me."

Why pass up working with Sinatra, Dean Martin, Sammy Davis, Jr., and Reprise's huge, unique roster? And I *had* given Mo my word before we had a contract. A handshake *was* a deal. I'd like to think my success through the years is due in part to my living by the same ethical code that served my dad so well. Your word has to mean something, and it's only as good as your commitment to back it up with deeds. One lesson I've learned in forty years in the record business: Be direct and tell it the way it us, even if it pisses people off and turns them against you. And honor your commitments. Good, bad, or indifferent, I stick to what I've agreed to. That's been the ethical foundation of my entire career. You can't do as much as I've done being full of it.

My mission at Reprise was to find hits for its roster, but I soon saw a major problem: one hundred–plus acts on the label, a huge, diverse cast of characters linked mainly by their ties to Sinatra—and by their failure to sell much product.

They had Alice Faye, Keely Smith, and Phil Harris; there were the McGuire Sisters, Rosemary Clooney, and Dinah Shore. Clint Eastwood and Doug McClure, stars of *Rawhide* on TV, had deals, and neither of them could sing. Despite all that class, Reprise's big hits in 1963 were Lou Monte's "Pepino the Italian Mouse" and Trini Lopez's live cover of "If I Had a Hammer." Something had to give.

When Reprise's head of A&R was fired, Mo told me, "We can't afford to hire a new guy, so you're the new department head. You're gonna have to take care of A&R yourself."

I knew what that meant: it was my job to tell Sinatra that a lot of his cronies had to be dropped. "Mo," I said, "we've gotta lose seventy or eighty. You can't make a living with them."

"*I'm* not going to tell somebody *he* signed—"

"Then I will. Get me an appointment."

I would have no problem delivering the news to Sinatra. I wasn't about to be intimidated by him. I was hired to do a job. He was the most celebrated and controversial pop singer of them all—but his albums were barely doing 100,000 units anymore. Dean Martin's had dwindled to 20,000 to 25,000—hardly legend material. I wasn't there to sit around in awe. I was twenty-five, I was new, I was there to shake things up. I knew the label was in the red and losing a couple of million early-sixties' dollars a year, a ton of money. Sinatra was rumored to be secretly flying into Chicago on weekends to borrow cash from friends such as mobster Sam Giancana—just to make payroll. Something was broke and needed fixin'.

On my day of reckoning a limo took me to Sinatra's desert home in Palm Springs. I waited a while before he came into the living room. He was very casual, nonchalant. "You want a drink?"

"Got any Jack Daniel's?" I knew he drank Jack. He poured, we sat down. "Now, tell me what you wanted to see me about, James."

"Well, Frank, Reprise is absolutely going to fail. It has no prayer whatsoever unless I get rid of seventy or eighty of your acts, acts that don't sell records."

He paused a second or two, no more, and looked directly at me. "All right, then, do it. What else?"

I couldn't believe his reaction. I fumbled around for an exit line. "Uhhh, guess that'll about get it for today."

"Thanks," he said, and it was over. I walked out, got back in the limo, and knew in that moment that I could work with him. If he knew you weren't afraid of or in awe of him, then he'd deal with you straight. If he sensed your fear, he'd back you up against the wall.

Sinatra had other things on his mind then. He was selling two-thirds of his stake in Reprise to Jack Warner, who wanted Sinatra to make movies for Warner Bros. Jack set Frank up in a half-million-dollar office complex on the Warner lot. Jack let Sinatra retain a third of Reprise—and threw in a third of Warner Bros. Records as a sweetener. He now had Sinatra, and Sinatra had what Capitol never gave him—control over his own subsidiary, but with Warners funding it.

Mo Ostin, a few other top Reprise executives, and myself were now switched over to Warner/Reprise. I began to strip the roster and update the label's image and sound by producing a few "hipper" acts—Jack Nitsche (1963's "Lonely Surfer") and, in early 1964, Jimmy Griffin, a young composer and guitarist. Neither went anywhere for us, but Jack worked with the Rolling Stones and scored film music; Jimmy made it big with Bread.

My own breakthrough at Reprise came when I got to work with the label's second-most-celebrated artist, Dean Martin. We recorded *Dean Tex Martin Rides Again,* a sequel of sorts to *Dean Tex Martin* from a few years back. I knew Dean loved country and was keen to do it. But there was nothing on the LP that radio would go for. So I told him, "Let me produce an album that has some hits on it for today's radio."

He agreed, but then he went straight to Vegas to play the Sands, where Sinatra's Rat Pack all worked. Dean would do his regular show and then hit the lounge. He'd have a drink and get up with a trio—bass, drum, piano—and do another set of old standards. These up-close, intimate shows thrilled his fans. Dean knew I wanted to cut some hits with him, but he said, "Pallie, I gotta do this first before we do that other album. I know this'll work. The timing's right." He was referring to an album of standards, which we called *Dream with Dean.*

By early 1964, when we went into the studio, I had a trusted ally in town, my boyhood buddy Don "Dirt" Lanier. On a swing east to Nashville with Johnny Burnette, I had stopped in Amarillo to visit Dirt. He was married, had a couple of young kids, and was working in some smelter or cement plant. And bowling. I tracked him down at an alley and told him to get his butt out to L.A. I told him he could make a good living in the wide-open music business.

By 1964 Dirt's marriage was on the rocks, and he was in L.A. His wife had tried to make a go of it in L.A., but she didn't like it and went home to Texas. Dirt stayed, and their marriage dissolved. I hired Dirt to be my contractor and book musicians on Dean's sessions. Soon Dirt was networking and on his way to becoming one of L.A.'s top contractors. It was great to be back together with an old friend.

We got together four or five musicians to re-create the lounge feel for Dean's studio sessions, including his longtime piano player, Ken Lane. The sessions went fast—Dean never needed more than a couple of takes to make a song his own. If anything slowed us down, it was having Ursula Andress come down to the studio. As muses go, she was as gorgeous as they get. Ursula and her husband at the time, John Derek, were friends with Dean and his wife, Jeanie. Those poor musicians could hardly follow their music charts.

The last session was winding down when Dean tossed out the twelfth song. It just wasn't coming off, but we still needed a song. Ken Lane started noodling something on piano and said, "Hey, how 'bout my song?"

I said, "Yeah, that's really pretty. What's it called?"

Ken started humming and singing, "Everybody loves somebody sometime." Dean seemed to know the song and liked it. I said, "Let's give it a try."

Ken scratched out a chord sheet for the musicians and lyrics for Dean. I went into the booth relating how Ken had just written this incredible song. Everybody laughed at me. Ken had composed it about twenty years earlier. I shrugged. What the hell did I know? I was only head of A&R.

We got a slow, moody version cut just as the session ended. I was elated, but still felt the song needed something. Then it hit me. I caught Dean and Mack Gray, who ran Dean's recording career as manager-roadie and confidant, and pulled Mack over. "My God, Mack, that's the song. But let's cut it with a big orchestra. I can make a record that'll work on radio."

Mack went over to Dean on the way out. "The kid thinks this is the song for you." Dean shrugged. "Sure. Let's give it a try." The "small" version would be included on the *Dream* album; the big-orchestra version would be released as a single *coinciding* with the *Dream* album, but included on Dean's next album.

Around this time I was producing—and dating—Reprise's wonderful jazz vocalist, Keely Smith, former wife and musical partner of trumpeter and bandleader-composer Louis Prima. After a couple of fifties' hits and nine years of marriage, they divorced in 1961. I met Keely when we began working on her new album. Immediately after the Dean sessions we flew for the weekend to Vegas, where she lived and performed. She told me Sinatra and Dinah Washington had both cut versions of "Everybody"—and played them for me. "I don't care," I told her. "With Dean it's a smash."

Back in L.A. I hired Ernie Freeman, a wonderful sessions piano player and arranger. I loved the way he wrote strings, especially on Johnny Burnette's "Dreamin'." Ernie had often recorded with producer Snuff Garrett, whom I had watched many times. I'd learned a lot by watching Snuff at United's Studio B. He'd pick out good songs, match them to the artist, bring Ernie in, bring out that great string sound, and put it with a rhythmic bottom and have it all captured by engineer Eddie Brackett. Eddie was brilliant at mixing live recordings, and his approach influenced me in the studio. Having also watched Phil Spector at Gold Star, I had witnessed the way he dictated and controlled the recordings and produced what was basically a "Phil Spector" record with his instantly identifiable sound. My studio method was, in a sense, a mix of their two styles.

Ten days later we went in to record a hit for Dean. I worked hard with Ernie to convey exactly what I had to have. Ernie was brilliant and just *got* it. I had the great Hal Blaine on drums and some strong studio guys. I wanted this version to have prominent piano triplets and some R&B bottom to go with the pop melody and strings on top. We ran everything through only three tracks with no overdubs or isolation rooms. There was "leakage" on the drums—meaning the mikes used for strings and horns also picked up the drums—but even that worked in our favor.

Eddie was working with no more than ten or twelve "pots," or knobs, at the mixing board. They weren't fancy faders like today, where you might have as many as eighty finely calibrated switches to slide up and back to get your EQ, or sound levels, sounding exact and wonderful. This was a dozen big old knobs for everything—with several string-section mikes coming into just two knobs. Today you'd have a dozen faders dedicated to strings alone. It took us two and a half hours just to get the mikes aimed and the sound mixed right. Eddie was terrific at working with what little EQ we had then. And as often happened then, we had to refine some arrangements to fit the miking, or they'd have thrown off the delicate balance.

Dean was patient, but the longer we fussed over the mikes, the mixing board, and the arrangements, the more scared I got that we'd lose him. Dean had run through the song a few times, but I told him not to wear himself out. I assured him several times we were almost rollin'. He was like, "Oh, no, go ahead, pallie."

Dean approached singing the way he approached acting. As he once told a Method actress who had wandered off to lapse "into character," "Excuse me, but you know as well as I do neither of us is gonna get an Oscar for this shit, so just come over here and say the lines. The director'll take care of the rest." He knew I was the "director" and didn't interfere.

We took a short break to get everyone's energy up and then it was time to roll. Sweat was pouring off Eddie because in those days you either captured it or you didn't. You either heard clinkers in that mass of sound or you didn't. The pressure of squeezing thirty or forty musicians into three or four tracks was awful. It wasn't like today where you work with a million bucks of electric digital gizmos that let you either get what you missed or improve what you got.

Dean nonchalantly stepped up to the mike and sang the hell out of that tune. When you nail it that good, everyone on hand knows it and feels they're a piece of it. After two takes I had it. We listened to playbacks in the big studio, where I had huge speakers set up. The track sounded fantastic. I told Eddie to get me an acetate to take home. I was then sharing a place way up in Bel Air with Dirt and an English friend of ours named Jack, Reprise's top promotion man. That night we broke out the whiskey and listened to that sucker all night long. When you've cut an exceptional record like that, there's nothing better.

•

Despite Dean's two minutes and forty seconds of magic, the timing couldn't have been worse. The British Invasion, launched by the Beatles' historic landing in late 1963, dominated pop music like nothing since Elvis in '56. In the first half of 1964 alone, as we mixed, mastered, and prepared to release Dean's single, the Beatles spit out close to twenty hits—most of them instant classics. They owned *Billboard*'s first or second chart position for *twenty weeks* during the first six months of 1964, ending the year with an astounding six No. 1 hits.

We were also on the front edge of the Motown explosion led by the Supremes. They had three No. 1s that year. There seemed to be no room at the top—certainly not for a middle-aged crooner. Perhaps history would be on our side: Dean's last big hit, "Memories Are Made of This," had held the No. 1 position for six weeks in 1956, the year Elvis exploded with five No. 1s.

Reprise tried to tell me it was crazy to put the same song on successive albums. I wanted to release the orchestrated single (from the later album) while the trio version appeared on *Dream*. I told the label, "Bullshit, who says you can't?"

By the end of June "Everybody" was on Warner's in-house priority-promo sheet—meaning it would be "worked" hardest. But it was dropped after two or three weeks, after getting turned down everywhere at radio.

Then two stations—in Massachussetts and Louisiana—added "Everybody," and local sales went through the roof. We suddenly had orders for 50,000 singles in one week. Radio's herd mentality worked for us, jumping all over that song.

Dean had a 1.5-million-selling gold monster that hit No. 1 that summer. The label, Dean, and Sinatra were thrilled. Deanomania had overtaken Beatlemania, however briefly.

As the summer wound down, the label's sales and promotion people were still fretting over having two albums out by one artist with two versions of a hit. They were concerned that radio listeners would buy the *Dream* album for the radio version and feel cheated by the lounge version. I told the label that anyone who called or wrote to complain could be referred to me.

The hit record pushed *Dream* well past a half-million sales, the first of more than a dozen gold albums Dean and I would do together. Tasting success, Reprise naturally switched gears and wanted *more* Dean product out there.

I got resourceful. I took a few things Dean already had in the can—some country-style tracks left off the *Rides Again* album—

and cut a few more new things. We rushed the *Everybody Loves Somebody* album while the single was still hot. In a three-month period Dean now had two gold albums—and not one record buyer had called in to complain.

I scrambled to find Dean a follow-up to "Everybody." Dirt and I were sitting up at night racking our brains. At three A.M. with both of us half drunk, Dirt, who'd collected hundreds and hundreds of songs in his head, grabbed his guitar and sang a lovely tune called "The Door Is Still Open to My Heart"—the obscure B-side of a 1955 Don Cornell single called "Most of All." Dirt's knack for pulling songs out of thin air blew my mind and made me think he could be a great "song man." I made him sing it well past sunup—and knew it was Dean's next single.

I dragged my butt over to see Dean on the Fox lot so that I could let him hear the song. I didn't have a demo, so I also had to drag Dirt with me. Dirt hauled his guitar and sang "The Door" live for Dean. He was all for it—and damn if we didn't have our next Top 10 hit in the fall.

The hits had a huge impact on Dean, Reprise, and me. His album sales were soaring past the half-million mark, serious tonnage for the late sixties. They got Dean and me on a roll: Dean charted another twenty times or so before the end of the sixties, though we never matched the success of those first two.

If you're a producer, you learn to strike while the artist is hot—and renegotiate your deal. After Dean's hits I "quit" for a couple of days as a ploy to get Reprise to give me a little more back-end cut. After "The Door" I went in to see Warner/Reprise president Mike Maitland and Ed West, his top finance guy and right-hand man. At one point West said, "I don't know why we should give you a bigger deal. Ernie Freeman's on every one of the hit records you're on. He's as important as you are."

That's not what I wanted to hear. I got up and announced, "Meeting's over."

I called Bill Justis in Nashville. Bill was an eccentric character with a southern-hipster edge. He was a jazz sax player and arranger-producer who had a giant instrumental hit in 1957 called "Raunchy." We had worked together a few times back then and I knew Bill to be a crazy man. He'd come out onstage dragging his sax behind him with a rope. Then he'd reel the sax in and play "Raunchy." He went on to produce some great music out of Memphis and Nashville. I asked if he'd fly in for my upcoming Dean sessions. "Oh, absolutely, baby, sweetheart, I'll be there."

By then Dirt and I had a song-hunting system down. I made trips to Nashville to meet with writers and publishers, but when the crunch came, it was me and Dirt, late at night, listening to dozens of demos, accompanied by our buddy Jack Daniel's. We had one radio hit, I felt, written by Warner's A&R head, Dick Glasser. It was called "I Will." We needed one more killer.

We were going over tunes with Lee Hazelwood, a writer-producer working with Nancy Sinatra for Reprise. Lee suggested his song "Houston," which he had produced for Sanford Clark years back for Warners. We decided to break into the label store-room at Warner/Reprise in the middle of the night. We rummaged around and found Clark's old single, making a huge mess. We cranked up the single on my office stereo, poured us some more toddies, and heard our second hit.

Justis didn't tell me that since we'd last spoken, he had had about a third of his stomach removed for treatment of an ulcer that came from a combination of drinking and nerves. "I'm at the Beverly Hills Hotel, baby," he said. "Come on up."

He had the approved song list and keys so that he could start arranging. He was propped up on his hotel-room bed with a tube in his stomach, draining out into a bag for pus, and a bottle of booze by his side. Justis was about as responsible as I was about following doctors' orders. He had a record player hooked up in the room, too, so that he could sit there and knock back a couple cocktails and go over the songs for Dean's *Houston* LP.

Justis showed up for the sessions, but unlike Ernie, who had every note on every music chart in place, Justis rushed in scribbling and shuffling score sheets. His notation system was a thing of wonder: instead of notes for, say, an electric-guitar solo, he'd simply indicate, *"Electric guitar, freak out!"*

During one session for trumpets and trombones Justis sent out for eight thirty-two-ounce bottles of beer. We drank what we could hold and emptied out what was left. Justis took rags or whatever he could find and wrapped them around the quart jugs and had the horn players jam them into the open ends of their instruments as makeshift mutes. I wasn't shocked when they made one of the strangest sounds I ever heard from a horn. But it worked.

On "Houston," Justis handed Dirt a bottle of scotch and a pencil and asked him to stand back in percussion. When I wasn't looking, Justis took a nip, struck the bottle with the pencil, took another sip, struck it again—then capped it up. "That sounds about right," he muttered to Dirt. He was *tuning* the bottle so that Dirt could beat it as a percussion instrument at the point in the song when Dean sings "Goin' back to Houston."

Justis not only arranged another gold album for Dean, he helped me arrange my new contract. When I had another meeting with Maitland and West, I said, "All right now, this album doesn't say Ernie Freeman anywhere, does it?" They shook their heads. "So let's just pick up where the last discussion left off."

Dean was hot. Four months after *Everybody, Dean Martin Hits Again* came out, then *I'm the One That Loves You* later that year. His comeback led to a TV variety show that debuted in the fall of 1965 and ran for nine seasons. Single album sales were pushing past 700,000. The sixties were turning into a very heady time.

While my salary had risen to $50,000 a year, my royalties for both singles and albums—and Dean had sold a few million LPs by then—rose from 1 percent at the outset to 1½, 2, on up to 3 points. This helped boost my income into the six-figure range, real decent money then.

Dean and I were a prolific team because he was so easygoing and casual. I was surprised by him, mostly because of the "lush" image he had cultivated. But you can't be drunk and do two albums a year—plus Vegas, a TV series, and movies. Dean got tipsy around me maybe twice, when four or five drinks became too much during an extra-long recording session. I'd have a bar set up for his scotch and water, but Dean couldn't hold a lot of booze. He'd nurse one drink for two hours, have another, and go home.

He always had his big silver mug on the set of his TV show, which fostered—rather convincingly—his lush image. But that drink would last him all afternoon. Guests assumed Dean was drunk, so *they'd* get bombed around him. Eddie Fisher got so stoned once, he fell clear through the set during a run-through. They cut the segment and ran a musical piece they had banked.

Soon after he saw me put his pal Dean back at the top of the charts, another Reprise artist called me one day to tell me he wanted to try to do the same thing for his own career. If I ever had doubts, I was now sure that lightning could strike twice.

"James, how are you?" Sinatra asked. "I'd like to talk to you about maybe doing a record with me. Can you come on over?"

I went to his office, but not before taking a quick look in my "good song" file, where I kept demos and acetates of songs I intended to cut when the right artist came along. I grabbed Matt Monro's English recording of "Softly, as I Leave You." Killer song.

"Have a drink, James," Sinatra said after welcoming me into his office. He poured a Jack Daniel's and as usual got right down to business. "If you're producing me," he said, "what would you do with me to get me hits?"

"Well," I said, "I wouldn't change or bastardize you, but I would change the music around you—dramatically. Bring you to the modern marketplace." That sounded about right to him. Sinatra paused a moment, then asked, "Got anything?"

Phew! I exhaled with relief. I walked over to the record player in his office and pulled out the "Softly" acetate. The song was as Sinatra as you could get. "Well," he said, "you think this is the one?"

It was one thing to pull off a comeback for cool, laid-back Dean. Now, as I sat there, the Chairman himself was asking the kid if he thought he could make that magic happen again.

I knew there was only one answer he wanted to hear.

"Yeah, I do. I think it'll get us started. It's a great song. We just gotta do it modern."

"Well, then," he said, "let's do it."

NINE

FRANK SINATRA never struck me as a show-business icon who thrives on other people's fear of him. He was an artist with an extraordinary instrument, and if you treated him as such, everything was cool.

After I booked studio time at United Recorders for a week or ten days ahead, people called to warn me about how rough it would be to work with him, how he'd take over and chew people up.

I stayed cool and focused on my job. The man had his pick of the greatest producers in the world to make Sinatra music for the ages. What he needed from me was a hit record, and "Softly" looked like a good bet.

The session was booked for eight P.M., and as always I called the orchestra for six. To get a lush, romantic sound, I had flutes and strings. We worked hard on the arrangement, fixing the charts before he arrived. Frank was extremely frugal with his time, whether in the studio or on the phone. I wanted everything ready. That was the way to go with him.

As I'd done with Dean, I invited several dozen trusted friends and associates to be there, to create an informal lounge setting. They were basically saloon singers who got turned on by atmosphere, by contact with an intimate audience. By the time Sinatra arrived, he was already warmed up and we were all set. Frank always did vocal exercises with his pianist, either at home or in an adjoining studio before the session. Dean was a stylist and more spontaneous. Frank had a precise, beautifully tuned vocal instrument that he played to perfection.

It didn't take more than a couple of run-throughs with the orchestra and we were ready. Sinatra sang it and went out to listen back. The playback was absolutely gorgeous.

"Well, James," he wondered, "do you think that will work?"

I had to be straight with him. "I think it'll get us about a No. 30 record. But it'll put us back on the charts, on the radio."

The news didn't seem to make him happy. Sinatra certainly didn't need a big hit for the money. But I understood the artist ego in him, especially after seeing Dean come out of nowhere and have one of the smash hits of the year. Top 30 must have seemed an anticlimax. He shrugged, "Oh, uh-huh, okay," he said, and off he went.

"Softly" was released in September 1964, and exceeded my expectations—by two notches on the charts. It got to No. 27 on the Top 100. That made me look pretty smart. Sinatra loved it when people didn't yes him but instead told him like it was. He may have wanted to hear me predict a No. 1 hit, but what he heard was what he got—and that got us off to a great start together.

To keep his momentum going, I needed that killer song to put Sinatra on top of the charts. I came across a piece of sound-track music by Bert Kaempfert that was used for a James Garner spy-spoof film called *A Man Could Get Killed*. It had been played for me by a friend named Hal Fine, who was also Bert's music publisher. One stretch of instrumental music caught my ear. I listened to it several times and flipped for it. I heard a song in there. "Get me a lyric on this," I told Hal. "This is for Sinatra."

Hal commissioned songwriters and twice submitted the melody with different sets of lyrics. Neither worked for me. They weren't for Sinatra. Then one night I found a package from Hal. It was a demo titled, "Strangers in the Night."

I cued it up in my office at home and sat down. It was the same melody, but these new lyrics hit the spot. They had been written by Charles Singleton and Eddie Snyder (Bert also gets credit), and I could now hear Sinatra all over this song.

I played the demo for Sinatra and he agreed it was beautiful and worth recording. I hired Ernie Freeman to do the arrangements, and Dirt booked an orchestra for a Monday-evening rehearsal at five P.M. Sinatra was due at eight.

After getting all the arrangements and miking just right for "Strangers," I called a break and headed over to Martoni's Restaurant nearby. Everything was falling into place, and I was sure we'd found the killer cut I'd promised to find.

I sat down and Jack Jones saw me and came by. As we chatted, he mentioned he had recorded a new single that had shipped Friday and was due out in a day or so. I asked him what it was called.

"It's a beautiful song called 'Strangers in the Night.' Bert Kaempfert wrote it."

I must have turned white. My heart started pounding. I mumbled something like, "Yeah, well, great. Good luck with it."

As Jones walked off, I became absolutely livid. I wanted to hire stranglers in the night to go after the bastards at the publishing company. Sinatra would be coming to the studio in thirty minutes thinking Top 10 breakthrough, but what we really had was a cover of a Jack Jones single. I was enraged. Hal hadn't told me that someone else at his publishing company had also pitched this song to Bobby Darin and to Jack. That was dumb, since I'd told Hal he had a shot at Sinatra cutting it.

I hustled out of Martoni's and shifted into overdrive.

Back at the studio I called some of my A&R staff and some friends and told them to round up about eight people with their own cars and have them ready to start working for me at United Recorders at around midnight. Asked what for, I said only, "To go back and forth to the airport." I asked one of those runners to fetch me seven or eight hundred dollars in $20 bills.

Then I decided not to tell Sinatra until we'd cut the song. I didn't want him changing his mind before we had it in the can.

I told Eddie Brackett to clear out the mastering room by ten o'clock and keep it free until ten the next morning. The mastering room was where you went from tape to disk. "What's up?"

"The asshole in New York gave Jack Jones 'Strangers,' and they've already shipped. It's landing today and tomorrow at radio. But they're not in a hurry. We are. I want to be nationwide by dark tomorrow with this Sinatra record."

Eddie stared at me like I was nuts. "Wow!"

The session went smoothly until we came to a half-tone change of key two-thirds of the way through. This was not the best time for us to hit a snag. I needed to get that sucker out on the street before Jones's cover. But Sinatra was having a tough time with the transition, and we didn't have the fancy gear you'd have today to make it work in the mix.

He picked up on the tension and got edgy himself. Frank never liked to look bad in front of people—and I had an audience of close to a hundred, plus orchestra. I was thinking, *My God, if he misses this thing one more time, he's goin' home.*

I had an idea. I left the booth and went into the studio: "Frank, sing it right up to the key change and cut. Then we'll give you a bell tone for the new key and we'll go from there in the new key to the end. We can pull it all together later."

He looked surprised. "You can do that?"

"Absolutely."

We cut the master tape up to the key change and stopped. Then I got everyone to be super silent and had Ernie ring the new key tone. The *bing!* rang through the recording studio loud and clear. Frank then kicked into the last verse in this new key and took it right on to the end. On this take, as on the prior ones, he added a spontaneous dooby-dooby-doo-type scat, something he had almost never done in his recording career.

Confident that we had enough to wrap, I broke the news to Frank that the publisher had also given the song to Jack Jones, that his single had shipped, and that I was racing the clock to beat him to the street. Jack was a nice guy, but this was a do-or-die scene with a pop legend—who was also my boss.

"No way I'm lettin' that son of a bitch beat us," I said. Sinatra looked a bit confused by how all this had come about—and how it would play out over the next twenty-four hours. But we both knew one thing for sure: That was my problem now.

About ten o'clock, after the orchestra, the audience, and Sinatra had gone home, Eddie Brackett and I went into the mixing room. We had to splice in Sinatra's key change, and Eddie put together a scat ending from the four or five takes Frank gave us. Then we mixed down from three tracks to mono, getting the vocal just right on top of the band, where it belonged. We went into the mastering room, where we cut the masters into metal and got those on their way to a pressing plant in northern California.

But because we were on a crash basis, we also cut acetate dubs—the kind I'd learned to cut in the Speech Department at West Texas. They looked like thick records, but you can only play them eight or ten times before they lose their sound quality.

By the time my people had all gathered at the studio, I had two lathes going simultaneously to cut the acetates—and a wad of twenties. Every three minutes we had another pair of acetates.

My promotion guy had phone numbers and addresses for every top jock in every major radio market. As the first pair of dubs came off the lathes, I put them in packages and gave them to him. He handed them off to runners. Two for Pittsburgh, two each for Cleveland, New York, Chicago, Boston. Each runner headed for the airport carrying acetates and crisp twenties.

The runners' assignment was to find the next flight to that city, give the packages to a friendly flight attendant along with a twenty or two, and ask her (few were men then) to hand over the package to our contact upon arrival.

Once the runner had the flight number, arrival time, and stewardess's name, he or she phoned our promotion guy who worked that city so that he could meet the plane and make the pickup. From there it was to go straight to the radio station and into the hands of the jock. We had the top fifty American radio markets targeted.

The acetates would start to lose their top-end clarity after the first few plays. But by breaking the record this way—with the breathless hand-delivery and hype of a new Sinatra acetate (and not a 45)—I was creating an *event*. This would get any deejay's attention. I also figured the jocks would tape their acetates right away and broadcast the taped version, ensuring top sound quality until vinyl 45s arrived.

This wasn't my first cover battle fought with guerilla tactics. I was once at United Studio B cutting a song when I heard a cover version in an upstairs mastering room. It had already been recorded and mixed down there. This got me angry. When the engineer and producer took a dinner break, I went into the mastering room, removed and hid two tubes from this big ol' piece of gear needed for mastering. This bought—no, *stole*—me some time to catch up and at least make it a fair fight to radio. We both hit the streets the same time a few days later.

By the end of the next afternoon, in early May 1966, we had hit all our markets. Jones's record had arrived in the mail and, as I figured, program directors took their time getting around to it. A hand-carried Sinatra acetate was unique, it was news—and it was an automatic playlist add.

By sundown Sinatra had an instant hit in cities across the country and we wiped poor Jack Jones off the map.

It was an expensive way to break a song, but "Strangers" became Sinatra's first No. 1 hit since "Learnin' the Blues" way back in 1955. The song stayed on the charts nearly four months and gave him the airplay breakthrough he had wanted so badly.

We were both elated. I could "quit" again and renegotiate with leverage. "Strangers" pushed my back-end deal to 3 percent and helped send my income into the $200,000 range.

It was never my desire—or expectation—to take over Sinatra's recording career. It was far too vast for one person. When

Sinatra was doing Sinatra, he didn't need me. When he did an album with the great Brazilian composer and guitarist Carlos Jobim, or *September of My Years,* one of his greatest albums ever, he didn't call me. He called Sonny Burke to produce. Which was absolutely the right call. Sinatra was totally in charge.

He only came to me when he wanted a hit record on the pop charts. Being the pro that he was, if he trusted and respected you, then he let you do your thing.

A couple of months after "Strangers," while Sinatra was rehearsing for a television show, he called me into his office and told me about a demo he had been listening to called "That's Life." He said he liked the feel of it so much—and other people's response to it—he was planning on singing it on the show. He played it for me and said, "I think we ought to make a record of this, James. What do you think?"

"Absolutely." I did agree with him on this. You knew he didn't respect you if he didn't ask you, but *told* you.

We booked the session for "That's Life" in what was then a new state-of-the-art eight-track facility at Western Recorders. Neither Eddie nor I had ever cut anything in eight tracks, so there was some tension and excitement going in.

I booked Frank for an hour later than the musicians. This gave Eddie and me time for the standard run-throughs for arrangements and mike placements. But when I arrived, Eddie, the best engineer for live recordings I ever worked with, was ashen. For reasons he couldn't explain, only the microphones for the rhythm section were coming into the tape machine. The entire string and horn sections and the background singers were not getting on tape. You could hear them in the headphones and out in the studio, but not through the board. Eddie later had three heart attacks; it's a wonder his first didn't happen then.

"It'll be okay, relax, Eddie. We've got the rhythm section. No problem."

I went out into the studio and moved the acoustic-guitar mike over to Sinatra's music stand. While Eddie's assistants were frantically trying to fix the eight-track board, I said, "Now Frank'll hear everybody except the acoustic guitar during playback. No problem."

I took the orchestra through the arrangements once or twice and was making some minor changes when in walked Sinatra—a half hour early. I was like, *What the hell're you* doin' *here, man?* But I said nothing. With him was his very young and beautiful future wife, Mia Farrow, with whom Sinatra was then having a much-gossiped-about affair. Mo Ostin, the label chief, and a few cronies also showed up. There was a veil of secrecy surrounding the Farrow affair, and a pesky paparazzo known for chasing people all over town had been hounded and run off by Sinatra's security people before the session started. Sinatra clearly didn't want to waste more than a few minutes at this session. When he was in a hurry, he wasn't thinking chart position.

"James," he said, "I gotta get this thing done. I got a dinner date I've gotta go to."

Oh, okay. I wisely decided not to tell him that the studio equipment was breaking down. But Sinatra was ready to go. He sang the song twice with the orchestra to get himself loose, because this arrangement was supposed to be stronger than the one he'd learned for the TV show.

When he had finished the second take, he took off his headphones and came straight in for a listen-back before I could even ask him in. I prepared him: "Frank, you have to understand this is a brand-new studio, with some kinks being worked out. The strings aren't on the tape, the vocals either. It'll be just you and the rhythm section. But don't worry. I'll put those on after you leave and it'll be just what you heard in the headphones."

He nodded indifferently and we listened back.

Something bothered me about the takes. They didn't work. They sounded too hip and pretty. I was after an arrangement with *balls*, with *bite*. When his voice came off pretty, the rhythm section backed off and calmed down with him. Aside from the fact that half the musicians were not being recorded, it just wasn't there for me.

When it ended, Sinatra looked over at Mo and asked him what he thought. "It's great, Frank." Then the cronies all nodded together. Frank shot me a look of impatience and put me on the spot. "Well, okay?"

I knew this wasn't going to go over real well, but I had to stick to my instincts. That was my job. "Well, *not* if we really want a killer hit, it isn't. We've got to cut it one more time and make it stronger on the bottom."

Dead silence for what seemed like a minute—but was probably fifteen seconds. Sinatra fixed those cold, steely-blue eyes on me during that silence. The cronies were cringing, thinking I'd lost my marbles. Frank broke the silence. "Let's do it," he mumbled, and headed back out into the studio.

I knew he was pissed. Nobody ever said no when he said, "That's it." But he'd have been more pissed if I'd backed down and put out a weak single that didn't turn anyone on. He was in my world now and trusted me enough to let me call it. If he was reputed to eat engineers or producers for dinner, it was probably because they let him. He was in control, but he had asked a question, and I answered honestly.

Still he was angry—and I only had one more crack at it.

The rhythm section had also come in for the playback. With my back against the wall, I told them, "Now, look, I want you to *stand* on this son of a bitch, put some goddamn *kick* in it like 'The Stripper.'" That was David Rose's 1962 instrumental hit with a hot brass section and a kick-butt drum bottom. That was the feel I wanted—only better. "This is Sinatra," I reminded them. "Let's don't be hip and cute."

They went back out and nailed it, just drove the song and gave Sinatra a huge energetic push. Frank was pissed, and you could hear him channeling it when he snarled, "That's life, that's what all the people say." He came off wonderfully intense, and when it ended, he signed off, "Ohh, yeahhh." The echo died, Ernie cut everyone off, I leaned into the talk-back mike and shouted, "Great. You got it."

Frank turned and walked out the back door. Never said "Thanks," "Good night," "Good job," nothing. His people were still staring at me like, *You have fucked up big-time.* My feeling was, *Screw it, I got what I wanted, which is what he wanted.*

While the musicians took a break, we moved the mikes around to get the horn, string, and backing vocal tracks I needed to fill in the tracks. Then someone in the band suggested an organ intro. Dirt called in a keyboardist, and within thirty minutes he was wheeling in an organ and setting up for what turned into a great organ intro.

I had never worked eight-track, so I didn't even know where to put all the stuff I had now. And there wasn't time to discuss it. I learned as I went along. I got the band down to two tracks and then pulled up the rough mix and had all this other space to lay in the overdubs. Suddenly it was obvious how great this would sound with the added clarity and textures of eight-track.

Dirt and I walked out of there with an acetate at about four A.M. I left another acetate to be hand-delivered to Sinatra's house at ten in the morning. Dirt and I went back to my house, sat up with a bottle of Jack Daniel's, and wore out that damn acetate until daybreak. When you come out of a grueling all-nighter at the studio with a killer song like that, you've got to hear it, get absorbed by it until you've played it clear out of your system. Listening back as night turns to dawn to a piece of music you've just created has always been one of the sweet rewards—and natural highs—that come with the record business.

Exhausted and pleasantly sloshed, I crashed sometime around seven A.M. and fell into a deep sleep.

When the phone rang, I stirred but didn't get up. Then my housekeeper shook me awake. I had no idea what time or day it was. But a woman was excitedly saying, "Mr. Sinatra on the phone."

Half asleep, I shuffled from the bed and croaked hello.

"James," he said, wasting no time, "it's just brilliant. Thanks." *Click.*

TEN

DECISIVE AND EFFICIENT though I was in stream-
lining Reprise's roster and reviving Dean and Sinatra, my personal life throughout the sixties was marked by turbulence and
calamity.

It makes sense, given how much I was drinking and how
much of my life then was spent in a close, windowless control
booth. It was easy to lose all sense of the outside world and not
know day from night. I had money, I was young, I was hanging
out with a fast party crowd. How was I supposed to know how to
go out into the world and find the right kind of *partner?* I never
learned much about dealing with the opposite sex living in Dumas, and since then my whole life had been focused on making
music. Surely my first marriage did not suggest I had a lock on
domestic bliss. It wasn't clear to me at all in the sixties, but I
would have years of trouble making intimate relationships work
with women. So, during that high-flying time at Reprise, there
was bound to be some turmoil in my personal life—moments I
would not be proud of, times when I was an irresponsible
drinker and a difficult companion to the women in my life.

Cutting through the big roster had taken time, and one of the
last acts I dealt with was the McGuire Sisters. The trio's big No 1
hits, "Sincerely" and "Sugartime," had come a decade earlier.
But, like other fifties casualties of the rock explosion who no
longer charted hits, the McGuires had been born-again as sixties
superstars in Vegas. After finding hits for Dean and Frank, I
wanted to take a good look at these acts and see if we could
strike gold again—before dropping them.

I took a *real* good look when I met Phyllis McGuire. She was good-looking, friendly, just past thirty—and very direct. We went out a couple times in Vegas, and the chemistry between us was obvious. I had every reason to believe she was unattached.

In L.A., Phyllis and I double-dated with Dirt and her older sister, Dorothy. We went club hopping—P.J.'s, Ciro's, dinner at Martoni's—among the stars and gossip columnists. Once the Jack Daniel's started flowing, Phyllis and I were all over each other.

But any plan of a smooth seduction back in her hotel room was soon dashed. I got so drunk, Phyllis had to tilt me upside down against a slantboard—a trendy thing to sober you up by forcing blood to your head. Instead, I had barf rushing to my head and made it to the bathroom just in time to heave. I was so embarrassed, I left.

Booze just might have saved my life that night. I went back to Vegas the next day to meet with Keely Smith, whose next record I was planning to produce. L.A.'s gossip columns had run items about Phyllis and our sexy night on the town. A friend of mine discreetly called to inform me that such high-profile club hopping was a big mistake: Miss McGuire, he said, was most definitely connected—romantically at least—to Chicago mobster Sam Giancana. I called to get Dirt up to speed: "Bowen, you son of a bitch. With my luck they'll send a hit man after us with bad aim and he'll try to take you out and get me instead."

A few days later I heard a knock at the door of Keely's house in Vegas and kind of froze when I opened up and stared at two giants of Italian-American heritage. "You Jimmy Bowen?" one asked.

"Why, yes, sir, I am."

"Do you understand that you are never to see Phyllis McGuire again?" *Plenty* of blood was rushing to my head now.

"Well, yes, sir."

"For as long as you live?"

"Yes, sir."

"If you wanna live."

"Absolutely, sir."

"You do understand us?"

"Never again."

"Thank you, Mr. Bowen."

The message had been delivered loud and clear. Sincerely. Giancana must have thought I was aware of his connection to Phyllis; but since I worked for Sinatra, he let me off light.

Just to be on the safe side, I decided to drop the McGuires from the label. That was *business.*

●

If I dodged a bullet with Phyllis, I soon found myself in a far more complex—and costly—situation with Keely Smith. The perfect word to describe it: marriage.

Keely was a wonderful singer with a great sexy look—the dark, intense eyes; the short black hair and Dutch-girl bangs. She was also five or so years older than I was, which was alluring. She and Prima had had their big hit, "That Old Black Magic," in 1958. They also had two young daughters, Toni and Luanne.

From the start sparks flew: one night Keely just seduced me—and I fought her off for maybe thirty seconds as I tussled with the ethics of mixing business and pleasure. Turned out they mixed real nicely—then. The lure was part older woman–younger guy, part artist-producer. I loved her voice, so full of emotion and fire. Keely was an accomplished, worldly, sexy woman. At her peak she was making well over a half-million dollars working Vegas three months a year. She was a class act full of sultry charm, and I was very drawn to her, simple as that.

We began dating around the time I was working with Dean. Dirt and I were sharing a place with a crazy Brit friend named Jack. Jack was nuts. His social life centered on his vibrator. Jack ran it through the AC wall socket. Batteries were kids' stuff. We knew when he had a girl in his bed. The lights would dim. At our house the hippie slogan would have been, Turn on, tune in, brown out. The motor rumbled through the house.

Dating Keely took me away from the bachelor-pad life, and gave my life some stability—or so I thought.

Another sign I was maturing: I decided to invest all that back-end profit so that I wouldn't go broke again. I acquired a 50 percent stake in a Beverly Hills jewelry store owned by a compulsive gambler. She had lost her husband, Bel Air house, and car in legalized poker tournaments. I came along just before she royal-flushed the jewelry business into the ground.

I did get a good deal on an engagement ring for Keely—using a big yellowish diamond that my partner said was worth $10,000 in 1965 money. Keely had it appraised and insured, and then stunned me when she announced, "It's a rare canary-yellow diamond worth $40,000."

No wonder our jewelry store was going under.

Another great business opportunity presented itself when I met a loan shark who was looking for a backer. He charged 25 percent interest to people who couldn't get credit from banks.

"You need cash in front," he explained as we sat up getting drunk, "so you can loan it out and collect big profits on the vigorish." Sounded like yet another solid return on my investment.

We did okay for a while until I learned how exposed my stake was to financial risk: while my loan shark and I were having dinner one night, he admitted he was having big problems collecting from a major Beverly Hills client. I asked what kind of problems. "Chick owns a jewelry store goin' down the toilet."

Whoa! This was incredible. I cracked up and told him of my jewelry-store deal. "Wait a minute, you're her partner?" he squealed. "Shit, that dame's already down a hundred grand, sellin' off all her better pieces at rock-bottom prices just to pay us back."

Yeah, right, my fiancée had one of them on her finger.

Amazing: I was fronting my jewelry partner cash to keep her gambling habit going and she was selling off our dwindling assets to pay the vig. When the loan shark couldn't collect from *her*, I couldn't collect from *him*. A bad double hit.

The next day I snapped into action. I went to our jewelry store with a large paper bag, locked the front door, and told my partner and her salesgirl, "Don't either of you goddamn move or scream." All I was missing was a stocking over my head and a gun. They stared in horror as I dumped all the shiny shit I could find into the bag. My eye naturally went to the cheap pearls and big costume pieces of junk and missed the tiny stuff.

I guessed I made off with $40,000 worth of shiny stuff. My loan guy wasn't so sure, and called in a squinty little fella with a magnifying glass wedged into one eye. The guy emptied the bag, gave it the once-over, and muttered, "Twenty-five hundred, maybe three grand, tops."

I lost my butt in the jewelry business, and got out of the loan-shark trade before going flat broke—vowing to stay aboveboard from now on in pursuit of big profit.

As omens go, the $10,000 ring should have told me something. Keely and I had our share of spats. One had to do with my dating Nancy Sinatra. I produced a song for Nancy, who was about twenty-five then and on the rebound from ex-husband Tommy Sands. Mo Ostin had asked me to work with her after she signed with Reprise. Our overdubbing had run well into the night. I was walking out to the parking lot with her when she caught me off guard. "So is this thing with Keely really serious or what?"

"Well, actually no, now that you mention it."

Before long, Nancy and I were hanging out together. She had a house at the bottom of Bel Air, but she was often up at the place Dirt and I had. I don't *know* if Frank knew his daughter was dating his A&R guy, who was engaged to one of his artists—but he probably did. I spent a weekend with her in Palm Springs, in one of the two bungalows her father had built for JFK's Secret Service detail at his place on the grounds of Tamarask Country Club. Kennedy had bunked in the main house when he visited as senator, but after 1960 his advisers recommended against hanging out with Frank, so he stayed instead with Bing Crosby. That pissed Frank off so badly, he became a Republican.

I didn't realize how involved Nancy was getting. She was a real neat, sweet kid, and being around her drew me in, though I was engaged. Maybe it was wanting what she couldn't have. Or the rebound thing. We were all bouncing around a wild L.A. scene, I was moving a hundred miles an hour every day, and someone's feelings could easily get lost in the shuffle.

Dating Nancy did convince me that I needed to break off with Keely. When I went to a party at Joe Smith's house in the Valley—Joe was now GM at Warner Bros. Records—I got to drinking and mulling over my love-life problems. Boozed up is a bad time to make big decisions. I was soon half bagged, with a private plane waiting at the airport, phoning Dirt to tell him we were going to Vegas. "The engagement's off. I'm not marrying her. I'm getting that damn ring back. It's worth forty grand."

I passed out as our tiny plane got tossed around in some heavy updrafts and bad weather. Dirt was white with terror. Still, we finally made it to Vegas. The next night I saw Keely in her suite at the Sands. I was there to end it and get the ring back. Dirt tracked down Keely's brother, Piggy, and lined up some girls for a party at Keely's to celebrate surviving the flight. Then they hit the tables.

I had Dirt and Piggy paged at the casino. Keely told Piggy to fetch the ring from her safe at home. Dirt got on: "I can't believe you talked her out of the goddamn ring," he said.

I said nothing. Dirt and Piggy then met us at the lounge in time for Keely's late set. When they sat down, I broke the news: "We're gettin' married. Tonight. Dirt, you're best man."

"Oh, *shit*. I've been lied to and misled by you before, Bowen, but this here's a biggie." He reached for an ice bucket, started pouring scotch, and got shit-faced.

Joe E. Brown told about two jokes and walked off. "That's it, folks," he said. "Post time. I'm goin' to a wedding." Then Keely did a short set and walked off. It was past midnight when we headed to a twenty-four-hour instant-marriage chapel on the Strip.

The ripped britches was a sign my first wedding was a mistake. This time Joe E. Brown took a piss in the chapel parking lot and spilled champagne all over the preacher. "If you don't get this guy away from me," the furious preacher seethed, "I'm not doing the ceremony."

I ignored these signs as well. I was in shock; my head still wasn't screwed on tight. Somewhere in the haze my agenda had gotten turned around. It hit me when I woke up and saw that ring poking up beneath the sheets on Keely's left hand. *Holy shit. This is my wife!*

Shortly past dawn Dirt beat it out of Vegas to do some damage control in Bel Air. But word had gotten back and the damage beat him there by twenty phone calls—all of them from Nancy. She was, Dirt said, "shattered" and stunned and "came unglued" as he tried to talk her down. Dirt called it the longest night of his life—and spent much of it wondering if Frank's henchmen, who we imagined were on top of Nancy's movements anyhow, were going to do us in. We weren't sure.

Dirt had seen enough craziness. He moved way the hell over in Glendale, went underground, and hid out for four months before surfacing again.

I probably should have gone with him. Instead, Keely and I settled in a house I bought in Toluca Lake, near the Warners office. She kept her Vegas house, but her two young daughters and other assorted family members gradually moved in with us. It was a nice piece of property for $129,000, but it soon got crowded with her mom, two brothers, two yapping poodles, and a Great Dane named Napoleon, who was big enough to run the damn Kentucky Derby.

Keely stopped working after our 1965 wedding. I never *asked* her not to work. The truth was, "I do" was the last thing in tune that came out of her mouth for three years. She did a few game shows, which paid her in gifts, not cash. One show sent her Polaroid film, which spoils after ninety days. We had enough for ninety *years*. She should've taken the $320 scale.

Having been a single working mom for several years, Keely wanted to stay home with her kids, which I understood. She was devoted to her girls, good sweet kids who have kept in touch with me through the years. But Keely and I were at each other all the time. We got crazy and had some terrible fights.

As if there weren't enough of us already, Keely started to talk about wanting another child. By then things were breaking down and I was fixin' to leave. Maybe she figured a child would help make things right with us. I had always assumed I would never have any children. But Keely kept at it.

I agreed to provide some sperm for a fertility specialist. We thought booze might have lowered my count or dulled my sperm. Keely took my "captured" sample to a doctor and came home thrilled. "He told me it looks great," she said. I was by the phone. "If you'll quit smokin' *and* drinkin' and lose about twenty pounds, your sperm count'll come back up and we can have a child."

I grabbed the phone and called our liquor store. "Send me a carton of Kools and a case of Jack Daniel's—and get 'em over here as fast as you can."

Keely was always a warm, loving mom to her kids—and has remained so to this day. As a singer her marvelous vocal gift could tap into the same passion and intensity that turned us on as lovers—or fighters. The less she sang, it seemed, the more that "chemistry" pushed us into loud, ugly fights. Keely had some fired-up Native American blood—a part of her that couldn't tolerate drinking. And I had my own problems drinking too much. Most of our worst brawls were set off by booze.

I moved out in 1968 and rented a rustic-looking house way up on top of Mulholland Drive near Laurel Canyon. I shared it with two guys, Tom Thacker, an old friend from Dumas who was in "the business"; and Bruce Hinton. Bruce, who was also going through a divorce, had become a close personal friend when he was head of promotion for Warner Reprise.

I was afraid Keely might ambush me up there, so I had a security-alarm system so tight, not even a bird could get past the front gate without setting something off. Plus, for extra measure I had a gas-station hose stretched across the driveway that dinged when a pair of car tires went over it. An early-warning system.

It was a great scene. Our place was a music-industry open house Friday nights. On any given night Glen Campbell, Duane Eddy, Mac Davis, Glen D Hardin, or James Burton—these last two played in Elvis's band—might come over and start jamming.

There was pot smoked around the house, but I was still only drinking.

In fact the drinking was bad enough that I hired a driver named Bud, who was pretty much on call around the clock. Bud often slept in his clothes on top of a bed in a small room off the kitchen. Some nights I'd come crash at five and need Bud to get me out on the golf course by seven.

No amount of security could fool the Indian scout in Keely. One night I was hanging out on the couch with a date and another couple. The house was locked up tight. Soft music, dim lights, a couple of toddies on ice—a warm, mellow evening.

Suddenly I saw Keely rise up from behind the couch, clutching a table lamp in her hand high over her head. I was too stunned to move, plus I'd been drinking for two or three hours, so my reflexes weren't real sharp.

Keely brought that damn lamp down right in my face, splitting my lip wide open. I was furious. My date was flipping out. This madness was supposed to be over.

I threw Keely down and sat over her until the cops arrived. I asked her how she'd gotten in. She had parked her car on the street, somehow got around the kitchen side, got down on all fours, and crawled through the damn doggy door.

The cops drove me to an Encino hospital to get my lip sewn up. I decided not to press charges.

When we finally had our day in court, Keely told the judge I had asked her to quit working, which I never did. Keely claimed I'd hit her, which I never did; I shook her a couple of times to get her attention. Keely told the judge I screwed around on her. Well, she did have the goods on me there. We had thrown a party, and as it wound down, I got wound up and, with Keely already in bed, I went home with a woman guest of ours and didn't come back till dawn. The woman ran into Keely at a bar soon afterward and decided to bring her up to date on that one.

I never did get the ring back, but my impulsive decision to fly to Vegas and try wound up costing me much, much more than that was worth. Keely got the Toluca Lake house, a car, two run-down rental properties I had in Venice, and $30,000 a year for three years. I paid the lawyers another $60,000.

There would be one final insult added to all that financial injury. I had set up my own company by then called Amos Productions. The lawyer I hired to handle my divorce was with the firm

I used for some business matters. His name was Bert Pines, a nerdy kind of guy with glasses, who lived two doors down from my bachelor pad. After the stress of the legal wrangling and finality of the divorce, I went out partying all night.

Two hours into a deep sleep I felt someone shaking me. "Get up, James," he was saying. It was guy in a suit and glasses. "Wake up and you can sign the papers. The divorce is final. We can collect our fees."

Bert was shoving legal papers in my face. "You son of a bitch," I yelled. "Don't you come to my house to get your goddamn money." Enraged, I got out of bed and chased him through my house, down the driveway, and halfway back to his own house up the street. Which was when I realized I was butt-naked.

End of story—or so I thought.

A few years later I was out late drinking with a golf buddy in his office on Sunset. I said good-bye, swung my car out of the underground parking, and headed for home on Sunset. I promptly ran over a No Left Turn sign while making a left turn. By the time I saw the sign, it was flat on the ground, and a bunch of sirens and flashing lights were coming my way.

"Walk this straight line," the officer said, pointing to a seam in the sidewalk. My head was spinning. "Forget it," I mumbled. "Take me in." I was booked for DWI and spent the night in jail. My new lawyer worked out a deal where I got off with a $1,500 fine, had the DWI scratched from my record, and agreed to go to traffic school. He had it all smoothed over.

He called me a couple of days later. "James, we've got some problem here and I really don't get it. I had everything worked out, but I just got your papers back and right on top it says, 'No Deals, B.P.' Now what the hell that's all about I don't know."

Oh, I knew. The city attorney of L.A. was now Bert Pines, a man with some good memory. He shot that deal down the moment he saw my name. It was Keely's ultimate revenge.

ELEVEN

MY FIRST TASTE of running my own company came in 1967 when I set up an independent deal through Warners called Amos Productions. I was still at the label, trying to look for hits for Sammy Davis, Jr., but I was tiring of the pressure of dealing with all the big names at Reprise and wanted to have more of my own show.

I hired as my in-house producer a young arranger-guitarist named Mike Post. I'd used Mike for a bunch of Dean Martin sessions and signed him as an artist to Reprise. Mike was only in his early twenties, but he had already played with Dick and Deedee, and on Sonny & Cher's mid-sixties' hits, such as "I Got You Babe." He was a brash, aggressive kid who you knew was going to make it.

Mike called his sound "folk-and-roll antiprotest music." I produced a couple of tracks with him, but nothing came of them. He was using his sessions money to produce demos on his own. He pitched one to a half-dozen labels before coming up to the big house on Kling Street in Toluca Lake. I was still with Keely, drinking way too much Jack Daniel's, and just starting my day when Mike showed up. It was three in the afternoon. He found me on the edge of the bed in my robe and houndstooth cap, hung over and flanked by a bucket of chicken and a couple of tuna sandwiches. I grumbled hello and asked, "So what've ya got?" It was a blues track.

"All right. Put the damn thing on."

When it was over, I said, "Well, that's pretty interesting. Did you produce that?" He said yes. "Well," I said, "here's the deal. I don't love this record, but you'd be a hell of a producer, and I've got my own deal with Warners now." Mike was waiting.

"I'll give you fifteen grand the first year, seventeen-five the second, and twenty the third—against *all* your producing, all your writing, and all your publishing." It was a great, lopsided deal—for me. Mike waited three seconds. "Deal!" he said.

I was amazed. "Don't you want to talk to a lawyer?"

"No. I'm tired of being a second-rate guitarist. I want to produce. You're the hottest producer in the business now and you just gave me the chance to break in."

I gave Mike three things right away to get him up to speed. One: a nickname, B.J., for Baby Jew. Two: I hooked him up to a twenty-four-hour hot line to me. Three: I gave him a year and a half to cut me a Top 20 record. Mike was okay with the nickname and the deadline. It was the phone that would drive him insane.

Days later he got a knock at the door and in walked a telephone guy holding a red phone with no dial. "I'm here to install the hot line," he announced.

Mike was dumbfounded. "The *hot* line? Isn't that, like, what goes between Khrushchev and Johnson?"

The guy looked down at his papers. "No, the work order here says this one goes between Bowen and Post. Right by Mr. Post's bed. Where's the bed?"

Mike shrugged. "Well, all right. Whatever."

My phone was in, so I knew when the installation was done. A hot line was great: no dialing. You picked up on one end, it rang on the other. I picked up my handset. Two seconds later I had Mike. "B.J.?" I said.

"Yeah?"

"Just wanted to know if this thing's working."

Click.

I'd kind of Sinatra'd Mike to welcome him on board. He had recently married and lived nearby in Studio City. I never thought twice about hot-lining Mike at midnight to do work or come over and play double gin and shoot pool. I was an after-dark drinker. I didn't start until the sun went down, then wouldn't stop until the sun was almost back up. Mike was often the only one strong enough to carry me upstairs and dump my body on the bed.

With Mike scrambling to make his Top 20 deadline, I turned my attention to Sammy. I was determined to get Sammy a hit record before I left Reprise. In 1968 I met with him in New York, where he was in a musical, to play him a song. Getting through Sammy's security was an ordeal. Sammy had been getting death threats, he said, and, given that he had converted to Judaism and married white Swedish actress May Britt, it was hard to know if they were from racial bigots, anti-Semites, or both. Besides, racial politics had gotten touchy in the late sixties. Militant black groups had been tugging on Sammy to help the "brothers" raise money for black racial or social causes. So things were tense around him.

Sammy's greatness as an entertainer—and his marvelous warmth and decency—were undeniable. If Sinatra was in a realm unto himself as pop-culture icon and entrepreneur, and if Dean was shy and aloof, then Sammy was Mr. Show Business. He had been singing and dancing from the age of three or four with his father and uncle in the Will Mastin Trio.

Because Sammy did Vegas, TV variety-show shtick, and middle-of-the-road music, his career trapped him culturally somewhere between the Black Panthers and the Rat Pack. But he was a fighter. He had endured racism all his life and then, in 1954, he lost his left eye in a car crash. Then he made a strong comeback with three hits a year later.

But now, in the late sixties, he had other issues. He spent freely and had, it was believed, million-dollar tax problems. And he had a new kind of identity crisis. After meeting with a radical black group in Chicago, he said something remarkable: "You know, Bowen, I worked all my life to be white and just about had it figured out—and now they tell me black is beautiful."

Somehow he kept it under control—the mansions, the VIP backstage parties, limos, entourages, women until all hours of the night. He drank wine coolers, but I never saw him drunk or incapacitated. If there was a heavy coke scene, as was later rumored, I never saw it. Sammy was simply a fireball who tore through life. Onstage he was incredible.

But Sammy had trouble hitting his stride in the studio—and we missed on the first three or four tracks we cut together.

Mike Post was way ahead of schedule. By the end of 1967 he was producing a debut album by a five-member folk-rock group he put together from the New Christy Minstrels, the First Edition. Mike had brought them to me to produce through Amos, and I released them on Reprise.

Mike felt the group's front man should be Mike Settle. To him the fourth most talented member—"an afterthought"—was a singer-bassist named Kenny Rogers. But the track that jumped off the First Edition LP was a killer late-sixties' Mickey Newbury song called "Just Dropped In (to See What Condition My Condition Was In)." Lead singer: Kenny Rogers. Mike had only let Kenny sing lead on it to appease him. The record was a Top 5 hit in early 1968. Mike beat my deadline by almost a year.

Mike got stubborn and still didn't hear Kenny as a great singer, but the hit gave Kenny some leverage—as in wanting to get rid of Mike as producer. But Mike insisted on releasing a follow-up by one of the other male singers, and the record didn't work at radio and the group lost its momentum.

Mike was just hitting stride himself. He came to the house late one night, on a creative rush with "something real special." It was mid-'68, and I was now in my final days with Keely. By midnight, as Mike liked to put it, I was "pretty well greased."

Mike found me in my office by the pool. It was summer and I was listening to some music with a couple of friends, as I always liked to do in the wee hours. "What've you got?" I asked in my this-better-be-good snarl.

"Well, just listen to this." Mike put on a reference disk and we listened. I reacted instantly. I pulled the disk off my turntable and snarled. "B.J., I can't hear any fucking melody in this." I marched outside and flung the thing into the pool.

Mike freaked. "Bowen, goddammit. That's my only copy."

"Aw, fuck, it ain't worth a shit," I grumbled. "Go back and cut somethin' with a damn melody."

The track was "Classical Gas," a pop-classical instrumental by acoustic guitarist Mason Williams, a composer and comedy writer for the Smothers Brothers. Joe Smith, head of Warner Bros., had liked Mike's arrangements on some other cuts and asked me to loan Mike out to produce and arrange Mason for Warners.

Mike came back the next day with a new "ref" and played it. When it was done, I said, "Jeez, good record. Really different."

"No shit, man. I wanted you to hear it when you weren't drunk." Mike definitely knew how to make a Mike Post record. He loved Mason's guitar playing, but talked Mason out of using a bass drum, guitar, and piano; he composed and added a weird bridge of Wagnerian horns to break up a tedious stretch of music.

These changes pissed Mason off. Then "Gas" shot to No. 2 and got Mike a Grammy for his crafty arrangements. Mason wouldn't work with Mike again—and ran out of gas himself when his next three singles didn't crack *Billboard*'s Top 90.

Mike's stock was starting to soar and I decided to put him with Sammy. Having pulled off being "white," Sammy felt he had to do an R&B record to assert his "blackness." Trouble was, black wasn't always beautiful when Sammy tried to sing it. We had a long rap about it and he was determined: "I'm black, I'm getting pressure to be black, I gotta do this."

Mike had grown up on blues and R&B greats; he was thrilled. "Two Jews makin' a soul album," I said. "Go for it."

But it didn't work out. When Sammy couldn't get some vocal lick down, they both got frustrated. Mike was upset at how unsoulful Sammy could sound, and Sammy picked up on it. "What's wrong with *you*?" he asked Mike.

"That's just not how it should go." Mike then sang a few bars—and put a lot of soul into it. Sammy was taken aback. "Like who *are* you, man? What's your story?"

"You mean, why is my skin white? Is that what you're trying to say?" They ended up talking all this out, with Mike finally producing *Sammy Steps Out*. But while doing the LP, Sammy's frustration peaked and he snapped. He broke down crying, slamming his fist against the wall and banging his head on the sound gobo, a portable device positioned around a mike stand for isolation baffling. "Oh, fuck it, fuck it, fuck it," he screamed. "You're blacker than I am."

"Yeah, okay, so what?" Mike said through the glass. "I grew up on Chuck Berry, Little Richard, and Ray Charles. You grew up studying Sinatra."

Toward the end of 1968 I met Sammy at his office on Sunset because I found him a song called "I've Gotta Be Me" from the Broadway show *Golden Rainbow*. Sammy was shooting pool when I walked in. Before I even mentioned the tune, he said, "Listen, man, this isn't like a *hit* song, but I got a thing I just gotta do—from a Broadway show. It's called 'I've Gotta Be Me.'"

That was a good omen, and we cut it. Nobody believed me when I said it could be a hit. But after mastering it, I sat up all night, played it, and knew it was a hit. To placate the label, we used that song as a B-side, and I chose another track as the single—but decided to call the album *I've Gotta Be Me*. This got by everyone.

When the single was ready, Mo came to me and asked, "Bowen, are you aware that Sammy's album title is a B-side, not the single?" He thought this might be an oversight.

"Oh, yeah, Mo, I did that. It absolutely fits Sammy Davis and the mood of the album." Mo paused, then said, "Oh, okay. Just wanted to make sure."

After slipping it by Mo we put the single out. On my own I hired a couple of independent promotion guys to work the B-side. One of them got a pop radio deejay at KRLA to flip the single and go on "I've Gotta Be Me." The song took off and became Sammy's biggest hit since 1955. My gamble paid off beautifully: driven by the title track's success, LP sales went through the roof.

As we did several LPs together, Sammy clicked and evolved into a terrific, self-assured vocalist. His greatest thrill, I believe, was when Sinatra heard him sing live in the early seventies and told him what a fine singer he'd become. Sammy puffed up to around five feet four inches for several weeks.

Still, finding hits for Sammy was hard. He had irons in all kinds of fires. Slowing him down long enough for a song meeting was difficult. And he always had his Rat Pack entourage and yes-men around. When he did show up for meetings or recordings, he was worn out or just pitifully unprepared. Poor preparation likely cost us one killer hit.

One of the talented songwriters I'd take pitches from was Mac Davis. Mac came to my house one night and sang something called "In the Ghetto." Immediately I thought it would be perfect for Sammy. I sent Mac to Lake Tahoe to play it live for him.

When Mac came back, he said, "Bowen, I don't know whether to thank ya or kill ya." He and his music publisher, Billy Strange, were the only white men in Sammy's dressing-room entourage, which included Jesse Jackson and some Black Power cronies. Mac found it uncomfortably tense.

I knew the feeling. At a meeting in Chicago once, Sammy jumped up and eagerly tried introducing me around to the "brothers," but the first two didn't even look at me or extend their hands. I got the hell outta there and waited for Sammy in my hotel room. If Mac was a little uneasy as he got out his acoustic guitar to sing "In the Ghetto," I understood.

But when he was finished, the brothers were in tears. Jesse Jackson sat in silence, then asked Mac to sing it over again. The next morning Jesse knocked on Mac's hotel room door and said, "I'm sorry, but you gotta sing that song for me a couple more times before you leave." When Mac told me this story, I knew Sammy had to cut it.

Unfortunately, we went into a big recording studio with a big orchestra and big entourage. Reverend Jackson loved "Ghetto"; he sat next to me at the board as if he were my first engineer. But Sammy showed up two and a half hours late and wasn't on it at all. He couldn't get the melody. Poor preparation and distraction blew the session.

Mac made out just fine with the song: "Ghetto" became one of two million-selling gold records Elvis had in 1969 ("Suspicious Minds" was the other)—a major comeback for the aging King.

If Sammy sometimes lost his way in the studio, he was brilliant onstage. I cut a couple of live albums with him in Vegas, and Sammy was always in supreme control. One night my engineer, Eddie Brackett, and I were way up on the third floor above the lounge in the Sands Hotel. We had a small remote-control board and two recorders working in sequence to get the full two-hour show. We snaked the mike cord from the base of the stand all through the lounge and up to our board. The orchestra started playing and a line of big-busted chorus girls came out kicking and dancing to fire up the audience.

Suddenly one of the girls caught our mike cord with her high heel and with one high kick yanked that sucker out of the mike stand. Our channel into the board went dead. Sammy's name was announced and he came trotting out. We were getting *nothing*.

I ran down and told one of Sammy's guys, who motioned to Sammy to stop. Unfazed, Sammy cut the music with a slash of his arm and, without missing a beat, cheerfully announced, "Ladies and gentlemen, I was going to let you know after this song, but I'll tell you now—we're taping this show for a live album. So let's give my producer a big welcome. Come on out here, Jimmy. Ladies and gentlemen, Mr. Jimmy Bowen!"

The crowd roared and a spot followed me out to Sammy at center stage. I was mortified. "There's some kind of problem, is that right?" Sammy just kept the patter flowing. The crew handed him a new mike and worked with Eddie to fix the other offstage. "Well," I said nervously, "one of those dancin' girls caught the mike cord with her heel." I sweated bullets out there while Sammy kept it going for five of the longest minutes of my life.

Finally the lights went down, Sammy walked offstage, I went back upstairs, the girls came out again, and as Sammy trotted out again, the crowd roared even louder. Nothing could stop Sammy. The stage had always been his home—the one constant in his life, one place where he knew exactly who he was.

•

Vegas was not a place where *I* could always keep my bearings. I did a lot of partying there through the Reprise years, more around Sammy than Dean or Sinatra.

Between the action at the blackjack tables and some of the most fabulous-looking hookers in the world, there was more than enough to keep you going all night long. Of course the major social buzzwords then were free love, not safe sex. Even when the love wasn't free, you didn't worry that it could kill you.

The casino was at once an exotic, tacky, risqué, edgy world. It blew my mind, for example, to learn that some of these great-looking all-American girls got into hooking to work off some kind of "fix" arranged through a shady underworld connection. Some fixes involved drug busts, but many involved secret abortions back when they were illegal and risky and had to be kept hush-hush. A girl who used an underworld network this way might be asked to repay the mob with this form of servitude for a specified time. They preyed on young girls, some of whom clearly made real good money in the process.

It was neat the way the pit bosses and dealers knew you by name and winked at you or said hello. When Frank or Dean performed, they'd come out after the show and get back behind a blackjack table and deal cards. You wanted to get in on that table because you knew they'd show you cards before you had to hit or not hit and let you win two or three grand that way. The pit boss didn't care; it drew a crowd, the odds were about 7 to 1 against you anyhow, and as soon as a few high rollers dropped by, they'd make it back real quick.

I gambled at blackjack when I had all those royalties rolling in. I'd take over a table and play $500 a hand. They played one deck and I got pretty sharp at counting cards—not to where I'd get banned. Now they play with four- or five-deck chutes. Counting brought the odds down to maybe 3 to 1 or 2 to 1.

The guy who really beat me at blackjack wasn't the dealer but the bartender. I was up once about $30,000 and just couldn't bring myself to quit, since as long as I was playing, they kept the free cocktails coming. Nothing clouds your judgment worse than booze. You can't win at the tables against Jack Daniel's. I left Vegas more than once with nothing in my pocket but ten dollars and a plane ticket home.

Mike Post produced a second First Edition album but it stiffed when it failed to get any radio play. By the time they were ready for their third LP, I knew we had to make some changes. I didn't want to lose an act like them to an outsider because I felt they still had the potential for big hits. So I hotlined Mike and told him to meet me at Martoni's.

"Mike," I said, "I'm going to hurt you. I know it."

"Go ahead."

"I've got to take this artist away from you. I have to produce them—"

"Hey," he said. "I understand a hundred percent. It's okay. I don't hold it against you."

"—and make Kenny the front man."

In my first session we cut "But You Know I Love You," with Kenny's lead vocal. It was a Top 20 hit that got them back in business. They loved working with me because I had the opposite approach from Mike. Mike was so dominant that he'd write out everybody's parts the way he heard them. My theory was— and always remained—that it's the artist's money, his or her life and music. If they've got a music to do, a music they believe in, then do it.

I learned the trick to recording Kenny was to use the first vocal or two. Kenny Rogers's test vocals were often his best. The more Kenny learned a song, the worse he sang it. He'd get bored and mess with it too much.

I was happy after two takes and moved on to the backing vocals. That's when I saw what condition their condition was in as a group. Which was not good. Kenny, Mike Settle, and Terry Williams got in a screaming argument over the harmony parts— Thelma Camacho sat it out—that turned into a fistfight. I was never wild about recording groups. Sooner or later they got on one another's nerves.

"Whoa-whoa, guys, that's enough of that," I yelled out. "Let's go home." I pulled Kenny over and asked him to come to the house at ten A.M. for a talk. When he got to my home, I said, "It makes no sense for you guys to have an album where you sing two or three, he sings two or three, *she* sings a couple. It's just dumb." Kenny kept listening.

"Look, your stuff's sellin', you gotta be the lead singer here, so from now on we're gonna start calling the act Kenny Rogers and the First Edition. And no more silly-ass fights. *Your* voice is the commercial one, *you're* the winner."

Kenny loved this. "Great. You gonna tell the group?"

"No, Kenny. *You* are." The blood left Kenny's face. "It'll never work unless you tell 'em yourself. Tell 'em *I* said this is what's happening, but *you've* gotta tell 'em."

He told them and, sure enough, all hell broke loose. Then they all came to their senses. This was the right way to go.

Kenny was one singer who knew what he wanted to do. He played me a Mel Tillis single called "Ruby, Don't Take Your Love to Town." He said he'd love to cut it. I said, "Hey, if you love it, let's do it."

We cut it for a summer 1969 release—the group's first with the new name. Radio resisted the song because its lyrics about a soldier coming home paralyzed were considered too controversial. This was at the height of Vietnam and the antiwar protest movement—and several weeks before Woodstock. It had been a Top 10 country hit two years earlier, but it looked like "Ruby" might backfire on pop radio.

Then we got a big break: Huntley and Brinkley did their "Good night, Chet. Good night, David" signoff and their broadcast ended as "Ruby" played over some dramatic footage of wounded GIs on stretchers being helicoptered out of the war zone. Next day that song hit radio all across the country. Everybody who wouldn't play it before played it immediately, and it got to No 6 on the pop charts.

By the time I finished my last record with the First Edition, Mac Davis's "Something's Burning," in early 1970, a lot had changed. I had left Warner/Reprise and, along with Amos Productions, was running Amos Records, with a distribution deal through Warners. My protégé, Mike Post, had become musical director of *The Andy Williams Show* in 1969. My days as a Rat Pack producer were all but over—as were my nights as a high roller at the blackjack tables.

After finishing one of my last projects with Sammy, I went to a casino cage to get two grand more in credit. I handed over my ID but the guy came back and told me my credit had been canceled. "Bad checks."

"Not possible," I said. "Go check again. I never write checks here and, besides, I don't write *bad* checks."

It was a case of mistaken identity—someone else with my name from L.A. had lost his shirt. I was pissed off, kept at it for forty-five minutes, and didn't get it straightened out until one of the hotel entertainment directors came down to vouch for me.

"So is this going to clear me up all over town?" I asked. No, the guy in the cage shrugged. Once you bellied up one place, you were bad news all over the Strip. And I thought, *Now, here's a sign I should pay attention to*. "You know what—fuck it. I don't *want* any more credit anyway." Still, I took my $2000, had my last big blowout weekend, and never did go back for casino credit again.

If I wanted high-stakes gambling, I didn't need Vegas anymore. I had my own record label instead. What I didn't know was that the odds of winning weren't necessarily going to be any better.

TWELVE

MY FIRST TWO EXPERIENCES running labels in the seventies were hardly auspicious. The first one proved that being "bankable" meant you could lose lots of *other* people's money as well as a fortune of your own; the second was a lesson in foreign ownership and poor management that convinced me to leave L.A. and run back to producing music.

When I started Amos Records, I got a half-million dollars from Ampex Tape and a half-million from British Decca for the foreign rights. I also put up close to a million dollars of my own. The deal got a boost when Ampex heard I was interested in recording one of its own early investors—Bing Crosby. I wasn't just being shrewd: I had always wanted to work with Bing, the top-selling crooner of them all.

Bing was pushing seventy and hadn't cut an album in years. Because the big song of 1968 was the Beatles' "Hey Jude," I thought an LP titled *Hey Jude/Hey Bing!*, with a cover version, would be a trip. (Bing's "White Christmas," cut in 1942, is still the most popular single ever recorded.)

Bing lived along the Pacific in northern California in a big old dusty mansion. When I went there for a song meeting, he led me to a small den that hadn't been disturbed in years. He played me some song ideas on the stereo system, but they all had a corny sound trapped deep in the past. "Bing," I said, "if we're going to sell records we have to make a modern album." Bing hadn't had a non-Christmas hit since "True Love" with Grace Kelly in 1956.

"Okay," he said. "What have you got?"

I played him three recent hits: "Both Sides Now," "Those Were the Days," and "Hey Jude." Bing shrugged, said okay.

Bing then walked us into a vast, long-abandoned ballroom so that we could set the vocal keys for our songs on the piano. Dust flew up as we moved across a hardwood floor. The piano probably hadn't been tuned since Roosevelt was president. I couldn't tell what keys we were in. "Well, when would you like to record?" he asked.

"Around two weeks from now, for two days?"

"Good. I'll fly down. I'd like to start at eight o'clock."

"We can do that. We usually start at six, but eight's fine."

"Gee," he said, "six is a little early. I meant eight in the morning. That's when the *tones* are there, you know."

"Bing, I was thinking eight at night. I don't know if I can *get* a band at eight in the morning." We agreed on nine A.M.

When the day came, I got to the studio at eight-fifty A.M. "Where you been?" he asked. He'd already been there an hour.

As we started cutting our first track, I heard a noise in the miking or board that was driving me nuts—a weird static I couldn't locate or remove. I stopped and asked my engineer to help me hunt it down. I walked out to Bing's mike stand to check if it was faulty. Standing beside Bing, I heard it clearly and looked down. "Bing, are you jiggling something in your pocket?"

He looked surprised. "Oh, is that causing a problem?"

For five minutes Bing unloaded about $34 in nickels, dimes, and quarters from his pants pocket. It was a nervous thing he did and didn't even know it.

We didn't get a hit from the LP, but sold about 50,000 albums. After selling 300 million records, Bing had all the pocket money he needed—plus the $34 we wrapped and shipped back to him after we finished.

By the beginning of the seventies a new, post-Beatles rock scene was emerging in L.A. The "L.A. sound" was a fusion of folk, country, and rock. One talented duo in that vein called itself Longbranch and Pennywhistle—formed by two kids named Glenn Frey and J. D. Souther. They got to me through Tom Thacker, my pal from Dumas High and bachelor-pad roommate.

Tom had signed Frey and Souther for publishing and recording with his own company. But when Don Lanier heard their demo, he urged me to bring Thacker in to Amos to get Glenn and J.D. on the label. When Tom brought them in to sing some songs, I thought they were just wonderful.

J.D., who was from Amarillo, was a bit on the surly, rebellious side. Glenn was an easygoing sweetheart. Their songs were squarely in that acoustic folk-country groove and it was fresh and upbeat, with just enough country to make me think back to the early Everlys. I really dug their stuff.

They were struggling young musicians, so Dirt pulled strings to get Frey and Souther into an apartment building in North Hollywood. They had no money, but I thought I'd give them a shot.

I made Tom a GM at Amos. He then brought me another terrific kid named Don Henley. He had his own country-rock-style gig called Shiloh with Jim Ed Norman. Tom and I made a stock swap between our companies: I gave him a piece of Amos's publishing and let him produce Longbranch and Pennywhistle's debut album.

Tom turned me on to more than talent. After the bachelor pad, I rented an A-frame way out in the Valley in Tarzana, just off the Ventura Freeway. Tom was smoking pot and was into the San Francisco rock scene. He was trying to get me off booze and thought pot might be a nice alternative. "You'll dig this shit. It's great with music."

One day he handed me a one-pound coffee can, packed to the brim with cleaned Colombian grass. No twigs, no seeds. I thought that's how you bought grass. I had no idea. At home I fumbled for thirty minutes trying to roll a joint. I finally lit up and smoked it all the way down like it was a Marlboro. Tom hadn't told me you took a hit or two and waited to get zonked.

When that shit kicked in, I went right past zonked and straight to superparanoid—absolutely certain the cops were going to burst in any minute and bust my ass. I freaked and decided I had to stash the grass.

I went outside and spotted a post-hole digger in the yard. It works like two little shovels that clamp together and gather dirt when you yank apart a pair of long handles. I started jabbin' and flexin', frantically racing to stay ahead of the "fuzz."

Tom had said I'd "dig this shit," but was this what he meant? Did he *know* this would happen? Was that the *joke?* The paranoia was intense. I buried my stash in a two-foot-deep hole, filled the hole with dirt, and dropped a large chunk of slate over it.

I was stoned out of my gourd. I went inside, opened the icebox, and stood there and ate till the damn light went out. It was like having an instant eating disorder. I thought about lighting another joint—but crashed before I could get it together.

I started *giving* that pot away—and it still lasted a year.

•

If our spirits at Amos stayed high throughout the year, our chart positions did not. Neither Longbranch, Pennywhistle, nor Shiloh got much airplay for Amos Records. We never found that one killer record that would get us going. I put out the first Kim Carnes album, but it didn't do well. I had an antiwar group called the West Coast Pop Art Experimental Band. *Real* experimental. We never nailed it.

Meanwhile, Ampex, which manufactured cassettes for the major labels, got into trouble when the labels saw they could save money by making their own. Ampex panicked, and one top executive decided to get the company into production so that they'd have product for their tape. They signed up a half-dozen independent producers like myself who also had their own small labels to give them product. I ended up in a deal to distribute Lee Hazelwood's label and some others through my own outlets.

But then, as I was about to bring out a record by an East L.A. garage band, I was sitting around drinking one night when I saw an enormous downside risk and panicked: If a record exploded, I'd be totally bankrupt. We had already spent most of our start-up money on salaries for a dozen staffers and recording budgets. Now, with a major hit, I'd have to press and ship, say, a million records. I'd have to pay the trucking lines within fifteen or thirty days and the pressing plant within thirty days. The independent distributors I was with sometimes didn't pay you for six months. Some of them didn't pay you *at all* unless you came up with another hit; then, at least, they had to buy that from you, so they'd finally settle up. A big hit then and I'd go under. I decided to fold the Amos tent.

As I dismantled Amos, my administrative assistant was looking over some papers and asked, "What are you going to do about this company?"

"I'm shutting down the record label."

"No, what about Amos Inventronics."

"What the hell is Amos Inventronics?" I had never heard of this company. She told me Thacker had set it up with an inventor. "Well, let's see him and find out what he's invented."

This older fellow had been one of the geniuses behind the original LP at Columbia way back. That invention changed the world as we knew it. What he created for Amos Inventronics didn't: a curved electric grapefruit-section knife.

"I'm startin' to think the only grapefruit around here is me," I said. "Now, what else you got?"

Elvis looked a little bit like this too when he was seven or eight. But only one of us ever learned to really *sing. (From the author's collection)*

My senior yearbook shot: Glee Club, Class President, National Honor Society President, Dance Band, Library Club—whatever got me out of class. *(From the author's collection)*

Graduation Day, Dumas High, 1955. My dad, Asa Bowen, got the Kirk Douglas chin; Class Prez did not. *(From the author's collection)*

All of Dumas came out to hear the Rhythm Orchids for our Homecoming in 1957—unless they thought the Demons had a basketball game that night. That's Dirt at right, and our sometime road drummer Dude Kahn. *(From the author's collection)*

At the Paramount, Times Square, 1957, for Alan Freed's show. I was so busy riding and spinning that big bass and making girls scream, I didn't bother to mike it. Instead, I asked a fellow in the house orchestra to play my parts. That's Buddy on the left and Dirt on the right. *(Courtesy of Buddy Knox and Dave Travis)*

I call this picture simply, "Gorgeous 8 x 10"—A Roulette glossy, circa '57, with my hair all puffed up and goofy. It got me two movie offers, but when they said I had to get up at 5 A.M., I passed. *(Courtesy of Puckett Studio, Dallas)*

It wasn't quite "Orchidmania," but Buddy Knox *(center)* and I each did a tune in our big movie break. Donnie "Dirt" Lanier *(right)* was our lead electric-guitar player. *(Courtesy of Showtime Music Archive [Toronto])*

Four decades after the release of my solo effort and our "arm wrestling" Rhythm Orchids album, they definitely qualify as collectors' items.
(Courtesy of Showtime Music Archive [Toronto])

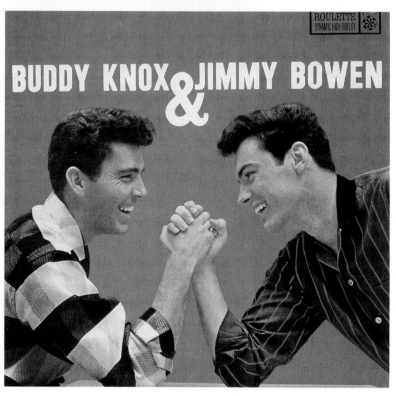

The Chairman of the Board with his producer and A&R guy at United Recorders on Sunset Boulevard, cutting "Softly, as I Leave You," in 1964. I was so busy predicting a hit for Frank I forgot to tighten my tie. Baseball legend Leo Durocher is on far left. *(Jasper Dailey/Michael Ochs Archives)*

Dean was always asking; "Where do I come in, pallie?" We had some great sessions at United, where we cut "Everybody Loves Somebody" in 1964. *(Jasper Dailey/Michael Ochs Archives)*

We may have jump-started Sammy Davis, Jr.'s, career for Reprise in the late sixties, but the goatee-and-leather-vest look obviously stalled out. *(Jasper Dailey/Michael Ochs Archives)*

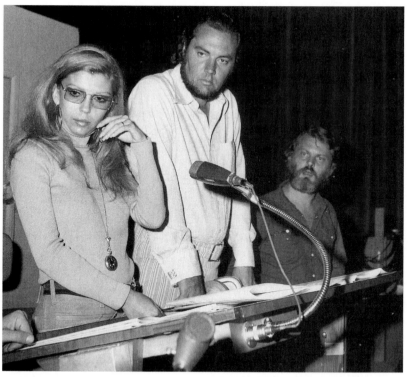

In 1967 I coproduced (with Lee Hazelwood) "Somethin' Stupid," Nancy Sinatra's duet with her famous dad. It stayed at No.1 for four weeks. Nancy and I remained friends and worked together again at RCA in the early seventies, when the above shot was taken. *(Jasper Dailey/Michael Ochs Archives)*

In the mid-seventies, C. W. McCall (Bill Fries) had his giant MGM hit, "Convoy." The novelty song did wonders for the CB-radio craze— but did nothing for the beard-with-no-mustache movement. *(Copyright © Alan L. Mayor)*

Conway Twitty and I shared a good laugh at a party for Twitty City around Christmas time in 1983, when he was on my Warner Bros. roster. Conway and I went way back together to his '58 classic, "It's Only Make Believe," which was maybe why I felt okay about telling him to change his sound—and his hair. *(Melody Lawrence)*

Hank Williams, Jr., and I took some time from his *Major Moves* sessions at Sound Stage in 1983 to chill out and try to look cool. *(Kenny Mims)*

I produced a couple hits for *Dukes of Hazzard* TV hunk John Schneider in 1984, helped by Dirt, the "song man" who found material for John. Dirt is shown bringing us some demos to my office. *(Don Putnam)*

I loved coproducing with George Strait at Front Stage, the room at Sound Stage with no glass wall between musicians and the control room. This was in the late eighties, during George's three-year run of No. 1 hits. At right, my old golfin' buddy Glen Campbell stopped by backstage at the Starwood in Nashville to say hi after one of George's 1987 shows. *(Beth Gwinn [above]; copyright © Alan L. Mayor [right])*

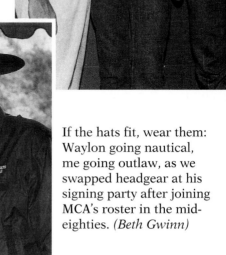

If the hats fit, wear them: Waylon going nautical, me going outlaw, as we swapped headgear at his signing party after joining MCA's roster in the mid-eighties. *(Beth Gwinn)*

Ginger, my Beautiful Texas Girl, above right, at our Whaler condominium on Maui in 1984, just after our December 1983 wedding. Ginger and I rededicated our vows five years later at the Kahala Hilton, above left, where we were originally married. Says something about the second time around! At right, with the beautiful wife—and not-so-beautiful Bill Haley spit curl—at the 1989 Universal Records showcase for Wild Rose, an all-female band, at Universal Studios in L.A. I ran the label as a joint venture with MCA Records. *(From the author's collection [above right]; Henry Diltz [right])*

Reba McEntire and me outside ASCAP on Music Row in 1987. It looks like I was saying, "I *told* you it wouldn't be easy." Actually, she had already been CMA Female Vocalist of the Year three years runnin'. *(Copyright © Alan L. Mayor)*

ABOVE: Party politics: MCA's shindig after the 1987 CMA awards was a black tie affair, but the two Texas mavericks on the right—me and Strait—forgot their tuxes. Bruce Hinton *(far left)* my V.P-G.M., Reba, and then-Senator Al Gore were all dressed for the occasion.

OPPOSITE, TOP: At the same party two years later the redhead's still in full party regalia—and I'm still not. That's Reba's husband, Narvel Blackstock, behind us. BOTTOM: George came over to chat with Ginger and me at the '89 post-CMA party. *(Copyright © Libby Leverett-Crew)*

In 1990 I invited our CEMA distribution people to watch a session at Emerald Sound so they could see how all that forty-eight-track digital hardware worked. *(Copyright © Alan L. Mayor)*

I handed Tanya Tucker her platinum CD for *What Do I Do with Me* in 1992 at Nashville's University Club. She had four Top 5 hits off the album. *(Copyright ©1992 John Lee Montgomery III/ NouVeau)*

At Fan Fair '94, Willie Nelson *(right)* and Charlie Daniels stopped by to say howdy to Liberty artist and onetime rodeo champ Chris LeDoux, the only real cowboy in the lot, on my left. *(Copyright © Alan L. Mayor)*

On Garth Brooks's tour bus in '94 with Garth *(right)* and Steven Curtis Chapman, a top-selling artist for Sparrow Records, Liberty's Christian offshoot. We didn't have to travel far—only to the Fairground for Liberty's Fan Fair Showcase. *(Copyright ©1994 John Lee Montgomery III/NouVeau)*

THE Billboard 200

TOP ALBUMS
FOR WEEK ENDING
SEPTEMBER 28, 1991

THIS WEEK	LAST WEEK	2 WKS AGO	WKS. ON CHART	ARTIST	TITLE	PEAK POSITION
1	NEW		1	**GARTH BROOKS** CAPITOL NASHVILLE	ROPIN' THE WIND	1
2	1	1	5	METALLICA ELEKTRA	METALLICA	1
3	2	2	14	NATALIE COLE ELE	UNFORGETTABLE	1
4	5	4	8	COLOR ME BADD	C.M.B.	3
5	4	3	12	BONNIE RAITT C	LUCK OF THE DRAW	2
6	6	5	18	BOYZ II MEN MO	COOLEYHIGHHARMONY	3
7	10	9	38	C&C MUSIC F MBIA	GONNA MAKE YOU SWEAT	2
8	9	8	21	MICHAEL BOL		
9	11	13	27	R.E.M. WARNER	TIME	1
10	3		2	RUSH ATLANTIC		3

In September 1991, Garth's *Ropin' the Wind* became the first country album to ever enter *Billboard's* Top 200 at No. 1. By then *Ropin'* was already triple platinum—so we did what any label would have done: gave him a plaque, threw him a party. *(Copyright © Alan L. Mayor)*

He had a machine that slowed down or sped up tape without changing the key. I said, Whoa, hang on a second here. That was cool. I kept him on for a couple of weeks until I learned it would cost a half-million dollars to get from manufacturing to market. I wished Mr. Wizard luck and cut him loose.

Carving up the music side was much more painful. I released Souther and Frey from their recording and publishing contracts to a young record-business hotshot named Irving Azoff. The price to buy their publishing contracts back was $7,500 each, whenever they had the money. They didn't have forty cents then. Henley was let go with Shiloh. Tom Thacker was so furious, I had to give *him* $12,500 in cash just to shut him up while I shut Amos down.

We were obviously just ahead of the curve. In 1971, Henley, Frey, Poco's Randy Meisner, and Bernie Leadon from the Flying Burrito Brothers formed a backing band for a young folk-rock singer from Arizona named Linda Ronstadt. They then broke off to form the Eagles. Their manager was none other than Irving Azoff, who got the band signed to Elektra/Asylum. Souther became a renowned songwriter in the seventies and had his own highly regarded Souther-Hillman-Furay Band with Chris Hillman and Richie Furay, of the Byrds and Buffalo Springfield respectively. Jim Ed Norman became a wonderful arranger-producer for the Eagles and others, then worked for me in A&R at Warners in Nashville in 1983 before taking over the label after I left.

Irving made out incredibly well with our deal, but he showed his gratitude several years later when he ran MCA in L.A. and needed someone to fix his flagging Nashville division.

I lost a million dollars of my own money and about that much again split equally between Ampex and British Decca. My debt was spread among suppliers—from the graphic artists who did my labels to printers, pressing plants, whatever. I still had about $50,000 to $60,000 a year coming in from various royalties, so I had *something*. But it took three years to get everyone off my back. If I owed someone twenty grand, we'd settled out for ten. I was still paying down some of the credit card accounts Keely had maxed out on, and was almost done paying her $30,000 a year.

While I still had Amos and its song-publishing business in the fall of 1969, I went to Nashville during what was then known as the annual deejay convention, the forerunner to today's high-

powered CMA Week organized by the Country Music Association in early October. As I had done throughout my years at
Reprise, I occasionally flew to Nashville to meet with writers,
publishers, and label people, since there was always strong material to be found there. I was also there to do business with the
man who ran Amos's publishing operation, Red Steagall.

Red was the same age as I was and an old buddy of Dirt's and
mine from Texas. He had come to L.A. in 1965, but went back
and forth between L.A. and Nashville. I was looking for Red to
make a deal to rep some major Nashville publishers through
Amos in the fast-growing L.A. music scene. Red was also a fine,
up-and-coming singer-songwriter for Dot Records in Nashville,
and we had worked on some tracks together in the studio.

The deejay convention was all one long industry schmooze,
the kind of thing I generally did an excellent job of avoiding. But
there was also a two-day celebrity golf tournament over the
weekend—reason enough right there to make the trip, the way I
saw it.

Red, meanwhile, had other notions of how I might enjoy myself. He got me a ticket to the kind of fancy industry banquet I'd
never attend on my own. This one I went to—and he made sure
to seat me right next to a stunning woman in her late twenties
named Dixie Amis. Dixie worked for Dot's Nashville division
chief, Jim Foglesong, and had become a good friend of Red's.

Red sat me down, made some introductions, and that was
that. Dixie and I hit it off right away—or at least well enough so
that I never did see Red again that night.

Not too long after that I returned to Nashville to finish up
with Red—and start up with Dixie again. Never one to dwell on
where a relationship was heading, I got her to move out to L.A.
and work for Amos. At least their names were a good fit.

Dixie's job was to not go down to the office, which she did
real well. I was now living in a great old horseshoe-shaped ranch
house that had been repossessed by the city of Thousand Oaks.
On one side was a golf course and the other a 500,000-acre national park. I told the city manager I'd rent it for $500 a month.
To my amazement he accepted.

So even after Amos collapsed, Dixie and I still had an afford-
able roof over our heads. With whatever was left after royalties
and paying down debts, we also had wheels—a pair of Mercedes
600s and a big ol' pickup truck—and a bunch of horses Dixie
loved. Not a bad lifestyle on a little money.

For most of the next three years I did very little but play golf at the Riviera Country Club with Dean, Campbell, and Dirt, cut a few records for Dean and Glen, and put together some record compilations for a company out of Chicago called Ronco, co-owned by Ron Popeil. Ron was a great TV pitchman who has sold everything from spray-on hair for balding men to juicers, a jerky-making machine, brooms, and things that shaved the hair off your arm. I did about one compilation package per quarter and got paid five or ten grand apiece, but it wasn't quite my gig.

I also made a third of my living gambling on the golf course. Playing for a big pot of money on the PGA circuit isn't my idea of pressure golf. Pressure golf is playing for money in your pocket that you ain't got. Many a day I teed off playing for $4000 or $5000 and had $1500 in my wallet. *That's* pressure. That's when you can't afford to hook a drive or take two shots to clear a trap. I loved that kind of pressure.

Dirt and I used to play these two good ol' boys in Thousand Oaks. One was an older fellow who, as Dirt put it, was "richer'n six foot up a bull's ass" and loved to gamble. He teamed up with a kid who'd turned pro, so they figured they'd nail us. Those two alone were usually good for three or four hundred a week.

By the end of 1973, it was time to get back to work: Dixie was pregnant and expecting our child in July 1974. I can't say our relationship was at a high point. I was still drinking heavily, I was wrapped up in whatever work I did, and was way too self-centered to feel I needed a child to complete my life. I thought that low sperm count from the Keely era would be my out. But Dixie may have felt a child would fix things between us. Her pregnancy was a big surprise. Whatever she and her fertility specialist cooked up, the voodoo worked. I was skeptical and felt it just wasn't meant to be. I know now my son, Christian, was.

Things started to change fast by May 1974. When I came off the Riviera course one afternoon, I had an "urgent" message to call Marty Machat, a lawyer in New York. Marty had settled our lawsuit against Morris Levy and Roulette in the late fifties, and his partner, Eric Kronfeld, put my Ronco deal together. Marty and Eric made things happen.

He wanted me to meet with the head of PolyGram about running their publishing unit. "You'd be great," Marty told me. "I'll set it up for you at four o'clock, Beverly Hills Hotel."

I had a couple of drinks, settled up my golf bets, and had my driver get me to the Beverly Hills Hotel. I met PolyGram's head of North America in one of the bungalows. We chatted for a half hour as he stroked me about my work with Reprise, with Dean and Sinatra. He said I'd be perfect for the job. "Well, would this be out here?"

"No, it would be in New York," he answered.

I stood, held out my hand, and said, "Hey, man, it's been nice meeting you, but I'm sorry I wasted your time. I just wouldn't be interested in New York City."

I headed for the door and he called out, "Wait a minute. Come back. Sit down." I stopped and waited to hear what he had to say. "We're also looking for somebody to run Polydor Records."

"Oh," I said, sitting again. We talked about that job awhile and then he said, "But that job's in New York too." I thanked him again, apologized, and got to the door, when he said, "Now, hold it, come back here a minute." I looked impatiently across the living room. "We also need a president of MGM Records."

"Is *that* out here?"

"Yeah, it is."

I walked back, sat down, and twenty minutes later I was the new president of MGM Records.

My job was to save a sinking label. My bosses kept me on a short leash. PolyGram was owned by Philips and Siemens, the Dutch and German industrial giants. They not only gave me a tight ten-year plan to turn the label around: because my predecessor, Mike Curb, apparently failed to earn their trust, and because they didn't trust any American executive, *every* piece of mail I sent out got opened in the mail room, copied, translated, and sent to corporate headquarters in both countries.

My first meeting as MGM president was in fact with Mike Curb. I had known Mike for years, having given him a production deal in 1963 when I was at Reprise and he was an eighteen-year-old kid who was just starting out in L.A. He wanted more than anything to produce a slot-car album. After the surf-music craze there was a brief six-month period where two or three albums had been done about these little-bitty cars that went around a track. I made a deal with him to produce a slot-car album. I think by the time he got it done, the fad was over.

Now we were record-company chiefs, so I said at our meeting, "Listen, I'm the president, but we both know who's got control here. It's you. So let's make us a good deal and go forward."

Mike had signed up all the Osmonds in various combinations—the Osmond Brothers; Donny; Marie; Donny & Marie; Jimmy, the little one; and any others. The Osmonds were about all the company had signed to make records, but they were all signed through Curb Productions, Mike's own company. Mike laughed and we then went forward.

One of my first big breaks at MGM got me back in business with Mike Post. Friends of Mike in Omaha had a huge regional hit for the small American Gramophone label. They hoped Mike could get it to a major. The driving force behind the record was Chip Davis, now of Mannheim Steamroller fame. This novelty record was called *Old Home Filler-Up an' Keep-On-a-Truckin' Cafe*. The artist was C. W. McCall, who was actually an Omaha ad executive named Bill Fries.

The "song" was a stretch version of a TV commercial for a bread company that Fries had created. It featured a truck-stop waitress named Mavis and a trucker. When Mike called, I told him to drop it off.

My listening sessions in the office usually started at nine P.M. after business was over, went until three A.M., and were fueled by booze. After Stan Moress, my right arm at MGM and today one of Nashville's top managers, and a couple of colleagues heard the song, I called Mike and woke him up. "Great song, B.J. I want to buy the master. I want you on the next plane to Omaha."

"Wait a second," Mike said. "You don't understand something. I don't work for you anymore and—"

"I don't care. Be on the next plane to Omaha, get me this record. *Please*."

"Bowen, I don't want to *go* to Omaha tomorrow. It's two in the morning."

"I have a watch. Now, come on, B.J."

"You should know Warners is also trying to buy the master."

"All right. Just sit tight. I'll call you back in a minute."

I called our lawyer and told him to prepare a contract for Mike to take out to Omaha. I had an assistant make plane reservations and then called Mike back. "Be here by nine to pick up the contract. And don't leave Omaha's airport without a signature on it—and call me before you leave." The last thing I wanted was to draw Warners into a bidding war for the song.

Mike called from Omaha at five P.M. When he said his friend, Don Sears, might want to talk to a lawyer first, I told Mike to put him on. A couple of minutes later Mike got the signature and flew in with the deal giving us C. W. McCall.

I gave Mike a finder's fee of one point.

A few days later I learned from inside sources that Warners

did indeed plan for a cover. I put a rush on and got several hundred records out to major country and pop stations. Four days after Omaha, we were getting airplay.

One reason MGM was struggling was that it was using the worst distribution system in America. It would have taken us another month to get records to our wholesalers. So I drop-shipped product all over the country by air overnight. It was costly, but if I didn't want Warners to beat me to the radio, I sure didn't want them to beat me to retail.

We won that cover battle—and got a Top 40 pop hit that crossed to Top 20 country. MGM was coming to life with the Mc-Call hits, a Top 5 duet by Donny & Marie Osmond, recording deals with the Osmonds, and solo projects by both Donny and Marie.

On July 5, 1974, Dixie gave birth to our son, Christian. I had gone through Lamaze with her and done my best to be the good husband with the breathing and the pillows and all. But when I took Dixie to the hospital and went to her bedside, this big old nurse walked in and said, "You move over, I'll handle this." I didn't do a thing but stand there in the corner for twenty-three hours.

Right after the birth I got a call from a top German executive in Europe, Kurt Kinkele. "Congratulations, Jimmy, on your new son," he said stiffly. "You will enjoy him very much. And *never* drop-ship records around our distribution system. We cannot allow that. Once again, congratulations on your son."

Click. I thought, *No wonder they lost two wars. They have no idea what they're doing.*

My deal with MGM took an unusual turn when the media giant lost the use of its MGM name to Kirk Kerkorian after he bought MGM's movie studio and film library. PolyGram flew me into New York, where I discussed my future with an executive for PolyGram-Worldwide. The plan was to move me up to the North American job in a year. "That's in New York, right?" I said. The executive nodded.

"Well, then, I'll have to have $500,000"—a nice bump from my current $75,000.

"For the three years, total."

"No. For *one* year. I'll also need a house in Connecticut, a flat here in town, a limo and driver at all times, and a helicopter to get me back and forth."

He never cracked a smile. "Are you trying to say you don't want the job?"

"Exactly. I cannot live in New York. I've said that before."

New York was only part of it. Running a pop label *and* making records, which was what turned me on most about music, was exhausting. If you're hands-on, it's twelve to eighteen hours a day. There was no time or energy left at the end of the day to produce. Plus, when was I supposed to spend time being a father to my infant son? This was rapidly becoming a concern for both Dixie and me.

To keep me busy, Polygram flew me back and forth to New York for six months to clean up Polydor's screwed-up A&R department. My own label was going strong, led by a big Gloria Gaynor disco hit called "Never Can Say Good-bye" and more bubble-gum music from Donny & Marie. Then Mike Post brought me what became his own career breakthrough—the theme from *The Rockford Files.* (Mike had teamed up with Pete Carpenter, a veteran arranger and trombonist, to compose for TV and film, and that wonderful partnership endured until Pete's death in the late eighties.)

The *Rockford* theme was so good, it got us a Top 10 hit and another Grammy for B.J. I knew the Europeans were weird when they got *pissed* at me for blowing their tidy ten-year plan by making $8 million more the first year than projected. *Rockford* marked the start of Mike's rise as the most successful composer-arranger in TV, with five Grammys and credits like *Hill Street Blues; Magnum, P.I.; Quantum Leap; L.A. Law; Law & Order; N.Y.P.D. Blue; The Commish; Murder One;* and many more.

Mike's hot these days. When a TV newsmagazine show needed a new theme, a producer called Mike. Mike didn't like the guy's attitude and tried to run him off, going on about not working for committees, he was too busy, it was only a theme, not a score, whatever. "That's cool, we still want you," the producer said. Mike told his agent, "Make up some outlandish fee for this damn thing and make it go away. I don't want it."

The agent called Mike back with a network offer of $75,000 for the minute-long intro theme. Mike said he'd do it for $100,000. The agent told Mike to stay put while he called the producer.

While Mike waited to hear back—about a minute and a half—he scribbled down a little melody line. By the time the agent called back to say they'd gone for the $100,000, Mike's theme was done. "Great," he said, "What do you think of this?" And he hummed the new theme over the phone. That little ditty came to more than a thousand dollars a second! Mike's come a long way since taking my low-ball offer to work at Amos.

By late 1974 we were looking strong. I had more than a dozen contracts out to sign artists and masters. I was going after Bob Marley & the Wailers; Charlie Daniels; a folksinger-songwriter named Stevie Nicks, who had done a terrific LP called *Buckingham-Nicks* the year before with her guitarist boyfriend Lindsey Buckingham (both later of Fleetwood Mac). Mike Post had just brought me the master of a neat song called "Third-Rate Romance" by the Amazing Rhythm Aces, and I wanted to sign them to record an album. It would have been one helluva roster.

But then I hit a wall: Kurt Kinkele marched into town and ordered me not to close any more deals for six months.

"We have a bunch in the works. Negotiated. Finalized."

"Cancel them," he said. "No deals for six months."

"It'll make us look like fools if we back out now."

"No deals!" I never saw such poor management and stupid business people in my entire career. The only thing the Germans knew about running a label was running it into the ground and losing $20 million in America.

In the spring of 1975, with MGM slated to become Polydor the following year, I quit. I had renegotiated my contract into a three-year deal—and my contract stipulated I could only be president of MGM Records and no *other* PolyGram company. So I had to be paid $75,000 a year throughout 1976 to *not* run the label. MGM got folded into Polydor, some people lost their jobs, and I had my freedom and almost two years' salary coming in.

At least I left the label on a roll: "Convoy," the Chip Davis–Bill Fries record that tapped the CB-radio craze, hit No. 1 at the end of the year on country charts, crossed over to No. 1 in pop, and wound up selling an incredible *seven* million records.

Once sprung from MGM, I began to get restless, sensing a big move was on the horizon. I wanted out of running labels. It left no time to produce music, which was what I loved most about the business. Also, the smog in L.A. was murder on my sinuses and allergies, and I didn't want my baby son to grow up breathing that awful air into his lungs.

But before I could seriously consider any major career directions, I had to make one crucial change: I had to quit drinking. There had been times in the early seventies when I'd surrendered to booze with a vengeance. I was drinking too much, too often, and didn't know when to stop. I would drink till I couldn't walk. Then I'd crash and need a day and a half to get it back together.

But if I was going to run a pop label, I wasn't going to have a day or two to sober up. So I backed off booze for forty-five days just as I was starting with MGM in 1974. I was doing real well for a few weeks, but then there were all those late-night listening sessions and I found myself getting through them with a couple of toddies. When we had some hits, that got the adrenaline and competitive juices flowing again, which drove me back to booze as well. Also, I was in New York hotels, alone and disgusted by what I had to deal with at Polydor during all that back-and-forth. Before I knew it, the Jack Daniel's was flowing through my life again.

But by March 1975 I was at the end of the line. I told myself, *This'll kill me if I don't stop now.* So I quit, went cold turkey. I didn't sign in anywhere; I just got on the wagon and pushed through it. It wasn't pleasant, wasn't easy, but it had to be done. It took me about a year, and I fell off the wagon a half dozen or so times. But I got myself straightened out.

Next on the agenda was figuring out what to do and where to do it. So I kicked back, traveled for a year, checked out places where I might start over and get back to what I dug most—making music.

I checked out Santa Fe and found it too desolate and close to what I had known growing up. I looked into the Seattle-Portland area, where a small music scene was building. I'd fly in, drive around, talk to people, try to see myself working there. But I couldn't stand the cold, gloomy, rainy weather. New York was out of the question. You have to drive an hour before you see a fairway, and the city always made me feel caged up.

I learned from traveling that California had nothing to do with the rest of America. You can get a distorted view of things if you never leave the West Coast. But when you do, you realize no one gives a damn about how hip you are. People are just living their ordinary daily Middle American lives and listening to music that is going to speak to that, not to what we thought was "happening" in California. It was like discovering a whole other country out there. And *country* seemed to be the music they loved most. Soon it dawned on me that the one thriving music center left to explore was Nashville.

•

Actually Nashville was a logical choice. For starters, I had no real alternative. Second, I was now a full-fledged adult, and country was adult music you could relate to. Rock was for kids, and the scene had gotten too goofy, coked up, and druggy for me to work there as a producer. I've always felt strongly that a musician, engineer, or producer can't do a great job unless he's turned on by the music, by the experience. Not much turned me on anymore in pop or rock, and I simply didn't produce jazz or urban music.

Another hook was that country was still cut "live" in the studio—everybody together. Pop was getting slick, computerized, mechanical; and it wasn't musicianship but drum machines and MIDI synthesizers that drove the disco sound of the mid-seventies.

Nashville was also familiar. I'd played the Opry in '57. I'd cut Johnny Burnette there in the early sixties. I'd had pitch meetings with great songwriters, like Joe South, Hank Cochran, and Roger Miller, while hunting songs for Dean. While running MGM in L.A. I had gotten to know Mel Tillis and Hank Williams, Jr., both of whom recorded for MGM's Nashville division. And I'd met Dixie there and worked with Red Steagall.

During one visit around 1970, I met a maverick artist-producer named Tompall Glaser. With his brothers, Jim and Chuck, they performed as Tompall & the Glaser Brothers. Their new studio on Music Row became headquarters for Nashville's "Outlaws." Tompall was friendly and open and said if I ever wanted to come in and cut a few tracks, I'd be welcome.

There were other signs pointing to Nashville. After quitting MGM, I produced a kid named Tom Bresh for a small L.A. label run by a pop promo guy I knew. We got a couple of decent country hits from the record in 1976. Then, when Tom asked me to do his next album in Nashville, I took Tompall up on his offer and also cut a single for Mel Tillis at Glaser's. When Mel's record became a Top 20 hit, I realized I could probably produce there.

The plan fell into place when I went to visit Dixie's folks in the tiny town of Blue Eye, Missouri, in the southwestern corner of the state. I took a half-hour drive into Eureka Springs, just across the border in Arkansas.

Eureka Springs was a unique little town—a third pot-smokin' hippies, a third local folks, a third transplanted retirees. The weather was good, the air was clean, the pace was right. I had my MGM money and royalties to ease the transition.

By July 1, 1976, we had pulled up stakes, left L.A., and moved to Eureka Springs, where I bought us a house. Nashville was now just a short hop by air from Springfield, Missouri.

I explored country music by getting in my beat-up old car and driving through the heartland—to Georgia and up through Oklahoma, from Arkansas down to Texas, across Missouri and back to Arkansas. I had never developed a taste for it and didn't have the least notion how to produce it. As I told Tillis in one of our sessions, I knew how to record thirty-five fiddles, but not how to make one sound any good. In town after town I punched the country stations on the car radio and talked to people about what turned them on about it.

Tompall tells of the time I came to see him not long after we moved to Eureka Springs. I showed up at his studio, set my briefcase on his office desk, and said, "Remember you told me that if I ever came to Nashville I had a home here? Well, here I am."

He smiled, shook my hand, and said, "Glad to have ya." Then he pointed. "You can have that office across the hall."

"Well, actually I kinda like this one," I said.

"No, this one is mine, see."

"Well, I like it."

"I'll tell ya what I'll do. I'll share it with ya."

Now, with a new home on Music Row, it was time to start building from the ground up again. Nashville was right where I wanted to be.

THIRTEEN

MY TIMING was perfect. Nashville's music business was in awful shape when I arrived.

My first two years in Nashville was an apprenticeship. I waded in and spent up to eighteen hours a day in Tompall's studio, listening, absorbing, producing. What were the roots of country? How did you engineer this hillbilly music? What were the dynamics, emotions, *textures* of a great country song? How did the *business* work?

Driven by an "extremist" or "addictive" personality, I became obsessed with learning what was wrong with Nashville and how it could be fixed. I wanted to make the music sound better, more modern and competitive with pop.

I learned right off that people treated you much nicer if they thought you were passing through than if you were a carpetbagger invading their turf. I moved in and out of town undercover, keeping my living arrangements vague. I rented the upstairs half of an out-of-the-way house near the Richland Country Club golf course and kept a low profile. I wore jeans and work shirts, drove a 1970 Buick beat up so bad, I left the key in it and still couldn't get anyone to steal it. I wasn't out to look flashy and draw anyone's attention.

Tompall was the best teacher, supporter, and friend I could have had. He'd say, "Bowen, you don't know how to make a mandolin or guitar sound country." I'd ask him to *play* me a great flattop guitar lick. He'd take me down to his office, the biggest mess I'd ever seen. He had tapes, 45s, and old LPs scattered all over, but he knew exactly where everything was. He'd pull out some old classic by Jimmie Rodgers or Bob Wills, cue it up, and go, "*There*, listen. Ya hear that? *That's* how it should sound."

Tompall was an outsider too, and as my ideas took shape, he knew they'd cut against the grain on Music Row. But he was supportive and urged me on. Nashville was a small town; one man could still have some impact.

Some things had to change. Producers had to spend more time—and money—in the studio. The average album was done in a couple of days and cost $15,000. And it sounded like it. Preproduction, the key to efficient recording, didn't exist. The story went that the great Billy Sherrill was famous for picking songs out at two o'clock for a session at four. Fine, but I couldn't work that way. Singers often didn't know what they were going to cut until the tape was running.

Artists had to take control of the creative process away from the producers and music publishers. And label heads had to be broken of the notion that album sales didn't matter. For years the producers and publishers had been counting up their penny royalties from radio play and missing millions in album-sales tonnage. I had a long uphill climb, but I was determined to shake things up.

Falling in love with country music was the breakthrough in getting swept up in this new challenge. I knew I had the musical instincts and technical skills. Now I had discovered a genuine passion for the music.

Other tastes changed for me while hanging out at Glaser's. I was soon smoking four or five joints a day. I saw people on both sides of the studio glass using coke and speed cut with baby laxative or strychnine and getting crazy behind it for three days before crashing hard. I never saw anything good from that drug. My energy was already intense; with my allergy and sinus problems, cocaine was never a serious option for me.

I couldn't drink anymore. I lapsed once with Tompall after a long session, and hit all the local dives. Got stone drunk and it nearly killed me. As he drove me home, I barfed out the window the whole way and thought I'd die.

But grass made me laid-back, persuasive, and a hundred percent focused. It helped me go from one studio to the other, clear my mind, and zero right back in. Drugs all affected the way I received music, so it was tricky. Jack Daniel's, being a depressant, dramatically dimmed the top end. Coke deadened it altogether. I experimented with it once and pushed the EQ up so bright, the top end hurt. Worst crap I ever recorded.

But grass magnified my ears, gave me detail in the tracks I might have missed. Or maybe that was just my excuse for getting high. But it worked. If Jack Daniel's fit the culture of Warner/Reprise, grass was the right hillbilly high.

I could handle the pot; what I couldn't handle was the doughnuts and cheese sandwiches in the studio. Grass made me so damn hungry, I was working twenty hours a day and eating eighteen. I must have gained forty pounds in my first couple of years in town.

I didn't tolerate a drunk or stoned artist—and over the years never saw a creative person who could handle cocaine. Tillis had a beer now and then, but if he had a hit off a joint, his stutter got worse. But he was always hysterically funny. Hank Jr. showed up a couple times with too much to drink, but he could still work. And he could be rowdy while stone-cold sober too.

And there was, of course, that *other* downside to drug use in the studio: The Law. I was working with Tompall's band at his studio one night in August 1977 when we got a call from a woman. She told us that Federal drug agents had just busted Waylon at Chips Moman's American Sound studio, where he was producing some Hank Jr. vocal overdubs. Apparently, DEA and local narcotics agents had been tipped that a shipment of cocaine was coming his way. One of Waylon's assistants had picked up the air-courier package and delivered it to him at the studio when they moved in. It seemed like a setup—and my caller was warning me that we might be next on a Music Row drug sweep because of Tompall's ties to Waylon and his own drug use.

I stopped the music to tell everyone what might go down within minutes. "Maybe we oughta take a ten-minute break," I said. There were four toilets there, and within seconds they were all flushing. Everyone was flushing whatever they had—pills, grass, blow, whatever. The water pressure in homes all around Music Row probably dropped 75 percent.

I had some potent organically grown grass that I was not inclined to flush. I raced to the tape vault which contained thousands of cardboard boxes in which two-inch master tapes were stored. One box had a strip of tape with the name of a gospel group handwritten on it. I pulled it down, opened it, slipped the grass inside, retaped the box, put the box back, and returned to the studio. I figured no way they'll check a gospel act.

It was just paranoia. They never showed. And Waylon never went to jail. The charges against him—possession and conspiracy to distribute—were eventually dropped.

I had come across Waylon for years here and there, but never worked with him until I signed him to MCA in the mid-eighties. He and I came from the same part of the country—Waylon's from Lubbock—and we're just a few months apart in age. So we were very much alike in many ways. I deeply respected and admired Waylon as one of the original Outlaws who broke the mold of the "Nashville Sound" in the seventies. He rebelled against the way the music scene had long been controlled by the Establishment.

When Waylon left RCA and told them to stick it, I jumped at the chance to sign him and work with him at MCA. But he had been messed up for years on cocaine and had recently gone cold turkey in the Arizona desert. By his own admission, coke was costing him up to $1,500 a day. He kicked it the hard way: no twelve-steps, no spas, just Waylon joined and supported by his remarkable wife, Jessi Colter. He had just been through the agony of sweating out his detox alone with her in Paradise Valley.

When we started his first MCA LP, Walyon was healthy, in great shape, right at that incredible point where his head was clearing and he was finally growing up. Many artists don't grow up because they never live in the real world. Still, when he went to the mike and opened his mouth to sing, I joked and said that "nothin' but dust" was coming out. The combination of cocaine use and years of smoking dries out the vocal cords and ruins careers. But Waylon had been to hell and back in his struggle for survival. He had a couple big hits for us on that first album, but my favorite was his wonderful audio-biography, *A Man Called Hoss*. Within two years that marvelous voice of his had returned.

One blond country queen who still hadn't made that journey came in to do her music the old-fashioned way—the producer telling her exactly what to do. My thing was to give the artist more responsibility over song selection and arrangements. But this big star, who sang some classic hits, couldn't deal with being her own coproducer and panicked. Once we were rolling, she was slurring and shaky.

I called a break and went out to see her—and realized why she needed three music stands. Two of them were for her pill bottles, airline liquor bottles, and nasal sprays. I should never have put her in that position. We got through that session, but I told her it just wasn't going to work out, and I quit the project. She agreed with my decision. The way I saw it, my job was to reveal and perfect the artists' music, not lay my trip on them. If they didn't want, or couldn't handle, that, why should I do it?

After L.A. it was easy to get drawn in by the camaraderie of Music Row. Most of the publishing, label, management, or agency offices were quaint old two- and three-story brick or frame houses converted for business use. The studios were all right there too. After L.A.'s slickness—and freeway madness—it was wonderfully laid-back and accessible. You parked out on the street or in a rear lot, walked in, settled into a big old armchair by a fireplace, set your feet on a table, popped a beer, poured some coffee, and talked music and artists.

But that same coziness masked much of what was holding the music back. Nashville was stuck in a technology time warp a full decade behind New York and L.A. Pop music was using sixteen- and twenty-four-track analog by the late seventies, and Nashville was still mostly on eight-track. Equipment gets obsolete fast, and with $15,000 production budgets and studios seeing only about 40 percent of that, they were barely staying open, much less upgrading to next-generation hardware.

New York and L.A. studios were supported by pop, rock, R&B, and disco superstars selling multiplatinum albums in the high-flying seventies; artists and labels were pouring small fortunes into recording budgets to achieve state-of-the-art sound quality. The artists demanded cutting-edge sound—at any cost.

Nashville's studios seemed frozen in time. I walked into a mix-down session at RCA and half the gear was still in boxes covered in dust. RCA's famous Studio B is now a museum. It was *then*. The board was awful and antiquated. The goal on Music Row wasn't recording the best-sounding music but keeping costs down. I was on a Hank Jr. session and couldn't get the EQ right on the echo chamber; no one else in the studio even knew where the settings were located. I had to unscrew two panels and crawl in there myself and readjust them. Eight years later I checked and they were still right where I'd left them.

One reason no one seemed to care about sound quality was that album sales were not viewed as a primary source of profit. That came from radio-performance royalties and tour income. Albums were so unimportant that in 1976, if you sold 100,000 copies, they threw you a party. There were country legends who had recorded twenty albums and still hadn't gone gold—*all combined*. In pop you got excited at a million to a million-five.

When Waylon and his wife, Jessi Colter, and Willie Nelson and Tompall cut their famous *Wanted: The Outlaws* in 1976, it was, incredibly, the first million-selling platinum LP ever produced out of Nashville. In those days if you said so-and-so had just gone platinum, you were more likely talking about hair, not hits.

I told people they couldn't expect a $15,000 LP to compete with a $300,000 LP—and charge the same for it in stores. They thought I was crazy. A pop-rock fan accustomed to crisp stereo FM sound would punch a country station and get a pinched mono sound from another era. Worse, the albums just weren't that good. You had a couple of decent tracks and the rest filler, songs that were included only because the producer or the guy running the artist's label had written them or had a piece of the publishing. The artist was often the last to hear what he or she would be recording—and often not until moments right before the sessions.

And people had gotten lazy. The songs often had the same intros, instruments, hooks, and fades. You could tell that maybe a half hour was spent cutting them, and then forty-five minutes mixing them down. Very little stood out. As long as the publishing people got their songs cut, they made their decent living and moved on. No one was thinking sales, marketing, mass merchandising.

Until the seventies, there were only 300 or so country radio stations, so country wasn't exactly blanketing the nation. Also, many retail outlets didn't even carry country; if they did, the LPs were all thrown together under *C*. The number of country-oriented stations had grown to maybe twelve hundred by the time I arrived in Nashville, but few were market-share leaders. Country was still largely "ghettoized"—rural, blue-collar, redneck music.

The Old Guard was still living, it seemed, in the glory days of Hank Williams, Patsy Cline, Wanda Jackson, Chet and Billy, George and Tammy, and no one was looking to stir things up. Artists, too, were trapped in the status quo. This was, after all, where they'd told me twenty years earlier, "We don't *play* drums at the Grand Ole Opry."

For years legends like Chet Atkins, Billy Sherrill, Owen Bradley, and Don Law formed an elite corps of executives who dominated Nashville. They weren't part of the Old Southern monied set living in Belle Meade mansions, but they'd done awfully well for themselves. Most of the land that became Music Row was owned at one time or another by rich executives in the music business. They had carved themselves out some prime real estate, a publishing industry, a record business with four or five divisions of the major pop labels. They were now sitting on bank boards and could steer money around to certain people and away from others, depending on who needed seed money for which studio near someone else's.

From the outside you got the idea that connections ran deep through land, money, and music. A couple of dozen people seemed to run the whole joint. The Country Music Association was the best-run trade organization I've ever seen. No one rocked the boat, and everybody got what they wanted. When it came time for the annual CMA awards show on network TV, I discovered it was as political as I had heard the Academy Awards were. When I ran my first label in town, I found out firsthand how block voting worked.

A couple of months before the awards I got calls from all the division heads in town, which was odd. The first one I spoke to said, "Well, this is the way we do this, you know." And it was like, "You don't have anyone in 'Best Group,' so give me your votes for such-and-such, and we don't have 'Male Vocalist,' so I'll give you mine for what's-his-name."

I said, "Deal!" I called them all back and sold my block of votes four or five times. Whatever they liked, I'd trade them. All the companies had 150 votes each—which included not only employees but distribution, L.A. office, mail room, aunts, uncles, whomever, to fill the count. They were supposed to sign and send back blank ballots to the label and then we'd fill them out according to the bartering you'd done.

Problem was, I didn't instruct anyone to fill out anything that first year. So I hadn't really traded at all. The truth was it was so small compared with today, with maybe two thousand voting members in all, that you really could stack votes and swing it one way or the other. And the show then was the only network TV outlet, so it was incredibly important for exposure and status. (The voting system has changed significantly, with many more CMA members and a more level playing field that doesn't favor the big labels.)

Country radio, since the early days of the Opry on WSM, had always been artist-driven. If you had a big hit, you became a star and radio played almost anything you put out—forever. Artists enjoyed longevity, fan loyalty, and unfailing support from radio. Pop radio had always been more hit-driven and thus more fickle.

That explained payola, the power of independent promotion, and cover battles. It was tougher and often dirtier, but it was a more wide open field.

It seemed thirty artists made all the music on country radio. And they conformed to the sound that got them airplay. Given the way label heads were allied with producers and publishers looking for outlets for their songs, the recording business became a vicious cycle that, I felt, denied artists control over their creative destinies. I decided that cycle had to be broken.

A singer lived and died by the hit record he or she happened to come upon in the studio. I was more interested in bringing along an artist who came to the studio with what I call "a music to do"—a vision of where they were going with their career.

One major artist looking to redirect his career destiny was Tillis. Mel was a good ol' Florida Panhandle boy, whose shuffling, country roots were close to the Texas music I knew. Mel had had a bunch of hits and been named CMA Entertainer of the Year for 1976. But he was smart enough to know his music was about to go away. With nothing to lose, he took a chance with me and asked me to cut an upcoming album. The award would mean momentum, TV exposure, more radio hits. It was time to push it.

Mel was a wonderful comedian, musician, singer, songwriter—and one of the naturally funniest people alive. He had worked Vegas, known Sinatra, and had been one of my artists when I ran MGM, so there was a natural affinity between us. His switch to MCA-Nashville created yet another link: MCA was run by Mike Maitland out of L.A., and Mike had been head of Warner/Reprise during my years there. So working with Mel was real comfortable, a perfect trial balloon.

I dropped my producer's fee from $20,000 to $5,000 for the album—$500 per song. When people told me that was outrageous, I figured they were praising my fairness. Wrong. That was still more than double the $150 to $250 a track most producers got. I also negotiated a 3 percent back-end deal on royalties.

I wanted to bring Mel into the modern world, give him a bolder, edgier sound. Despite his hits, Mel's music sounded dated, stale. If he wanted to sell more than his usual 40,000 LPs, he'd have to take some risks.

I learned it didn't take much to ruffle people's feathers and piss them off in the studio. I remember one early session where the drums were off in a small enclosure and the guitar out in the big room. I told my engineer, Ron Treat, "You dumb-ass hillbilly, get the drums out in the studio, where they can breathe, open 'em up. And put the acoustic guitar in the little room." He told me nobody had ever wanted the drums out there before. I told him I didn't care what people did before me.

People still assumed no one wanted to hear drums in country. My view was, Go for it. Come to the modern world. I put fifteen mikes on one set of drums, and people again thought I was crazy.

Things were done differently in Nashville. No one worked off sheet music and charts. Nashville's top session guys followed handwritten numerical codes denoting chord changes. In the key of G, for instance, G, C, and D chords were shown as I, IV, and V. A-minor was II-minor, and so on. My understanding was this system had come out of gospel music, and it allowed for fast key changes.

Then there was the problem of the "leader." For Tillis I had some big studio names. Harold Bradley, whose brother, Owen, was one of the powers at RCA, was the session leader on guitar, meaning he got paid double for being the intermediary between the producer and the musicians. I was used to calling the shots in a session, even with Sinatra. I didn't need a leader between me and my players.

I told Harold to take a seat so that I could get a sound check on his acoustic guitar. That pissed him off. I'd screwed with his routine. Suddenly I was a gruff Yankee intruding on a group of hunting and fishing buddies. Then he sat down.

The drummer, Buddy Harmon, one of the best, refused to play the kick-drum pattern I wanted in the verses and damn near got belligerent. I'd stand right in front of him and show him what I wanted, and he still refused, like, Who was I to tell him how to play? Grady Martin, a marvelous session player on electric, was half full of vodka and burned out on four sessions a day for fifteen years. He was playing a riff on "Heart Healer" that I'd heard on some other Tillis album. They all repeated their licks. When I told Grady to try something different, he started poutin', and Tillis had to go over and put his arm around him and ask, "Wh . . . wh . . . what's wrong, uh . . . Grady?"

"Aw, this son of a bitch wants me to play 1956." I overheard this peculiar remark and retorted: "Gee, Grady, didn't mean to hurt your feelin's. Move it up to '57 if it makes you feel better." I was being humorous. But he only got more pissed.

Then I went to Pete Drake, the great pedal-steel ace who had invented a device that made the steel "talk." He had it talking as we ran down "Heart Healer." When Pete, a sweetheart of a man, asked me what I wanted him to do, I said, "Anything but make that damn thing talk. Tillis is the only one using words on this session." I was just trying to lighten the mood, but the ones who were irritated took me literally. It became a hostile environment.

Acoustics were a mess in most Nashville studios back then. Studio gear was still used in ways bordering on primitive. A good limiter controls recording levels. It holds back a vocal or instrumental surge and prevents distortion. It's not designed to squash and deaden textures. But when engineers were cutting a song every forty minutes, the limiter just stayed at a constant setting and squished the life out of Tillis, Grady, or anyone who got a little out of hand.

I took the time and trouble to make the best use of all the gadgetry. Except for some dividers around the drums, everyone was out in the open in one big room. When Mel sang, the limiter, which controls the recording level, was set at about 35 dB, ten times normal for a singer. The needle just shot up and stuck in the red zone. If he'd whispered or screamed, it would have been the same. Cutting way back to almost no limiting, you can achieve a much purer vocal, but then you have to work harder and ride the faders up for the soft sections, and back for the loud ones. No one seemed to care. They set the limiters and left them there.

I cut Mel's way back, which gave him a warmer, softer sound, not quite as hard and pointed. Everything went wrong on those sessions, and nothing good should have come of them.

That kind of sloppy engineering is what gave so much of country what I called its honk factor. Honk, to me, gave country a sound that was difficult to bring to the mass consumer. It hurt your ears and turned off pop-music lovers. It was often a matter of overlimiting the vocals.

I offended a good number of folks early on when I told an interviewer they must have had one helluva rug sale because of all the carpeting on the walls and floors of every studio. It was supposed to reduce "leakage" from one instrument to another, but it deadened everything. Scream or belch, it'd all get sucked up in the pile and soundproofing.

We did the padding thing in pop and moved on. Nashville was still Carpet City. "Let the note ring," I'd say, "The more of it you can catch, the longer, bigger, richer it'll sound."

One article a few years later called me the Prophet of Music

Row. The truth was I didn't have a crystal ball. I was just apply-
ing what I'd already lived in the world of pop. I knew it was coming our way in Nashville.

Mel's album cost about $36,000 to produce. I did it the way I
usually produced records: Once I had all the basic tracks, with
all the sweetening from the instrumentation and backing vocals,
I made what is called a rough mix in about a half hour. A rough
mix is never meant to be a finished product; it simply gives you
enough of a sense of what you've got so you can live with it for a
few days and get used to it. Then I went in and spent a full day
on the final mix.

When I saw Tillis at his office a couple of weeks later, he had
all the bills on his desk and he was so stunned he could barely
stutter.

"Bowen . . . Bowen . . . Bow . . . h-h-how can . . . ? I c-c-can't
believe this." When Mel got really mad or scared, he couldn't talk
at all. But he knew he was funny and played off it. I almost fell
off the couch. "You . . . you . . . s-son. . . . of a bitch."

He told his assistant, Maggie, to ask me for him. "Mel wants
to know," she said, "how you can spend thirty-six thousand five
hundred dollars on an album."

"Well, what did you spend on the last one?"

"I think fifteen thousand."

"But what did the last one sell?" I asked back.

She checked and came back. "Forty thousand."

"Well, let's wait and see if it was worth it."

Mel held up one bill and waved it. "Explain this. What's . . .
cartage?"

"Mel, that's French for cartage. That's the guy that carried
Larry's drums up to the second floor and set 'em up so that he'd
be fresh and ready to play. Drummers don't haul their own stuff
in New York and L.A. Only here."

The first single off Mel's *Heart Healer* LP was the title track—
and it hit No. 1 in early 1977. He had two or three more Top 10
hits that year, which helped push LP sales to 140,000 units.
"That's great," he said. Me, I loved these numbers.

"No, Tillis," I answered. "Anything under five hundred thousand is bullshit. Unless you were also the publisher of three Top
10s off the album and made thirty thousand dollars on each
from performance, as an artist you'd be lucky to break even selling a hundred thousand. You've got to sell a million LPs to make
any real money."

A few years later George Strait said the joke up and down Music Row had been that I came to Nashville and taught him how to make a $30,000 record for $150,000. Maybe so, but George also had a wall full of gold and platinum LPs to show for those budgets.

Heart Healer got Tillis and me on a hot streak. In four years I produced three or four albums; fourteen singles in a row reached the Top 10. I updated Mel's sound by moving the drums way up in the mix, experimenting with new instruments and textures—and with preproduction.

For one ballad, "I Believe in You," I flew the great Jim Horn in from L.A. to play flute and added a string section. Took time, cost money, absolutely. Tillis loved the song and wanted to pull it off just right. It was part of my plan to broaden his appeal—and sound—and to sell more albums. He came in four or five times and did twenty-four takes before he nailed it. I also did something Nashville wasn't doing then—vocal "comps." I'd take a line or word from one vocal performance and put it on another, until you were using only the best phrases. I knew it had to be really good for Mel to work on a ballad with strings and flute.

Then my promotion man, Nick Hunter, panicked: "You can't put strings and flute on a Tillis single; two stations have said they'll never play it."

"Nick," I said, "if we don't push the envelope here and if we don't quit runnin' because radio is afraid of something, this music is never going to change or broaden or become exciting enough to sell millions of records. I still believe in it, and your people are just going to have to work harder on it. Prove it one place—and the herd will follow."

That's exactly what happened. The song went to No. 1 in the middle of 1978.

I was determined to change the way songs were recorded. Instead of cutting four songs in a three-hour session, I'd do one or two. You couldn't work faster than that and do it right. Look at the way background vocals were done, for example. Before, the singers listened two times and taped. If the syntax was right on or not, if they sang flat or sharp, no one cared. Producers just buried the vocals in echo and stuck them back in the mix. I hated that.

Background singers and musicians loved working with me. We took our time to get everything just right. If I took three times longer, they made more money on the clock. Musicians liked me because they took pride in their musicianship; I slowed the pace down and encouraged them to give me their best work.

My point was that everybody wins: if you *spent* more money, you made better music, sold more albums, and *made* more money. It was all about breaking bad habits in the creative process. The talent and music were there. The trick was setting them free.

But what was making Mel a lot of money in the studio was killin' him onstage. Every time I added a new sound, Mel would hire a musician to re-create it in concert. One night I ran into him at the studio. "Bowen," he glared, "do me . . . a fuckin' . . . favor and don't put no more new . . . shit on m-m-m-my records."

I asked why. "Cause I'm up to two buses, a truck, and . . . a fifteen-piece orchestra. It's . . . a-breakin' me . . . on the road."

With Tillis I began to get a solid, if grudging, reputation. On one of his No. 1 hits Mel was credited as coproducer. My feeling was that he—and most every other artist—would feel more connected to the creative process by also coproducing. It may have seemed subversive then, but it was all for the good. As I've told artists for thirty years, "You take care of the music and the music will take care of the rest."

I was taking such good care of other people's music that my personal life was beginning to play like a broken record. The commuting between Eureka Springs and Nashville got old real quick. Dixie visited me in Nashville a couple of times, picked out some furniture and painted a couple of rooms at my place. But she didn't much care for Nashville and loved where she and Christian were living.

By October 1977, just before the first Tillis album, Dixie and I decided to call it quits. One big reason: Dixie Two.

I met Dixie Gamble at Tree Publishing, where I was just hunting down some good songs for Tillis, not a new wife. Dixie Two was a thirty-year-old woman who worked for a couple of song pluggers at Tree and did some song pitching herself. Before long she was hanging out at the Glasers' studio and we ended up getting together. She was divorced and the mother of two young sons, Garon and Shannon, but it was clear she was really into songs, songwriters, and the making of music. We started going out for real in the summer, and by October 1, 1977, we moved in together. I gave Dixie One Arkansas and I kept Tennessee, is how we ended it. It was a fair deal.

Between Tillis records I cut some tracks for Red Steagall and Roy Head, both on ABC Dot. Roy's rock career went south after his big 1965 hit, "Treat Her Right." He switched to country but hadn't had much luck. I didn't get a hit for Red, but two of the singles I did with Roy broke the Top 20 in 1978.

I was beginning to wonder, though, if I was becoming a victim of my own early successes. Mel had come to me. Jim Foglesong at ABC Dot had only hired me because Red and Roy had asked him to and he didn't want to fight them. But the big boys at RCA and CBS, the leading divisions, were *never* going to hire me to produce acts. And that scared me to death.

A friend who had attended an industry party told me, "Bowen, you ain't got a prayer here. I overheard a top guy at CBS last night say, 'Bowen'll never work for us. He spends too much and he's too damn opinionated.'"

If you had a big mouth, spent a bunch of money, *and* happened to be right about stuff, you really pissed off the good ol' boys. I was turning into just another Outlaw.

There *was* a solution: Run my own label. Again. Mr. Outside had to come inside. I'd never change the system without the power of a division behind me.

I didn't know how soon that chance would come.

FOURTEEN

I N THE SPRING OF 1978 I was in L.A., visiting Mike Maitland, now president of MCA Records. Having worked for Mike when he was head of Warner/Reprise in the sixties, I felt comfortable telling him his Nashville division, little more than a distant outpost for giant MCA, was poorly run.

The roster was a mix of big stars like Tillis, Conway Twitty, Loretta Lynn, and Tanya Tucker, thrown in with aging veterans like Cal Smith, Nat Stuckey, and Bill Anderson. Sales and market share lagged way behind RCA and CBS.

"Well, would you want to run it?" he asked out of the blue.

I was flattered but said I had come to Nashville to make music. I did suggest Jim Foglesong, who I felt would bring in good people from ABC Dot and turn MCA into a strong label. Since I'd already produced some hits for Jim's ABC artists, I'd stand to benefit by working with the MCA roster.

Later Mike and Jim apparently struck a deal, but Jim, despite an offer rumored at $125,000, backed off at the last minute. I was disappointed. I'd had it all worked out. "Why *don't* you do it?" Mike asked when we talked next, this time more insistent.

I mulled it over. "Can you pay me a hundred and a half?"

"Absolutely."

"Deal."

In June 1978, I went to work as vice president–general manager of MCA Records–Nashville—and immediately started cleaning house. Many I let go weren't "record people," so I replaced them with people whose music sense could build a viable, competitive division.

Now that I was inside, I saw clearly how the good-ol'-boy system worked. I hired Billy Strange, a jack of all musical trades I knew from L.A., to clean up the A&R department. Billy had come to town before me and knew his way around.

A couple of weeks later he came into my office laughing. "Take a look at this," he said, shaking his head. He had the paperwork showing how one of Nashville's top producers owned all the songs on one of our artists' albums; owned the studio where it (and most things he produced) was cut; made himself the A.F. of M. and AFTRA leader on the session contracts; *and* took a 2 percent producer's fee. Not illegal, but ethically wrong—and bad business. The artist was being screwed by self-interest and greed.

It was the artist's recoupable advance that financed the recording. Only after the label earned back its negative costs did royalties kick in. This arrangement was more or less the status quo, but it was bad because it took control away from the performer and concentrated it in the hands of the producer-publisher.

Since no one was selling many albums, people scrambled to control as many links in the creative chain as possible. As leader on *two* union contracts, you made maybe $300 per session, times the number of sessions per album, *plus* a producer's fee for each album track—*and* producer and publisher royalties. Over time you could earn a lot of green without ever selling gold.

I called the producer in and sat him down. "What I just found out could ruin you if anybody knew about it," I said bluntly. "This artist cut *your* songs, in *your* studio, with *you* as session leader—twice—and producer. That would look terrible on the street, you doin' that to some poor artist." He look stunned. "So I'm taking you off as leader on these contracts and I don't want to see it again. Don't be rippin' the artist off. I'll keep this between us. You can't have anyone find this out."

Shaken, he left and thanked me for sparing his reputation.

Of course I then let it out all up and down Music Row—not his name but the nature of our confrontation and how it had to stop.

After restaffing, I attacked the roster. It's hard to let a great old-timer go, but it's business that has to get done. In deciding which artists and employees went or stayed, I researched the situation. To get a fix on salespeople, for instance, I'd call retail and find out who takes care of business and follows up and who doesn't. With A&R I'd check roster signings, the label's musical direction, examine the artists' output and sales. With promotion you call radio and see who works product aggressively, who doesn't. You can also check numbers on airplay, station adds, bullets, and record charts.

With artists you call stations to see if they work with radio or cop an attitude. You call honky-tonks to see if they keep people dancing and drinking or show up late and short-change the crowd. You can attend a show undercover, or bring them in and talk. If it's a pay-or-play deal, and they haven't played, you can pay them five grand or so and let them go away.

Decisions are also based on intangible "people" factors: Does a staffer fit in with the label's "culture" and direction? Is an artist someone the VPs will get behind with plenty of "give a shit" energy and passion? Bottom line: There are no secrets in the music biz—a record's Top 10 or it isn't; it stiffs or it doesn't. People produce—or they don't.

I dropped more than a dozen acts—and this was before Branson gave old hillbillies an afterlife onstage. Conway and Loretta had three kids between them signed to MCA just to keep them happy. Dropping them was business and they understood. Life goes on. There are political signings—favors—and they often go. It was a wild first month. General Sherman and I would have scored about the same in a job-approval poll.

Keeping a superstar like Conway was a no-brainer, but I thought he might be ready for a good long talk. So I had my head of sales, Chick Doherty, arrange a meeting with him and his agent, Jimmy Jay. I also asked Chick to prepare a graph showing how, despite a terrific run of No. 1 radio hits, Conway's LP sales had been declining. There had been some weak singles released, and Conway sometimes sounded dated. The music was changing; Conway wasn't. I had known him since the fifties, when he hit No. 1 with "It's Only Make Believe," one of the classic rock ballads of all time. His switch to country had made him a giant in Nashville, but I still felt it was time to stir things up. If I see a storm coming, I go indoors, not wait out in the open until it hits me.

It was great to see Conway. We hadn't run into each other too often, but there was an artist-to-artist ease and respect between us. We sat down, and Conway, a genuine superstar in country, asked, "Well, Jimmy, what is it you want to see me about?"

"Well, Conway, your career's about over."

A nervous grin broke across Conway's rugged face and he looked over at his agent. "Anyway," I continued solemnly, "I thought you might wanna do something about it."

I kept a straight face. Everyone broke into a jittery laugh to see if I was joking around. Jimmy Jay looked like he was going to have a heart attack. Conway was the biggest act he'd ever had. I went on. "Now, I've known you off and on for, what, twenty-some years. You haven't changed your hairstyle, your band, the kind of songs you write and sing, haven't change anything." He still had that slicked-back, late-fifties rock-and-roll pompadour. "It's *time,* man. Everything's changed around you. What you're doin' is old. You're too good. You could fix all that if you really wanted to."

Conway was shocked, but he was also the ultimate pro. To him "Conway Twitty" was not a person but an enterprise—a creation of Harold Jenkins's imagination. It was as if you were talking about a third person sitting in the office named Conway. "I'm not asking you to talk about it now," I said, to ease him through the moment. "I'm just tellin' you. Think it over and give me a call."

One of my first official duties at MCA was producing an hour-long showcase of the label's top artists at Opryland during Country Music Week in late September. I had told my people, "If we're gonna do this, let's do it right." The sound system for amplified electric instruments was awful at Opryland, which was built for esthetics, not acoustics. They couldn't handle what I had in mind, so I brought in outside sound. I staged the showcase with a fifty-piece orchestra and a half-dozen computerized screens flashing pictures of the artist synched up to the music. It was very high-tech and cutting-edge, and Music Row again thought I was nuts. Country acts tended to just open the curtains, stand there, and sing.

All my acts ran through brief soundchecks—and then Tanya Tucker rolled in an hour late with her new rock-and-roll band from California. She had just been signed to MCA and her *TNT* LP was due out with a rough, driving rock sound. I let them rehearse awhile, then I told them this had gone on long enough. The audience had been sitting through all this since ten A.M., *and* they'd heard two other label showcases already. It was not good to test their patience and goodwill for another hour. The crowd was hollerin', I was pissed at Tanya, and I finally got her offstage. We got under way fifty minutes late.

I went back to the control board as the show began. Out came our first act, Bill Monroe, the venerable "Father of Bluegrass." I never liked country as a kid, and bluegrass sounded to me like singing through your nose. Bill had his quartet and his mandolin and some acoustic instruments with four mike stands. Having set the sound for another much-louder electric act, I figured these ol' bluegrass boys needed a boost with the sound. So I jammed those mike faders way up.

But when Bill & Co. bore down on some bluegrass ditty in that high, lonesome wail of theirs, I didn't believe the noise that came through those stacks: the first twenty rows you could see people's hair blowin' back, it was so loud and screechy. People got up and made for the exits, hands over their ears.

I was tickled to death. Hell with 'em, I said. They were irritated with us, I got even with them. They came for country, they *got* country. After that first song I eased it back down to human levels. I'd never heard anything like it in my life. Bluegrass could be hazardous to your health at those levels.

Then Tanya came out with the rock-and-roll hair, tight leather pants, and halter top. She was awfully cute when she put her mind to it. She started off with two old hits and her fans loved them. But then she did a cut off her new, rock-influenced album. Now, when you're seventy-eight years old and country, you don't necessarily want to hear a three-minute guitar solo with ear-splitting feedback. *Another* two hundred folks filed out. By the middle of Tanya's next track off *TNT,* the whole front center section had been evacuated.

Unfortunately poor Tillis had to follow Tanya and faced a nearly half-empty hall. Mel got so mad at me, he came by and just sputtered. Then he went out and did his set. It was not the most spectacular debut as a Nashville division chief.

By the end of the summer Mike Maitland had been diagnosed with what we would now call early Alzheimer's disease. Mike was only in his early fifties but was having severe memory lapses. He would come into town for meetings and leave his briefcase behind five different times. It was sad to watch. I had never heard of this disease until then.

When he could no longer serve as president, MCA stuck him in a windowless office to avoid a costly buyout. Then they named their head of marketing, Robert Siner, to replace Mike. My gut reaction was: *No way this'll fly. Marketing and music didn't always mix well.* And I was upset by the way MCA had treated Mike.

I needed Siner's assurance of total autonomy—or the hell with the deal. I called him at home on a Sunday. "I hate to bother you," I lied, "but I don't think I'll be running MCA here come tomorrow evening unless you can fly in tonight and convince me to stay." No incoming chief wants to face losing a high-level guy. It looks like a no-confidence vote on the street.

Siner flew in with the best of intentions—but it was a bad tactical move. I knew I had him. He should've had *me* fly out to *his* headquarters.

For a couple of hours my Nashville lawyer, Dick Frank, and I sat with Bob while I reiterated my need for a free hand in signings, firings, budgets, and so on. He gave in so thoroughly that when he left, he would almost need my permission to visit us again. In wanting to win me over, he gave me more than any division chief in Nashville had ever had. "That was brilliant, the way you handled him," Dick said after Bob left. I told him to have a seat.

"Why? What's goin' on?"

"I want you to draft me a letter of resignation."

"What?" He stared at me in disbelief. I wasn't thinking of Siner, but of his boss, Sid Sheinberg, the powerful head of MCA, Inc., Worldwide, the entertainment conglomerate. "If Bob tells Sheinberg what he gave up down here, he'll be furious. Siner wasn't that bad a kid. Why sacrifice him?" We got the letter done in an hour, and I overnighted it. Then I called Siner's secretary and urged her to tell him not to discuss our meeting with Sheinberg until he'd read the letter.

The resignation wasn't a threat. I knew I couldn't stay at MCA. There was the Maitland thing; and I also felt I could not build a division when the main company was in turmoil. After two hours I could tell Bob was a marketing guy who knew little about running a record company. There was no sense getting him in trouble over me. I wasn't his real problem. His real problems would be with Elton John, Olivia Newton-John, and the other high-flying pop-rock artists he had just inherited. Another issue: It was not an especially exciting place, and I wanted out.

Once Siner read the letter I was gone, but no one knew it yet. The next day I got a visit from Conway, who had not only thought over our last talk; it seemed he'd been to the hairdresser. Instead of the slick fifties do, he had a late-seventies do, blow-dried and all puffed up. We had a good laugh over the way I had presented the situation. "Bowen, you got your point across real well. I *heard* you. I'm gonna make some changes, gonna fix things."

"Conway, I couldn't be more glad to hear you say that, but I've got somethin' to tell you. I'm making some changes too. I'm outta here tomorrow."

"Say what?" Conway gave me a nervous half-grin.

I told him I was leaving, but wanted him to know I felt he should keep the faith—and the hair. "I don't want to see it be over for you, man. You're on the right track. Modernize your music. Just go and do it."

My resignation was announced on Wednesday, in mid-October. People who were only angry at me before were now bewildered. This wasn't how things were done on Music Row. In less than four months I'd fired a couple of dozen employees and artists, most of whom had kids, spouses, road bands, and crews to support. My enemies list was growing by the hour. Having just derailed a bunch of careers, I quit and was out of a job myself.

But I wasn't about to leave anyone enough time to gloat.

FIFTEEN

T WO DAYS AFTER my resignation, Dick Frank got a call from my friend, Joe Smith, then heading Elektra/Asylum in L.A. Through the seventies Elektra/Asylum was a boutique pop label with the Eagles, Joni Mitchell, Linda Ronstadt, Jackson Browne, and Warren Zevon, among others. But its Nashville division had only one major artist, Eddie Rabbitt, a dismal 2 percent market share, and losses the year before of a couple of million dollars.

Joe was calling to say he wanted me to run the label.

On Saturday, I flew to Dallas, where he was attending the premiere of Clint Eastwood's movie *Every Which Way but Loose,* for which Elektra had the sound track. Joe and I met in his hotel room, where I agreed to be VP-GM and in-house producer. I accepted a slight pay cut to $125,000, but won an extra royalty point on what I produced for the label. I was betting that the point would be worth more than the $25,000 drop in salary.

I wasted no time making that happen. The day after the screening, on Sunday, I sat in the Beverly Hills home of Mike Curb, who now had his own company, and signed a third-party deal to get Hank Williams, Jr.

Back home I cleaned house again and restaffed without raiding the MCA crew I had just put in place. My temperament was geared to building, not destroying. I got as much satisfaction from leaving a label with a strong, intact organization as I did from building a new one.

•

Not long after I took over, in late 1978, Dixie Two and I got married. I hated fancy big-ass weddings, so we had a small ceremony in the front yard of the house we were renting. But as with each of my previous marriages, I had a bad omen right before I took my vows: this time it was chiggers. As I stood by a big tree pledging to stay with Dixie in sickness and in health, I got attacked by a bunch of damn chiggers.

We had moved into the beautiful three-bedroom house on Golf Club Lane in Green Hills owned by newly elected Lamar Alexander, who had moved into the governor's mansion. Dixie had quit Tree but wanted to get back into the business. One of my less popular moves as label head was setting up a new department, Elektra Publishing, and hiring my wife to run it.

Elektra was one of two Nashville divisions owned by the New York–based Warner Communications (the other being Warner Bros.) in the sprawling Warner/Elektra/Atlantic realm. But they'd never made a nickel off Elektra-Nashville. A big album for them was 150,000 units, which was what Eddie Rabbitt sold. But promotion and sales weren't really on the job, and WEA's powerful distribution muscle wasn't flexing on their behalf compared with its pop-rock labels. That had to change. Still, I made an outrageous prediction to Joe: "I'm going to turn this label into a $30-million operation within four years."

With his backing I went after and signed Eddie Raven, Conway, and, in 1982, Crystal Gayle. I knew the Bellamy Brothers— Howard and David—were leaving Warners (they were signed through Curb), and Curb wanted to take them to CBS. But they visited me at Elektra against Curb's wishes and talked about their career directions. The Bellamys were wary, frustrated, and disillusioned: they were songwriters who'd had many big radio hits and toured two hundred days a year, but weren't album artists. They said I was a "total renegade" who, as an *album* producer and label head, could bump them to the next dimension.

They were renegades as well. They lived with their wives, kids, and parents way off in Florida and had just produced a pricey $220,000 LP themselves at Criterion in Miami. Warners rejected the album, they said, and booted them. But I believed in them, signed them, brought out the album (*Restless*) and got a few big hits from it.

Picking winners is no science. If it were, no one would make records that stiffed. Best you can do is hope you're right more than wrong.

I remember passing on one aspiring singer when I was just

making my move from L.A. to Nashville. She had just been discovered by my buddy, Red Steagall. Red had heard her belt out
"The Star-Spangled Banner" at the 1974 National Finals Rodeo
in Oklahoma City. The singer had worked in a family trio but, I
guess as a fallback, was still studying elementary education at
Southeastern Oklahoma State University. She must have figured
she had a better shot at becoming a schoolteacher than a country singer then.

But Red heard something in her voice and agreed to help her
get a record deal. She came to Nashville, cut a demo with four
songs, and Red pitched her all over town. But no one seemed to
want another "girl singer" in Nashville then and he couldn't get
anyone excited enough to sign her.

I was one of the producers Red was hoping to win over. He
had cowritten one of the songs on the demo and was acting as
her manager, but I still respected and trusted Red's opinion. We
had worked together in publishing for a decade, and I had
recorded him as an artist. If it was in his best interests to get her
signed, it was also in my best interests as a producer looking to
break into country to get hooked up with a promising new
singer. But I didn't hear it. She simply didn't work for me.

"Sounds too country," I told him, "for where radio's going
now."

She was pure country, all right. That red-headed Okie girl
never did become a schoolteacher, but she sure taught me a lesson about picking talent—namely, that you never *really* know.

The singer's name: Reba McEntire.

In trimming rosters, there are always some tough calls. Vern
Gosdin was one of them. Vern was a purist with a marvelous vocal instrument. But the trend in country was toward vanilla
"crossover" music with pop arrangements, and Vern's sales unfortunately did not reflect his natural gifts. (He later ran up more
than a dozen Top 10s for various labels when the pop thing faded
later in the eighties.)

Some decisions are easier. I remember when Elektra's people
urged me to go to a label showcase to hear three acts in Houston.
This kind of cheerleading goes on all the time. Fortunately, I was
able to sit in the back of the club, just in case I had to make an
early exit. The first act was just terrible. Then came Wood New-
ton, a songwriter signed to record, but who was as un-artist as
you could get. The headliner was David Houston, who'd had a
bunch of hits for Epic and then stalled out.

He was about forty then and came out wearing blue jeans

with a big ol' gut hangin' over it, a T-shirt with holes in it, an out-of-tune guitar, and a high, off-pitch tenor voice that had long since left him. I made it through about four songs and split.

It was the worst show I'd ever seen. Next day I dropped all three acts. As for the people who sent me down there to see the future of Elektra, they were history.

Another act I had no second thoughts about dropping was Jerry Lee Lewis. "Killer" had switched to country in the mid-sixties. Joe had signed him just before I arrived. It was a good deal for Jerry Lee, bad for me: seven albums "firm." I was stuck for a few more years, at about $300,000 per record. My approach was: Never give that long a deal, and leave your options open.

What Killer needed more than a record deal was a rehab program. He was messed up and at times incoherent on booze and pills, and no fun to work with. I cut one thing with him real fast and never wanted to do it again. He was acting like white trash, wild and crazy, shootin' guns off. So I made his manager a generous offer: "I'll give you three hundred fifty thousand dollars to make him go away."

It worked. Then, before he left, Jerry Lee had a Top 5 hit with "Thirty-nine and Holding." But it was still a good drop.

Not long afterward I was singing a different tune: .38 and holding. Killer got pissed off for being dumped, so I sent two of my top guys on a house call to make peace. Letting him down easy was hard: Killer pulled a gun and scared the hell out of them. Then he muttered something about killing me.

A week later I was at Sound Stage late. Dixie's brother, who was visiting South Carolina, decided to stop by the studio. He had a beard and was about my size. He borrowed my Caddie and must've found one of my sailor's caps on the front seat. Though younger, he probably looked exactly like me at midnight.

As he got out of the car, he was set upon by two guys at knifepoint. He fought them off, but got cut up pretty bad. When he pressed the security buzzer, I got to the door and found him bleeding heavily. His attackers ran off and I rushed my brother-in-law to the hospital.

In the wake of this bizarre and suspicious assault, the label put a twenty-four-hour security tail on me—the private detective, the vans parked near the house, the secret surveillance cameras, the works. The security guy found a tap on the phone line, but couldn't tell if it had been put on from when Lamar lived there. But they did theorize that the mugging may have been Killer's payback, although we never confirmed this.

There was an upside to all the intrigue: I could stay in the house all winter and start my car with a remote-ignition gizmo. It's not easy to find people to start your car for you when you imagine it could blow up.

Instead of feeling like a duck waiting for hunting season to open, I went on the offensive to get something on tape that we could use against Jerry Lee. My security guy went to where Jerry Lee lived and climbed a telephone pole to tap his line. Just then two Feds came out of nowhere and busted him. He told them what he was doing and they told him, "We're already listening in. You can't mess ours up." They saw he was a pro, so they let him go. Jerry Lee ended up with a tax-evasion rap but was ultimately cleared of the charges.

I settled things myself with Killer when I had a friend explain to him in no uncertain terms that whatever might happen to me would also happen to every member of his family. That was the end of that.

Elektra's fortunes picked up soon after I arrived. Eddie Rabbitt hit it big with "Every Which Way but Loose," the Eastwood-movie theme song. It was Eddie's big breakthrough, staying at No. 1 for three weeks. Still, his albums only reached the 150,000 to 175,000 range despite his radio success. Eddie's "team"— manager Stan Moress, my onetime number-two guy at MGM, and cowriters Even Stevens and David Malloy, who produced him—all hoped that my arrival would lift his LP sales.

The synergy between records and film worked wonders in 1980 with *Urban Cowboy*—the John Travolta–Debra Winger movie featuring long-neck beers and Gilley's mechanical bull. The double LP came out on Irving Azoff's Full Moon label.

Irving had acquired the rights to journalist Aaron Latham's *Esquire* article on Gilley's honky-tonk near Houston. He called me and said it was an incredible crossover LP with country *and* pop hits by Boz Scaggs, Bob Seger, Mickey Gilley, and an obscure singer named Johnny Lee, a house act at Gilley's.

Urban Cowboy probably did $30 million in LPs and cassettes. The breakout No. 1 hit was Johnny's "Lookin' for Love" in the summer of 1980; it crossed over to *Billboard*'s Top 100 at No. 5 and went gold. The song's demo had been pitched all over town and rejected by twenty-one artists before it got picked for the sound track. It made Johnny Lee a star overnight.

Hollywood's impact on record sales was shown clearly when Eddie cut a song for *Roadie* that year. The movie was a stiff; the song, "Drivin' My Life Away," hit No. 1 country and Top 5 pop. It was Eddie's second No. 1 in a row after "Gone Too Far" off his *Loveline* LP.

At the end of 1980 he released "I Love a Rainy Night," and *that* went gold *and* hit No. 1 country and pop. Eddie cut four more No. 1s that went Top 40 over the next two years.

All these crossover records kicked sales of his LPs to just short of 2 million each. Eddie and his team knew that pop-country groove as well as anyone then; out of the dozen or so singles he released for us before we merged with Warners in early 1983, ten of them went to No. 1.

Crossing over was becoming an obsession on Music Row. Kenny Rogers did it beautifully—with "You Decorated My Life," "Love the World Away," and, in 1980, "Lady"—because he had started in pop and knew what he was doing. But then the wannabes in Nashville tried to ride the trend going the other way. With so many songwriters, producers, and A&R taking aim at two charts, a lot of Nashville music straddled both genres but sounded like neither. We got to hear some of the worst, most plastic music ever to come out of Nashville.

The desperate grab for crossover left some ugly stretch marks in town. Travolta's movie briefly boosted sales of western wear and mechanical bulls; but to this day the term *urban cowboy* on Music Row has come to stand for all that slick, corny crap with too many strings and no edge created in a dumb-ass quest for Top 40.

The irony of "urban cowboy" music was that when a good-looking *real-life* cattle roper and rancher named George Strait came along in 1981 with a pure, Texas swing sound, no one took him seriously. He was almost an outcast because he wasn't crossover material. Artists like Vern Gosdin, Reba, and Strait were all still a little "too country" for the urban-cowboy era.

That silly craze faded, but its effect was deeply hurtful to country. Nashville had a couple of slumping, aimless years before the pendulum swung back to country's "New Traditional" roots, sparked by purists like Ricky Skaggs, then Strait, and, in 1985–86, Reba and Randy Travis. Travis blew the doors open with his *Storms of Life* debut LP, featuring great songs like "1982" and "On the Other Hand." Once that first LP did 2, then 3 million, the country-music industry was virtually reborn.

Long before that revival I had a wonderful opportunity to get back to the roots of country by hooking up with two very unurban cowboys.

The initial tracks I cut with Merle Haggard were recorded at Glaser's studio in late 1978. The first was "The Bull and the Beaver," a fun duet with Leona Williams. Then we did "Red Bandanna" in early 1979, and both went Top 10. My new deal with Elektra allowed me to produce acts on other labels, which in this case was MCA. Leona had just become Merle's third wife. Wife number two, his backup singer, Bonnie Owen, was a bridesmaid who still toured with him. Nothing about "Hag" was ordinary.

Like Waylon, Haggard was just months apart from me in age, and we'd met now and then through the years but never really hung out together. He was a wary veteran who always seemed to be fighting with record people, worried someone was taking advantage of him. He had been in the business for some fifteen years and was, by any measure, a legend: between 1967 and 1977 virtually all of Haggard's three-dozen-odd singles went Top 10, including an amazing twenty-three No. 1s. If we hit it off right away, it was because he sensed I was on the side of the artist, not out to exploit him.

The sessions just fell into place and I never even got paid for them. Merle then disappeared for a good part of 1979, living on his houseboat on Lake Shasta way up in northern California.

Merle was going through a traumatic time of midlife self-examination, having just turned forty. I went and visited him out there. He had a beautiful house on a hill. From there it was a short way to the lake, where he had the houseboat and an old nightclub. We talked for a couple of hours about his life and career. I told him to modernize his road band, the Strangers, because they'd been with him forever and played from another generation.

We went out on his boat and I talked him through a lot of what was troubling him. We talked about him worrying about it being over for him. He was very emotional about turning forty, losing his edge. He didn't know if he could really write anymore. I assured him he had a lot yet to write and sing about. He talked about getting screwed out of a lot of money by this one and that one, and he'd reached a point where he didn't know if he really wanted to go forward or the hell with it. We talked about recording together again when he was ready.

Hag struck me as an extremely emotional, brooding, inward man. He had spent three hard years at San Quentin in the late fifties for burglary and had always been tough to get close to. He is not by nature a talker, an orator. He has always been a killer songwriter, who speaks most eloquently and forcefully through his music. I believe Merle knows he is one of our finest rural poets in this century and he has struggled with the demons that come with that awesome gift, that burden. He has a wonderful sense of humor, but he was also a deep, very serious artist.

When he felt recharged, Haggard got back to work. He came to me and talked about how he could sell a lot of albums. One way, I said, was to replace his road band with great, studio-wise sessions pickers with a modern sound. His band's sloppiness, which worked onstage, got exaggerated in a studio. A studio player's a whole other animal from a road musician. One's got to be good for three minutes and retain only that much music at a time. The other's got to ham it up for an hour and a half and remember a whole show's music. Most live guys get jammed up playing while wearing headphones, hemmed in by the silence and isolation of the studio. They thrive on contact and energy. It's two different art forms.

Hag himself was terribly uncomfortable in the studio and did some of his greatest recordings onstage. He was not sloppy. His phrasings were utterly original; he was a great stylist on the order of a Bing or a Dean, with wonderfully subtle and expressive vocal dynamics.

The studio guys I hired loved the challenge of simulating the Strangers—but with discipline and finesse. It was a new thing for them, instead of the same licks session after session. They got into it.

Haggard had a place in town, but he'd pull his tour bus up behind the apartment and sleep in the bus. He loved being on the road, which has been his real home for thirty years now. I asked him why he did that and he said, "My suite back there is the same size as my cell at San Quentin. The only place I feel safe is at the back of that bus."

We're not likely ever to see another Haggard come along in country. His is a bygone era. Country singers today don't come from San Quentin. Garth Brooks studied marketing at Oklahoma State. Mary-Chapin Carpenter got an Ivy League degree. Today's instant superstars have handlers in Beverly Hills. With Hag there was a powerful mystique around the man that defined the essence of what country had once been about.

Yet he remained aloof, never courted Nashville. He also never won many CMA awards. I think Hag came to hate Nashville because he felt the Establishment always got something from him without ever giving anything back. He didn't trust easily.

But whenever he rolled into town and word hit the street that he was cutting a record, it became an event. An entourage gathered—the songwriters, publishers, promotion people, the Nashville insiders who kept his world afloat. And artists who wanted, simply, to pay their respects.

Things moved a little slowly around Hag because there were always people stopping in to say hi, pitch tunes, ask a favor, whatever. Hag was a magnetic, charismatic star, who, if he showed up a little late, didn't make a big drama out of it.

At one session I made some enemies on Music Row when the venerable songwriter Hank Cochran showed up drunk and obnoxious. He busted in, pitching tunes to Haggard. People had been indulging this kind of thing for years. Back in those days the great writers just busted into a session to play a song for an artist even as he was recording.

I just took Hank out on the second-floor landing and we had a talk. "If I walked into your house while you were settin' there writin' one of your great songs, I'd shut the fuck up and let you finish it. Now, stay out of here and respect what we're doing."

A while later I was behind the control board with the music so loud, I couldn't hear anything, but I *sensed* eyes burning through me from behind. I turned around and there was poor Hank, with Mel Tillis, sitting on the floor cross-legged. They were there to watch and hear Haggard record. Hank pointed to Tillis and mumbled. "Bowen, he made me come back in here."

Tillis turned to him and said, "Hank, uhh, uhh, shut . . . the fuck . . . up. You're . . . in here on a p-p-pass . . . as it is."

That cracked everyone up. They spent the rest of the night cross-legged on that control-room floor, being real quiet.

Hag was nervous meeting all my musicians. But once he trusted me and loosened up, recording with these pickers was a wonderful experience, and he was thrilled with the results. After the first run-through and a test track, he came in and put earphones on for a playback. A big smile broke across his face. "Sounds just like the Strangers," he said. He brought his road band in for a listen. They loved it. Hag's guitarist, Roy Nichols, a wonderful stylist, had had a few drinks as we listened. At one point he grinned, and I overheard him tell one of the Strangers, "Huh, I don't remember *playing* that."

We had a terrific single that Hag had written called "I Think I'll Just Stay Here and Drink"—which was four and a half minutes of terrific picking. MCA wanted me to edit it down to three minutes, but I just couldn't bring myself to cut any of the great solos at the end or fade it any sooner. I called Merle and said, "This is ridiculous. Let radio fade it on any of these solos when they want to. But let's *us* not mess with a great piece of music."

I sent the same message to MCA. "You guys aren't thinkin'. Give radio a time, like three-ten, on the label copy, and let 'em fade it when they want." Haggard wouldn't agree to the editing anyway, so MCA reluctantly agreed.

The song came out in January 1981, aired at four-forty or so, and of course became Merle's first No. 1 in four years. I explained to Haggard the reason his song's length *really* worked at radio. "I was in radio. We always loved these long records 'cause we could put 'em on and hit the john."

That album was an important kick in the britches for Hag, and it helped to keep his music going during the second half of his life. I felt it was one of his best albums ever. It was also the beginning of a long and durable friendship. We never cut an album together after that, but he did ask me to mix a couple more records for him around that time. One was an album of live tracks recorded at three venues—a sports stadium, a small hall, and a Texas club. He wanted all the tracks to sound live and as if they were done at the same place. That was interesting. I took about twelve seconds of "ambience" from Anaheim Stadium—whooshing, murmuring crowd sounds—and looped it so that I could splice in behind the crowds at the other places to equalize the aural dimensions of the three venues between songs.

Then I sampled light and medium applause and wild crowd roars and put them all on "triggers" to make them happen where they fit the sequence and flow of the show. If Hag kicked into, say, "Okie from Muskogee," or some other famous song of his, and his fans erupted with recognition, I triggered wild applause.

Incredibly, he got a Top 5 hit, "Rainbow Stew," from all that trickery.

I was eager to bring Hag over to Elektra when he left MCA that year. But Merle's manager, Tex Whitson, a longtime buddy from the San Quentin days, felt the bigger CBS machine would be better for Merle. I was sure for a day or two I had him. I met with Merle and Tex in the bus behind Merle's Nashville apartment when it got to where Elektra and Merle were only $25,000 apart. To break the stalemate, I told them, "Look, since everything else is agreed upon, let's just flip for it."

I took out a half-dollar and they agreed. He won the toss, we shook on it, and I was sure we had a deal. A few days later Merle called and told me, "Tex feels strongly about me goin' over there. I love you, man, and I'd like to be with you. But, you know, Tex feels the bigger company can sell more records."

As our friendship evolved, I helped Merle in other ways. He had money and tax problems all throughout his career. Hag was obviously not a savvy businessman. Every time he came to town from Bakersfield, it seemed he got screwed one way or another. And there were rumors about Hag's vices being costly, and he had fifty-some-odd people on his road payroll and felt responsible for feeding his longtime friends. If he short-changed anyone, it was Internal Revenue, so he had his troubles.

A couple of years ago he called me, as he often did when in his darker moments. It wasn't about not having charted since 1990—almost no one from his generation was getting airplay anymore. This call was about money. He had borrowed money from a Nashville bank and put up his vast publishing catalog and royalties as collateral. But he owed the IRS and couldn't pay back the bank note. The bank wanted to foreclose. Tree Publishing was circling to acquire Merle's publishing from the bank at a fraction of its real value. It was an awful scenario.

"Bowen," he asked, "would you be interested in buying the publishing company at the right price?"

I told him, "Of course I would, but that's not the point." Instead I urged him to declare bankruptcy in order to tie everything up. Merle took my advice, saved his precious catalog, and, once under protection, he was able to get the right price for it. He not only got out of debt, he had a few bucks left.

It was especially gratifying for Hag when the CMA finally got around to inducting him into its Hall of Fame in October 1994. I was surprised when, in his speech, the lone industry person he named for helping him get there was me.

I know Hag has considered me a genuine, trustworthy friend ever since those first sessions at Glaser's. I guess he never associated me with "Nashville"—and that was his own way of saying thanks for sticking by him. I'd stirred up such a stink in town for so many years by then that it was a validation for me as well—as if he was saying, "Bowen and I, we're a lot alike. We're both crazy sons of bitches."

A major part of Elektra's turnaround was due to another purist who, like Hag, stuck to his guns and became a giant.

When I signed Hank Williams, Jr., I saw him as a country-music treasure. But he was recording the wrong songs in the wrong style. He had struggled all his life to find his voice and escape the long, dark shadow of Hank Sr., a godlike figure considered the greatest country singer of all time.

Hank's first hit as a teenager was for MGM, his father's label, and it was a cover of Hank Sr.'s 1950 No. 1 hit "Long Gone Lonesome Blues." He overdubbed duets with his father's tracks and sang the theme for the film biography *Your Cheatin' Heart*. Red Foley was once reputed to have told young Hank at the Opry, "You're nothin' but a ghost of your daddy."

Hank idolized his father and tried for years to emulate his sound with a smooth and classic country voice. But he also hated trading off the legend; besides, his own passions ran to R&B and blues. So he fell in between the cracks: he was too bluesy for rock and too rock for country, but country was too pop for him. His search for an artistic identity was driving him nuts. In the process, though, he had cut some damn good songs.

Hank had some hits for MGM in the seventies, but I knew he wasn't where he wanted to be. He was drinking, depressed, divorced, and on a self-destructive tear. To get his life together, he left Nashville for northern Alabama.

While I was at MGM in L.A., I had hired Dick Glasser to shape up our small Nashville office. On one visit to see Mel Tillis, I came upon Hank, who was waiting to see Dick. He was pouting and negative. I asked him what was up.

"I can't just be me. Everybody wants me to be Hank Senior."

I went in and told Glasser, "Let that kid be whoever the hell he wants. He doesn't want to be, and will never be, his dad. Can you blame him? Let him be happy."

Glasser took Hank down to experiment with a new sound in Muscle Shoals, Alabama, home of great seventies southern rock. Hank cut a hard-edged breakaway album called *Hank Williams, Jr., and Friends*. The record helped Hank move out from his father's shadow, but it didn't cut it in a town looking for bland, "countrypolitan" music. I didn't care: I wanted to sign Hank to my own deal someday.

Then, in August 1975, just as the *Friends* LP came out, Hank took off for a climbing and hunting trek in Montana. While stepping across the side of a high ravine, his footing gave way and he bounced a couple of hundred feet down a craggy mountainside, crashing against the rocks and landing face first. It was a miracle he even survived.

The fall shattered bones all through Hank's body and virtually tore his face off, cracking his skull in two places. The front of his face was split straight down the center, from top to bottom. He underwent major reconstructive surgery and has worn dark shades ever since to hide his disfigured eyes.

Other injuries directly changed Hank's music. He lost almost half his hearing in both ears and compensated for his deafness by singing much louder and stronger. Having cheated death, he endured a long rehabilitation and came through it tougher, more confident, more determined to be Hank, Jr.

Hank's producer was Ray Ruff, who, I felt, was matching Hank poorly with material. Ray was a good promotion man but a terrible producer, and he knew I knew it. Hank was cutting Jackson Browne and Bee Gee covers, the Bobbie Fuller Four's "I Fought the Law," singing with choirs and strings. Made no sense. I wanted to produce him so that I could capture his fusion of pure country roots, the best blues voice around, and his intense Outlaw energy. I got my chance when I came to Elektra and signed Hank through Curb.

I also had to sign Ray Ruff's wife, Susie Allanson, in order to close the deal. That's how Curb operated: if you wanted something real bad, he made you take something else to get it. I got them both for recording costs and a percentage of profits. Susie had a couple of nice little records and was a good kid but not a great singer. A very small price to pay to get Hank.

Hank's previous album sales were a weak 25,000. I negotiated a producer's fee of $15,000 per LP and three royalty percentage points against it. (Royalties roughly doubled in value when fourteen- and fifteen-dollar CDs became the industry standard.) I knew Hank could go through the roof.

Hank's manager asked me to help him with an album he had cut in California but now hated. I met Hank in Muscle Shoals to discuss recording some new tracks to replace the bad ones.

I had asked Don Sessions to book five Muscle Shoals sessions guys Hank liked. I flew in and we met at the studio. As we chatted and caught up, it was apparent Hank had a big chip on his shoulder, sounding almost bitter. But then he hadn't had a big hit in five years.

Then I asked, "Well, have you got any songs for us to record? We got a great rhythm section in there."

He shrugged and snarled, "Nobody's interested in my songs."

"Well, then, we're in a lot of trouble, pal, because I didn't bring any songs for you. You must have something, you're a damn good writer." He seemed wary, on edge, mistrustful.

He got out his acoustic guitar. "I do have this one thing," he said, tuning it up. "It's called 'Family Tradition.'" I heard it once and said, "That'll do it. Come on."

When I was done mastering "Family Tradition," I knew we had a career record. I remixed a couple of California cuts we would keep, finished up four others from Muscle Shoals, and released *Family Tradition* as an album title in June 1979.

My head of promotion, Nick Hunter, burst into my office and said what I already knew: "We've got a monster. Radio's all over it." Within three or four weeks it exploded.

Hank was clearly an artist with a music to do—but he hadn't done it yet. I called him in for an hour-long talk to get him to trust me, to let me help him be the best Hank possible. He hated labels, the business, radio, hated *everybody*. He was an angry guy who didn't trust anyone. Nashville was a bunch of bad memories. I had to get him past his fear and resentment.

"You've got a smash here," I said. "But I'm in the album business."

He nodded. "That's the business I wanna be in." Maybe the chip was off the shoulder. Hank was ready.

"When we do an album again," I said, "I want forty minutes of magic, not three. You have the chance to do that." He nodded.

"We're going to tape your live show and get who you really are. If your road-band guys aren't good enough for the studio, I'll put a band together for you. They'll be your *road* band in the studio. It'll be *your* music. You just have to give me a consistent flow of material. Nobody writes songs like you."

Hank was no fool. He'd been up and down the charts fifty times. He asked questions, told me what he hated about "the business." "It's a new day here," I assured him. "We're gonna make great music, get on radio, get into retail. You're gonna be a superstar." We shook on it. He never backed down on any of it.

"Family Tradition" had a pure-country sound that bucked the vanilla trend and went Top 5 in the summer of 1979, and despite my decision not to release a follow-up single, *Family Tradition* went gold. Hank was starting to get on a roll.

I went out to Reading, California, to tape Hank's show live. His road band was technically awful—out of tune, out of sync, one of the worst bands I'd ever heard. But Hank's energy and charisma still got a *thing* happening with the crowd—and that's what I wanted to isolate in the studio and surround with great players on the first full album I did with him.

I played Hank's live tape for my session guys and brought

Hank in to work out all his own arrangements. Then the musicians refined what they heard and did their tracks. Hank loved this. Once we had the basic instrumental track, I'd have Hank sing the song three or four more times, then I'd piece together phrase by phrase one killer vocal. Hank couldn't write music, so at the end I'd have him sing into an open track—we were now up to twenty-four and thirty-two tracks—whatever he heard in his head, whether it was horns, electric-guitar solo, harmony vocals, and so forth. Then I overdubbed these people later.

Hank's first single off that terrific album was the title track, "Whiskey Bent and Hell Bound," and it made it to No. 2. Whatever he heard in his head now came through on record. I wasn't imposing my thoughts, but helping him capture his own. The transformation was dramatic: he got turned on, wrote killer songs, and went at it with all the passion and desire that had been bottled up inside him for so long. Hank was playing the game now—and winning big.

Our third album was *A Country Boy Can Survive,* and it's one of the best things he and I ever did. Interestingly the title cut, like "Family Tradition," didn't go to No. 1. It stuck at No. 2 for three weeks. But both songs were milestones for Hank—and for country. They were far more important than, say, "Honky Tonkin'," which did get to No. 1. Given the goofy methodology used to determine chart positions, I've always felt No. 1 records don't mean nearly as much as one might think.

George Strait once came to me all upset when, after a long string of No. 1s, some record of his fell just short. I told him what counts in the real world is not chart position but *rotation*—light, medium, heavy. It's about how many times the consumer hears your song on the car radio or FM at home, not where it's sittin' on some Top 100. Besides, the only people who read the trades don't *buy* records; they get 'em free.

I also told him how, back before computers reflected actual airplay, labels could manipulate the hell out of the charts anyway. The trades relied on tracking stations for their reporting. There were P1, P2, and P3 stations, based on population, with a major P1 market weighted equal to, say, three P3s in compiling playlist "adds." The stations based their decisions on "call-out" listener research—"I'm tired of it," "Still love it," "Great new song," and so on. Promotion people would beg and scream and trade favors with programmers so that they could accrue enough radio-station adds to reflect movement up the charts; this way label-promotion people could keep a new song's all-important chart "bullet" for when the trade papers called those stations. In lieu of outright payola in country, it was all part of the numbers-game fluff. Thus, while having a No. 1 hit sounded great, it wasn't often the artist's greatest work.

So I told George, "I tell you what. For two months you go out onstage and introduce your number-two record as your latest number-one hit and I'll give you a hundred dollars for every fan who jumps up and yells, 'Bullshit, George, it stopped at two!'"

George never came around to collect.

While *Urban Cowboy* was dominating radio, Hank and I went on to record some rowdy, hard-driving country hits like "Women I've Never Had," "Kaw-Liga," which his dad had recorded, and a ballad, "Old Habits." We were off and rockin'. Despite early warnings I'd received about Hank's attitude, he was terrific. We hit it off, he showed up on time, and was a total pro.

Hank had been a heavy drinker and had done some cocaine before I worked with him. One song he did was about him almost OD'ing. But he had gotten past all that. Still, even without the excesses he could be loud, rowdy, and intimidating; there was still some of the old, wilder Hank left in him.

One night he showed up at the studio packin' a .38 loaded with blanks. I knew Hank had an extensive handgun collection; I'd seen them—hundreds of them—at his home in Alabama. I was inside the studio and heard some gunshots. Hank was shooting his blanks at the trash basket and the ceiling. He was just a big kid raisin' hell. Someone came in to let me know. "No problem," I said calmly.

I reached into my briefcase and set my own .38 Smith & Wesson on the recording board. When Hank busted into the studio, he saw the piece and stopped.

"Whoa, sir, what have we got here?"

"We've got a thirty-eight-caliber Smith and Wesson, and these aren't blanks."

When it came to his actual work in the studio, however, Hank wasn't firing blanks. His bullets were all over the country charts. Five of our next six singles—including the wonderful "All My Rowdy Friends Have Settled Down"—all hit No. 1. Hank's amazing comeback sent his album sales close to the one-million range. My feeling was that in twenty years young artists would be cutting remakes of Hank's best songs, just the way his generation did with his father's.

We made a good team: We did eleven studio LPs—among

them *Whiskey Bent, Rowdy, Man of Steel, Habits Old and New,* and *Major Moves*—and three greatest-hits packages. All but one went to Top 5, and all have been certified gold or platinum.

One genuinely rewarding moment for me was when I re-signed Hank to Elektra down at his home in Alabama. I had the label publicity department round up press and photographers for when I handed Hank a big ol' advance check for $1 million.

Hank had climbed back to the top of the mountain—living proof that he could be, like his dad, one of the all-time greats.

With Hank and Rabbitt, Elektra got on a terrific ride. At times it seemed we couldn't miss. Tompall and his brothers hadn't had a big hit in a decade, but when I cut a song with them on the label in 1981, it hit No. 2. It was a remake of the great Kris Kristofferson song, "Lovin' Her Was Easier (Than Anything I'll Ever Do Again)." It was a nice way to repay Tompall for being my guide on Music Row.

I thoroughly enjoyed working with the Bellamy Brothers. When I hooked up with them, the LPs were selling 150,000 or so units, but they had never made it huge. Their sound *was* a bit wimpy, I thought—what I call bubblegum-country—to move a ton of albums. That's what needed fixin'.

They respected my view that you change the music first—and hype the artist after. As I was always saying, Take care of the music, and the music takes care of the rest.

Working with Howard and David was a kick. Both were personable, hardworking Florida boys who smoked some grass but didn't get crazy behind booze and other hard drugs. They lived the good life on a big farm outside of Tampa. When they asked if they could cut their first Elektra LP there, I said I'd give it a try. I figured on playing some golf there too, but Tampa being the lightning capital of the world, it didn't go well: I got run off the course twice by lightning and once by alligators. 'Gators can really mess up your short game.

The Brothers each had a house at the compound, and their parents lived next door. Frances Bellamy was a warm, wonderful lady whom I had gotten to know in Nashville. She had really taken to my precocious son, Christian, who, at age six, could make conversation with a rock. They became buddies and, when I decided to go to Florida, Frances invited him along. He was living with his mom, but he loved going down there.

I urged the brothers to shop around for more substantial material, and that probably kicked them in the butt to write better songs on their own. We worked on giving them a meatier sound. We produced three quick No. 1 hits with them—"For All the Wrong Reasons," "When I'm Away from You," and "Redneck Girl." (I gave this last single to Warners to help them satisfy their obligations to their former label. I frankly didn't think it would work as a single.)

I hired a remote-recording truck out of Atlanta and parked it just outside a twenty-by-forty foot wooden shed where they and their road band taped demos and rehearsals on cheap equipment. I ran all the mikes from there into the truck; the speakers were in the shed; and we cut the *When We Were Boys* album crammed in that place without any idea how anything was going to sound.

Back at Sound Stage in Nashville, the Brothers, who coproduced, helped me get some mike noise out, and clean up and mix the tracks. Those three early hits marked the beginning of a great working and personal relationship that would go another six or seven years and bring Howard and David another half-dozen Top 10 hits.

The Bellamys were good-humored guys with whom I shared a load of laughs. They once walked into my house, turned into the living room, and Howard started conversing, thinking he saw me on a couch in a big picture window. After a minute or two he stopped when "I" didn't seem to be responding.

"Damn," he said as he started to freak out. "That's not Bowen." Then he heard me yell, "C'mon in the kitchen, boys." Howard had been speaking to a lifelike dummy propped up on the couch that bore a faint resemblance to me. "Damn, Bowen," he said, "I thought you'd lost a lot of weight there for a minute."

I cracked up. "Yeah, I put that out there for Jerry Lee to take shots at."

I bought Eddie Raven's contract from Dimension Records, a label owned by Ken Stilts. Ken would become one of my closest friends, and manager of the Judds. Eddie's career had been stalled, but I produced a couple of Top 20 hits with him. But then he left Elektra for RCA and put together a dozen or so consecutive Top 10 winners. The trouble we had with Eddie wasn't his studio work. He was a solid songwriter, easy to work with, with a real good voice. Eddie's problem was performing, and it was common enough all over town: a lot of country acts simply had terrible live shows. True, some just have a knack for the stage and holding an audience, but most don't.

I once told George Strait he might try to liven up his stage act just a touch—and he did: he waved his cowboy hat a few times during the show. But George could get away with just standing there looking and sounding terrific. Most can't.

Eddie Raven was a big, tall Cajun kid who dressed kinda gawky. He gave a dull show with not a lot of heart in it. It was a show that didn't stir up sales. Eddie's LPs probably did around 50,000 units. I tried to get this across to a lot of those hillbillies: A certain percentage of people who leave a great show will buy that new album. They connect to you, and want to relive the experience. You're supporting album sales. If you're dull and boring, why would fans want to relive it? That forces an artist to live from incredible single to incredible single in order to sell LPs.

A strong live show can also turn on your own promotion, sales, and publicity people. Garth Brooks was brilliant that way. You want your people to walk away proud, pumped up to have an artist on the label. If they don't, where's the "give a shit" going to come from at the office? I've let a lot of artists go so that they could find better luck elsewhere. Eddie found it with RCA.

Toward the end of 1982 I had a luncheon with Crystal Gayle and her husband, Bill Gatzimos, a lawyer who also helped Crystal run her career. I wanted to bring her over from Columbia. We argued over my policy of paying some musicians double scale. Crystal didn't believe in double scale, which added recording costs that had to be recouped with album sales. I argued that it got you better music.

I asked Bill, "Do all lawyers charge the same?" I asked Crystal, "Do all artists have the same deal?" They said no.

"Then can you tell me," I said, "why a kid who just fell off the turnip truck with his guitar is supposed to get paid the same as a brilliant picker like Reggie Young, who's played on three or four hundred hits?" They said they'd talk it over.

The discussion, which showed my commitment to getting her the best musicians possible, helped persuade her to sign. Some people have accused me of using her move to Elektra to replace Allen Reynolds, who'd produced her for ten years—and causing a rift between Allen and me. Neither is true.

Crystal's first LP for us was *True Love*. When I heard it, I told both of them it needed three more tracks to really work. Allen reportedly wasn't thrilled she had left Columbia anyway and didn't agree. He felt she shouldn't give in, and declined to produce any more cuts. But it wasn't a bitter feud. He and I talked at the time and he understood that things run their course and end. It's rarely the label that fails to deliver the hit; hits are created or not created in the studio, and sometimes your gut tells you it's time to change the formula in order to get more hits. They had had a slew of them together. But that's how I got to record her—to finish *True Love*.

I went to publishers myself to hunt songs for Crystal, and played her ten or fifteen before we went in to cut the new tracks. I played her Rodney Crowell's "'Till I Gain Control Again." Rodney is a superb writer. Crystal liked the song but didn't hear it as being for her. I got her to reconsider, and she came around. It went to No. 1 for us just as Elektra and Warners were merging in early 1983. (Crystal's first Elektra release was her duet with Rabbitt, "You and I," which had gone to No. 1 at the end of 1982.) Rodney's song was the first of a half-dozen Top 10 hits we had together through 1984.

Crystal and I did her *Cage the Songbird* LP throughout the summer of 1983, and it remains one of my favorite Nashville projects. She not only sang wonderfully in the sessions, it became literally a labor of love. Crystal was pregnant with daughter Catherine Claire and in fact went into labor while we were mixing "I Don't Wanna Lose Your Love." All her creative energies were flowing. That song went to No. 2, and "Turning Away" went to the top in 1984. It was a great little rock-type song that some people thought would scare away Crystal's fans at radio. They were wrong.

Crystal was a terrific vocalist as well as a sweet, soft-spoken woman. I enjoyed our work together very much. If anything kept her from being a Reba or a Dolly—she's *had* almost three dozen Top 10 hits—it was that she never had much *showbiz* going for her. She just went out there and sang.

When people bitched that Garth didn't sound country enough, you had to watch him onstage to understand how he got fired up. That's why he was King of the Hill. He burns so hot and intense for his audience, there's no way he's not going to sell records.

I had a great time bringing Conway over from MCA, which didn't want to lose him. Conway had more No. 1 hits—there are forty of them—than anyone in country history. He was also head of a vast business enterprise and, like me, was a hybrid of artist and businessman. He had a CEO's ego. He came to our meeting with his lawyer, CPA, agent, and business manager, Dee Henry, a trusted adviser whom he later married. The issue was, Should Conway jump ship?

I prepared a presentation to show off Elektra's success. Just before the meeting, I got a visual aid money couldn't buy: a TV news item about MCA's parent company being sued by the star of a popular TV series over monies he claimed were owed him. MCA's president, Sid Sheinberg, was asked on air if he felt bad about his corporate Goliath taking on the actor. Sid's answer was along the lines of, like, "No, I don't. He's a big boy, he's got top lawyers. He didn't just come in from Nashville." In other words he's no dumb-ass hillbilly.

I loved it. I got a copy of the sound bite for our meeting. I told Conway, Inc., that, yes, it's better when an artist has longevity at a label and stays where his catalog is, especially when it's a gold mine like Conway's. But I said this was a new day in Nashville, and L.A. wasn't hip to it. L.A., I went on, was too damn big and elitist to give a damn. They look down their noses at Music Row. "Here," I said, "I'll prove it."

I popped in the cassette, cued up to Sheinberg's interview, and once it played, I knew I had 'em. Conway signed on.

When we got together to record, we had a great time. I assured Conway and Dee I wasn't going to run the show but rather let Conway be himself and keep growing. He'd done awfully well without me. Then Conway stunned me by saying he wanted to cover the Pointer Sisters' ballad, "Slow Hand." Its two writers had pitched it around Nashville, but no one wanted it. Then the Pointer Sisters had a huge pop hit with it the year before.

I laughed and said I'd be accused of ruining Conway's career because I let him do it. I was all for Conway pushing the envelope. He had steamy lyrics in songs like "You've Never Been This Far Before," "I See the Want to in Your Eyes," and "Tight-Fittin' Jeans"—and they all got to No. 1.

"Slow Hand" was the first one we did together for Conway's *Southern Comfort* LP, but "The Clown" was released before it, in April 1982. On "Clown" I had to go to the West Coast while we were mastering. The song was over four minutes long and I phoned in an editing change I felt was needed to Glenn Meadows at Masterfonics. But whoever took the call didn't hear me right, and we somehow ended up with a two-minute version. Nick Hunter called me in L.A. and was all excited. "Hey, Bowen," he said, "what a great short record!"

I immediately told him, "Stop shipment." I then called Glenn and ordered the correct edit redone.

Both singles got to No. 1.

Conway wanted to do another cover of a pop hit, Bette Midler's "The Rose," as the title track of that first Elektra LP. He loved the song and I was all for it. But he had a lot of trouble getting the first verse down just right. So I called a short break and went to the bathroom just up the hall.

I left the door to the control room open and could hear Conway start to sing the song—and then stop. As I washed my hands and was walking back, I heard him *talking* the first verse that goes "They say love is like a river. . . ." My engineer thought Conway was joking around and stopped the tape.

I heard Conway tell him from out in the studio, "No, no, no, wrong, back up, that's how I'm gonna do it." The engineer apologized, and rolled again.

As I walked in and Conway spotted me, he finished speaking the first verse—and then sang the rest of the song, obviously thinking I hadn't heard him or would never approve. But the truth was I loved it.

That solution did work. "The Rose" was out by the end of the year and hit No. 1 a few weeks later, helping push his debut LP for us toward a half million.

After four years Elektra had turned around, and so had my career. I was producer on more Top 20 hits and gold records than anyone in town—*and* a record executive who got things done. I had vowed to change Elektra from a tiny outpost operating in the red to a $30-million-a-year contender—and had done it. Almost.

Incredibly, as 1982 drew to a close, I had fallen short by only $1 million. Elektra had gone from a $6 million gross with a $2 million loss to $29 million gross and an $8 million profit. Our market share had jumped ninefold—from barely 2 percent to a very respectable 18 percent.

The bottom line wasn't the only thing grabbing my attention as we approached 1983. The other major turnaround in my life was taking shape right across the hall at Elektra—and it involved a very attractive young woman on our staff.

But she was one employee I didn't fire. I *married* her.

SIXTEEN

MY OFFICE AT ELEKTRA was on the second floor of our cramped two-story building. I used the entrance off the rear parking lot. I never saw much of the first floor. I was also in and out of studios so much, I never saw that much of the second floor either.

Another reason not to hang out there: Dixie Two was running Elektra Publishing in an office downstairs, and we didn't always get along.

I noticed something different on the second floor at the end of 1980. Looking across the hallway into the office of my GM, I had a straight shot at his very cute, very young assistant. When I finally attended a staff meeting, I got a closer look and a formal introduction: her name was Ginger Tillisch, and she had piercing blue eyes, a great smile, a great sense of humor—and, it seemed, a great husband. He was a good, young engineer I had begun to use named Steve Tillisch.

Ginger was a West Texas girl from Amarillo. She had come to Elektra in May 1980, after working in publicity at Capricorn Records in Macon, Georgia. Capricorn folded and she and Steve went to live in Colorado. Ginger called a Capricorn colleague named Mike Hyland. Mike had worked at Elektra Records before I got there, and she figured he could help get her work. Figured wrong: "I just got fired by Jimmy Bowen," Mike told her.

But Mike did put her in touch with Martha Sharpe, my new assistant (who would go on to a great career in A&R). They hit it off by phone, Martha hired Ginger as a receptionist, and for several months in 1980, Ginger answered phones downstairs.

She and Martha became good friends and, because Martha and Dixie were friends, the three women would hang out around our big pool on weekends. In the fall Ginger came upstairs to work for Ewell Rousell, my GM, and eventually became director of administrations.

By then my own marriage showed every sign of not making it. I wasn't much of a father to Dixie's boys, but then, I never intended to be. I was straight about that from day one. I didn't want the responsibility—and my work life didn't allow for it.

Life at home got more complicated when Christian moved in with us for a year when he was six or seven. After I left Dixie One, Christian got screwed up trying to take my place as man of the house. He did as he pleased, bossed Dixie around, took no discipline. He'd ask, "Did you take your keys? Lock the doors?" He was like an adult personality trapped inside a child's body.

He had attended a Montessori first grade in Eureka Springs, where if you acted up and got wild, they sent you home—which happened on the average of three times a week. Through the second half of the school year Dixie worked as a runner for a TV series filmed near their home, but she moved Christian out of Montessori and into a public school closer to her job. Now, when he raised hell, he went to the principal's office. As a result, he was in trouble all the time.

One day he went to Dixie and announced, "It's time for me to get to know and live with my dad some." He was a lot to handle; I figured she was glad to get him off her hands for a while.

When he showed up—Dixie Two's sons were a few years older—he had to repeat first grade. This embarrassed him and damaged his self-esteem. He was sometimes obnoxious if Dixie tried to rein him in. She once asked Christian to do a chore and he snapped back, "Women don't tell men what to do. Men tell women what to do." The little guy needed help badly.

I had him with me a lot, but I also needed to leave him with baby-sitters. I'd take him down to Elektra with me, where I was more than happy to share him with staffers, Ginger among them. He was like another artist on the roster, a handsome handful of a kid. The women found him adorable, charming, and a royal pain. They helped me control him.

But Dixie Two's boys didn't deal well with him. I encouraged ties to their own father, which the boys sought out, but he disappointed them badly. They resented—and envied—Christian for having a father. Dixie did the best she could. But she was also doing her thing at the label. So the kids were often left with our housekeeper, Annie Mae. It was a hellish time for them and us, and after a year Christian went back to Dixie One.

By the beginning of 1983 the pop-music industry had been hit by a devastating recession after the heady growth of the seventies. By the early eighties rosters had swelled and recording costs had shot through the roof; but sales were peaking, the hype on punk and new wave fizzled, and labels were hit with severe downsizing.

In New York, WCI, looking to cut costs, decided to merge its two Nashville divisions—Elektra, which was thriving, and Warner Bros., which was losing money. I flew in for a top-secret meeting with Warners' boss, Mo Ostin, in January 1983, in which he asked me to put the labels together. Warners was doing $7 million to $8 million in business and struggling. They had John Anderson, who just had his first No. 1 hits, "Wild and Blue," and "Swingin'," and great singers like Emmylou Harris and Gary Morris, but they didn't have major star power.

With the merger, I was suddenly running one of Nashville's Big Four, along with RCA, CBS, and MCA, which by then had acquired ABC Dot. The balance of power was shifting on Music Row. The new Warner Bros. had two full staffs and fifty-four acts—which meant more firings, more enemies. It meant new shiny jackets—and a larger office space. That meant spending a lot more time with my blond, blue-eyed director of administration.

I let most of the Warners staff go and kept my own department heads and staff. I didn't need two of everything and wasn't inclined to get rid of people I was winning with, in favor of people who were on a losing team. I dropped more than half of the fifty-four artists on the combined roster.

It was a crazy pace. We had two or three staff meetings a week, and I had several albums going. Everyone had access to me at home or at the studios. Every studio I was working at had a meeting room for me to conduct business with VPs, artists, or managers. That way I could run the label without interrupting the creative flow in the studio. But I wound up producing a bit less that year. Part of the reason was getting the labels together; another part was getting together with Ginger Tillisch.

Ginger was in charge of the office move in May 1983. First we took over two small buildings connected to a church; then we rented and gutted the Florence Crittenden Home for Unwed Mothers and built a space five times larger than where we'd been. Planning the move threw us together more and more. It was clear we liked each other.

Dixie was starting to drive me nuts. She wanted to go more into producing and had worked with Hag's wife, Leona; she had also gone to L.A. to do a pop record and video with Pam Tillis. I heard from various sources that she had begun to exploit and misuse the fact that she was the label head's wife; she was pushing friends and colleagues away—including Martha and Ginger.

Ginger's marriage, meanwhile, seemed secure, despite her long hours. Steve *was* a fine engineer, who I was beginning to keep real busy at night on more projects. Funny how that worked. He had moved up as one of my first engineers on a bunch of albums.

One night while Dixie was in L.A. I stopped back at the office at about ten. Ginger was just fixin' to leave. I asked her to come get a bit to eat and she accepted.

Fed up with life at home and burned out by work, I did something with Ginger I didn't do often: I opened up to her. It was real easy and comfortable being with her. "It's too bad I'm happily married," she said, catching me off guard. "Sounds like you need someone just like me."

I knew she was just teasing. She had described Steve as her best friend and their marriage as a strong, mutually satisfying relationship. I came back with, "I couldn't marry you anyway. You have cats, I have allergies." I didn't know what else to say.

"The cats could go."

This *was* getting interesting. Ginger has since said she was "just blabbering" and never felt anything was going on between us beyond the flirtatious bantering.

We lingered and bantered for three hours. I drove Ginger back to the parking lot. As she went to open the door, I reached over and lightly touched the back of her head. We both felt a jolt of sexual electricity. Ginger blurted out, "I'd better get out of the car now, Bowen. I've already sinned enough for one night."

I thought, *Now that's cute.* Nothing had actually *happened,* but the boundary that had kept us at a safe distance from each other had been crossed.

I called her first thing in the morning. She'd been awake all night. "We've got to talk," I said.

I went to the office, picked her up, and drove out to Love Circle, a street that ends in a favorite local parking spot on a hill. The agenda was pretty simple: parking's pretty much always the same, even in adulthood. The Circle was deserted at ten A.M. and offered one helluva view in daylight.

Ginger walked into the office later with her cute white and pink outfit all wrinkled up. One of my VPs couldn't resist: "Jeez, Ginger," he said, "looks like you slept in your clothes."

That was the day I told Ginger, "I want to marry you." It was also the day Ginger replied, "*Excuse* me, I'm happily married, you know. This is *crazy*. It's not gonna *happen!*"

The next day, Saturday, we met at the Maxwell House Hotel. I made sure to keep Steve busy in the studio, with Ginger making plans to meet him later in the day, as if nothing was up. The hotel was out on Metro Center Boulevard, a ways from Music Row, where we'd almost certainly have been spotted at, say, the high-profile Spence Manor Hotel.

To make this sin look semi-legit, I went through the charade of buying three pieces of cheap army-surplus luggage. The pieces fit inside one another and were an ugly red plaid.

The bell captain must have thought I was one strong sucker when I checked in hauling that big-ass suitcase without a grunt. He offered to help, but I waved him off. If he'd grabbed it and felt how light it was, he could only have figured I was about to commit murder or adultery.

I signed into the Presidential Suite and went upstairs. I stood at the window and watched Ginger's tiny golf-cart-size Toyota pull in off Metro Boulevard. From way up top I could see only one free parking pace in the first three rows of cars and drew a line with my eye between the car and the space. I guided her in as I muttered, "Come on, come on, over here." She paused once and nearly settled for a spot farther away, but then she continued and, as I focused on the spot, she pulled right in.

Bingo. Communication. Done deal.

She came in smiling. "The whole time comin' over here," she said, "I'm going, 'The one thing Mother always said was never ever fool around with your boss, *ever*. Worst thing you can do.'"

I wrapped my arms around her and pulled her close. "Thank God for your mother." She got it.

"You mean, maybe *that's* why I'm here—'cause she told me not to?"

By the time we checked out that same afternoon, both of us knew we were meant to end up together.

When I booked some L.A. musicians to come in for sessions, I figured I'd save money by renting apartments instead of putting them up in costly hotels. So I rented a one-bedroom place off West End Avenue, a couple of miles from Music Row. But I didn't put any musicians in there. I put us in there.

We got more brazen in mid-June and spent a weekend together in L.A. I had some Elektra business; Ginger went furniture shopping. I stayed at the Westwood Marquis, she checked into the Beverly Garland, near Elektra's office. Then she came by and spent the weekend with me, checking in to get any messages from Steve.

Both of us came away with a bad feeling about the sneaking around and the hurt it would cause. I knew Ginger was giving my track record with women—and how I could throw up a wall, or simply bail out—serious thought. By the time we flew into Dallas for connecting flights, we agreed it had to end. "We can't keep doing this," I said. "It's just no good this way." Ginger then flew to Amarillo to see her family; I headed back to Nashville.

Ginger was back home at the movies with her brother and sister when she got up to call me at a Nashville studio. I was mixing a Hank Jr. track with her husband. She wanted to let me know it was me, not him, she was missing; but it was Steve, not me, who answered. Twice. She hung up both times.

Finally, when Steve answered again, they chatted a while. Then Ginger asked for me. "I have to talk to Bowen about office furniture."

"Yeah, right," he snapped. "Why don't you talk to him about the casting couch?" She knew right then it couldn't go on.

"I've been tryin' to call. I miss you," she told me. "This isn't gonna work this way."

"I know. Forget whatever we agreed to in Dallas."

We finally decided to end our charades and deceptions over July Fourth weekend. Dixie and I had already begun talking about going our separate ways. She was on her way to New England for a week away with her two sons. I was heading to Kauai. Word was out that I was not taking Dixie, but no one suspected Ginger was the Other Woman.

Steve was due home from Muscle Shoals on Saturday morning, July 2nd. Our flight to Hawaii was noon that day. When he walked in the door at ten A.M. Ginger was waiting to tell him—with her bags already packed.

"Looks like you're going somewhere," he said.

"I am."

"Where?"

"Hawaii."

"And who with?"

"Bowen."

Ginger met me at Martha Sharpe's home, where I had assembled all my top executives to break the news myself so that every-one heard it straight from me, not the street. They were in shock. Then we took off.

Our first couple of days on Kauai, Ginger and I caught the tail end of a giant hurricane and saw nothing but torrential rains. I badgered the front desk until one accommodating staffer lined up a room for us at the Whaler Condominiums on Maui, where she assured me, we'd have some sunshine. We flew to Maui and drove clear across the island, arrived at the Whaler, and went up to Apartment 1051. We stepped out on the balcony, took in spectacular views of the Pacific, the white beaches, and the islands of Lanai and Molokai rising out of the ocean in the west.

Paradise.

We were a long way from the mess we'd left behind. I got hold of Dixie at our Golf Club Lane house after her vacation and told her I wanted a divorce and that Ginger and I were going to get married. I told her I wanted the house but that anything in it she wanted was hers.

When Steve and I had it out after Hawaii, he asked me, "How could you have done this to me?" I said he was just an innocent party who got hurt by something beyond our control. Falling in love with his wife, I said, wasn't something I *did* to *him*. Two peo-ple came together—that was it. These things just happen in life, I said. He sank into a bad state for a while, but we were able to get past any bitterness and become decent friends again, often working together in the studio.

Dixie moved out to a townhouse somewhere in town and we settled up by the end of the year. It's fair to say I took pretty good care of her.

News of my love affair didn't go down well in Eureka Springs. Dixie One pulled up in a pickup truck to say she wanted Christ-ian to come back home with her for a couple of weeks before second grade started. I said fine. He was all for it.

But when she called at the end of summer, she announced that she was keeping him because he didn't want to come back with me. "He's staying here, your life is too crazy." Part of this, naturally, was wanting her son with her; part of it may have been an attempt to continue getting support from me.

Christian, still the little man of the house, got on the line and said, "I need to stay here, Dad. She needs me here." Dixie then moved up to Tulsa, where her sister and some family lived, and put him in a private school there.

It was strange that Christian was going through just what I had experienced at the same age my parents split. (My father had too, for that matter.) It was ironic to be reliving it through my son. There were times I considered going up there and bringing him back. But that would create constant hassles with his mother. It would put him in the middle, where I'd always been. I decided to sit back, see how it went.

With Christian away and most all the furniture gone with Dixie Two, Ginger felt lost inside the big, empty Golf Club Lane house. It also needed some renovation since, as she noted, I'd shared it with another wife. She wanted us to start fresh. "Let's get rid of it," I said.

We sold the place and got something much smaller just inside the fringe of Belle Meade, the Bel Air of Nashville. It was like a shoe box, but Ginger fixed it up nice and cozy, and if she was happy, I was happy. She did a great job with the bathroom, putting a big old tub in so that I could soak my bad back. The huge bed we'd gotten for Golf Club Lane after Dixie moved out took up the whole floor of the tiny bedroom, leaving just enough space to walk around it.

As we made plans for a December 1983 wedding on Maui, I came to see why the fit with Ginger was so right. I had an aversion to clinging, dependent women, and Ginger was strong, assertive, and free-spirited. I didn't need for her to shape her life around mine—and it was a relief to see that wasn't even an option. Ginger wanted to work on her painting and pursue friendships on her own. We both hated Nashville's dress-up party crowd. The only times I ever wore ties were to funerals and weddings, and I never had much fun at either. When I asked if she liked to cook, she was smart enough not to lie; she hated to cook.

"Great!" I said. Another big plus. "I hate that about marriage—a woman slavin' for three hours over a meal I didn't want in the first place. I like menus, I like choices." And my late studio work made scheduling a home-cooked meal a real trap.

The fifteen-year age gap wasn't an issue and neither was having children, which was key. Her brother and sister came along ten and fifteen years after she did; when her mother then went to work, Ginger did the potty training, diapering, and her share of caretaking. Been there, done that.

One thing I knew for sure about Ginger: She was no gold digger. When we decided to be together, I was technically $40,000 in the hole—owing to the recent split. Sure, I had my royalties coming in over time, but, as many gold records as I had produced, in my domestic affairs I'd been split more times than AT&T stock.

I made Ginger a promise early on: I'll make the money; you see if you can hang on to it. The artist part of me has never worried about money. I've never been materialistic and always had enough. But when I had too much, I could always find ways to make it vanish. What was unique with Ginger was that it felt like a genuine partnership based on equality and sharing. That was a breakthrough for me. And there was chemistry, humor, intimacy, friendship. We were genuinely compatible.

On December 11, 1983, we got married. We flew to Honolulu, where Reverend Takamori, dressed in a white robe, performed a simple ceremony by the waterfall and dolphin pool of the Kahala Hilton. It was the way we wanted it: not a soul around we knew. Our wedding was witnessed only by the minister's daughter and a guy with an electric guitar and a tiny amplifier. They sang "The Hawaiian Wedding Song," served a big wedding cake, took some pictures of us, and that was it. This one was perfect.

I had come to believe there were big odds against any two people staying together forever. It's a rough game when three strikes doesn't even get you out. You just keep swinging. I had never been out in the world trying to satisfy my vision of my perfect partner. If she didn't come and find me, nothing happened.

It took me five times before the right somebody found me—right across the hall. I want to run Ginger off once or twice a month, but it passes quickly. Next day comes, I still dig her. Before, if I ever got that way, it was over. I was gone.

I had gotten so used to getting married every five or so years that I decided to keep pace—and keep marrying Ginger. In 1988 and 1993 we returned to the minister in Honolulu to reaffirm our vows by the waterfall and dolphin pool. Now that we live on Maui year-round, it'll be real easy in 1998.

My father—who always loved Dumas—called me from Santa Barbara, where he and Frances have lived for years. When I told him Ginger was a Texas Panhandle girl, he said, "Well, son, now that you've married a girl from *America,* maybe this one'll work."

To him a Panhandle girl was the ultimate catch. I believe there's something to the fact that Ginger and I come from the same corner of the world. For years I'd heard all that talk about finding your soul mate and always dismissed it as nonsense.

Not anymore I don't.

SEVENTEEN

MY TWO PRINCIPAL CRUSADES in Nashville were to put the artist in control of the music and to improve the sound quality of the music itself. After three or four years as a label chief and producer in town, it was obvious to me that progress could be made faster in ways other than working with one artist, one record at a time.

But to speed things up, both the culture of country and its music-making hardware had to change.

The generational split in Nashville was widening between the Old Guard and the new wave. One group resisted change; the other felt disenfranchised, as though they were on the outside looking in. When their demos got rejected, it was simpler for an aspiring artist to use the Establishment as a convenient scapegoat than it was to write better material or make better masters. The upstarts could hide behind a wary "us and them" stance. What they needed was an energy point, a forum not linked to the powerful Country Music Association.

That was one motive behind my founding the Nashville Music Association with a small corps of dedicated music-business people, including Mike Hyland, Bob Beckham, and Dale Franklin Cornelius, our executive director. (She later dropped her husband's name when they divorced.) The labels contributed a couple of thousand dollars each to cover Dale's salary and to fund some community activities. We charged dues and built up a strong membership numbering several hundred.

Some saw the NMA as a hotbed of crossover networking, others as a monthly bitch session to work issues out about video, copyrights, breaking in to the business. It was like a hipper, alternative CMA.

Another motive behind the NMA was to bring the business and creative communities of Nashville together despite a history of mutual mistrust, if not loathing. The blueblood snobs of Belle Meade looked down at all music people as drunk, pill-poppin' hillbillies. And the creative community resented that Fan Fair in the spring pumped more than $5 million into the local economy through the tourists it brought and that CMA week in the fall was good for another few million. From our view on Music Row, it was all take, take, take—but no give from business leaders.

I remember going to an executive at First American Bank in 1978, who bluntly told me, "We don't loan money in the music business. They're a bad risk. I got a basement full of guitars, an organ, and a tour bus out back."

"Is that because they're bad risks or you're a bad banker?"

He didn't like that. I told him he sounded like California bankers in the early sixties. They didn't want to hear about musicians then either; but once those young rock-and-roll kids had checks for $3 million and $4 million to deposit someplace, it was amazing how quickly the suits started loving rock and roll. "You watch, same thing's gonna happen here," I said, "but only for the banks that come to the party early."

Dale Franklin was the heart of the NMA, a dynamic, generous woman who spearheaded our trade show—Music Expo—for a couple of years as a bridge to business. It was quite effective. All the labels and publishers, such as Tree and Combine, had booths; the mayor, the governor, and other officials cut some ribbons and posed for photo ops with country's movers and shakers. This led to meetings with banks, the chamber of commerce, the offices of the mayor and the governor, the tourism commission. We were in business.

My days were so frantic, I sometimes didn't know which end of that bridge I was crossing. One morning, thinking I was rolling into a mix-down session, I took four or five long hits of some strong grass in my car to get ready for the music. Then my driver and security man, Mike Jones, pulled into BMI's lot. I asked why. "Well, you're addressing some big NMA thing today."

Oooohh, I thought, *this is going to be interesting.*

I walked in wearing blue jeans, work shirt, sneakers, and dark glasses under my whaler's cap. The cap became my trademark; I wore it to keep overhead studio lights from driving me nuts. I immediately found Dale and asked her what we were doing. "Rap number two," she said quietly in our private code. I knew that meant the subject was: "Nashville, Entertainment City, Not Just Music." Dale and I had done so may meet 'n' greets that I could go on autopilot and give one of my three or four prefab raps, tailored to my audience.

I looked around at a sea of several dozen dark suits and realized that the mayor, the governor and the chamber of commerce had every top Nashville executive or one of their representatives on hand. I wasn't in any shape to address them, so I poured some strong coffee, focused my mind, and welcomed them. I said it was important for everyone on hand to stand and introduce themselves and explain exactly what they do. I knew that with these politicians, I had just bought myself thirty-five or forty-five minutes.

When it came back to me, I was still awfully high, but I went into my rap: "This meeting is very simple. We have to recognize one another's contribution. We represent the second largest industry in the state of Tennessee and we've ignored one another too long. It's time we move forward with a mutually beneficial relationship," ya-da-ya-da-ya-da.

When the *Tennessean* ran a morning headline hailing music as the state's second-biggest industry, people at the label asked me what the *first-biggest* was. "I have no idea. But I do know you never claim you're the biggest, because people can challenge you. No one challenges someone who only claims number two."

But it did have a nice ring to it. Ten years later people were still calling country the state's second-biggest industry.

The NMA was a magic little time for me and I served as chairman for four years. The CMA had its eye on us because they saw we were catching on for a while. We were never a serious threat, but membership grew, we got good press, and we stirred things up on Music Row.

And the guys in suits started showing up at the party.

If Nashville was bent on attracting pop's audiences, it would have to give them a modern sound to match what they were used to on pop and rock FM. Otherwise we'd never compete. That meant embracing emerging studio technology.

One mistake I had made in L.A. was not messing more with the engineering of music. I had my hands full making three-track recordings with forty-piece orchestras. We'd use maybe twelve inputs for fifty pieces, adjusting the same dial, or fader, for flutes, acoustic guitar, and chimes. With luck your arranger scored the work so that they didn't all play at the same time. Otherwise their volumes would clash, they would leak into one another. I watched the score sheets from the booth, cuing my engineer so that he would know precisely when to move the fader up or back. It was painstaking, demanding work, but I devised a system that worked.

When eight- and sixteen-track came in, I still had my three-track thing down—and didn't move with the times. That was the mistake. When I saw Nashville trapped in a technological time warp ten years later, I saw an opportunity for change.

There were three ways to make music better: pay the top studio guys double scale; make the best music possible with whatever gear we already had; push studios into digital.

I had started double scale in L.A. as a way to lock in the best players and not get them worn out. The best guys never say no, but they get booked to death, playing four or five sessions a day, running from one studio to another all over town, six, seven days a week, until they are just fried. How can they stay sharp and inventive like that?

If I wanted a musician for two three-hour sessions—two-to-five and six-to-nine—I didn't want him or her somewhere else for four hours in front of me or holding back and pacing himself for a session behind me. But I could pay him for four sessions and have him to myself for the two, with his energy focused on *my* tracks.

The musicians' union in town said, "You can't do that." The reason: "It's never been done down here before." Everybody went crazy. Today it's not uncommon for the best pickers to earn triple or even quadruple scale when recording pop, and double with country.

Most studios worked with eight- or sixteen-track. Tompall got a twenty-four-track mixing board pretty early. As LP sales increased, album budgets inched up, more money flowed into the studios, and by the early eighties they were ready for the major leap to digital.

I got my first glimpse of the future while mixing one of Hank Jr.'s albums. Glenn Meadows, one of the few tech-heads in town, owned Masterfonics, a terrific mastering facility. He always had some new piece of gear to check out. One night Glenn brought me a two-track digital recording machine to Back Stage, where I was working. I used it to mix down from twenty-four tracks of an analog machine to two-track stereo, which the consumer would hear at home, on a Walkman or car system. I did it analog as well.

I then AB'd the mixes, switching from analog to digital and back as I studied every nuance.

"Screw analog, this is it," I said. There was no hum, no hiss, no "transience busting"—the sound of music hitting analog tape. When sound hits analog, it distorts and plays back different. The impact subtly changes the music's color. It adds hiss and alters the top and bottom end. Hiss increases over time.

But in digital what I heard going into the machine was perfectly reproduced coming back out. You could send crystal-clear sonic purity to the digital machine and receive it the same way. It was as thrilling as seeing television for the first time, only it happened to your ears. There was no noise added, no distortion. Digital captures the natural sound of music. It takes what you give it and stores it without altering it. The era of wobbly vinyl and stretchy tape would soon be over.

Analog did make for *warmer* music, the main reason lots of people couldn't stand digital. There was a harsh, brittle "glare" to the sound. My feeling was, if you want warmth, *put it in*. But don't give it to me with all kinds of other sonic debris, such as hiss that I can't control or get rid of. There are machines that will *give* you hiss and distortion if you want them, but you can't get rid of them if you don't.

I knew Nashville would never catch New York or L.A. with analog. But we had a chance to blow right past them with digital. Rock-and-roll guitarists weren't jumping on digital because a prominent feature of their metal-guitar sound was the transience collision of guitar licks with analog tape. It was a texture built into the music, and their fans were hooked to it. And they liked it that way.

Digital told you exactly what musicians were sending you through the glass partition. I was an instant convert. It became my mission to bring Music Row into the digital age.

I called Glenn the next morning. "This is incredible," I said. "But I'm going to need more than one because I got three or four albums going at once." Glenn got a couple more digital two-tracks for me to lease for mix-downs.

My digital crusade got a boost during a vacation in Hawaii. I met with Tom Headley, an engineer who had designed studios in L.A. and elsewhere in the sixties and seventies. I always thought he was ahead of his time. We talked about some problems I'd had with his Westlake Studios room, such as the big metal cabinets with EQ and other stuff in them right behind the chairs in the control room. Sound from the playback speakers would hit that metal and reverberate all around your head until you wanted to scream. Tom admitted he had learned a lot from mistakes he'd made with design and equipment, but was ready for a challenge.

I was going out on a limb, but it was worth the gamble. Tom was still years ahead of Nashville's sound technicians. Many were clueless about basics such as building a room where you could cleanly record a bass drum, or how to build nonparallel walls. They threw up four walls, carpeted everything, hung two speakers from the ceiling, and called it a control room.

"We need *tomorrow's* studios," I told Tom. "You made every mistake known to man building them before. You should be ready to make great ones now." Tom listened warily. I knew my approach could have backfired. Tom had the good life in the Hawaiian sun; he wasn't exactly burning with ambition. I was deliberately trying to fire him up.

I flew Tom in to meet with Ron Kerr, the majority stockholder of Sound Stage Studio. I asked Ron to let Tom build him a new studio with no wall between the musicians and the control room. I told Ron I'd lease it for a year and use it five days a week. That way he could show a bank that as much as $1,600 would be flowing into the studio each day—and get the capital to invest in the rebuilding.

Ron didn't redo both rooms at Sound Stage; Ron and Tom created a big, beautiful room called Front Stage. Top did a great job. The new place had thick concrete slabs separated by just the right number of inches of air that truly soundproofs—either between two studios or from the outside. (Sound passes through solid concrete.) Front Stage would have been a great bomb shelter. Sitting at the board you couldn't hear a thunderstorm outside.

After I went to MCA-Nashville in 1984, I helped swing a similar leasing arrangement with the new owner of Emerald Studios: I promised to use the studio every day for six months if he'd hire Tom to build a new control room. Emerald needed one. I was the first label chief in town to commit to recording digitally. Soon almost every CD we put out had to have the word DIGITAL on the front.

When Glenn Meadows saw what was happening, he went to

198 JIMMY BOWEN *and* JIM JEROME

Tom on his own and got him to build what became an incredible mix-down room at Masterfonics to go with his two mastering rooms. Mix-down gets from twenty-four tracks (or thirty-two, forty-eight, etc.) to two tracks; mastering is when you prepare your two-track recording for cassettes, CDs, or LPs. Then Tom redesigned Glenn's two mastering rooms and playback systems, using a Japanese manufacturer and his own stuff. Tom's speakers are the best I have ever heard.

Having cracked the door to digital, Tom blasted through it and never looked back. He moved to upstate New York for a while, then to Switzerland, building thirty to forty studios throughout Europe that are among the finest in the world.

He left his mark on Music Row—and gave *me* a chance to make country records that would compete sonically with all other forms of music being cut, from London to Los Angeles. We had three studios converted to digital, with up-to-the-minute thirty-two-track Mitsubishi digital recorders, SSL control boards, super mix-down and mastering facilities at Glenn's place, and all the outboard gear—the limiters, compressors, EQ—whatever we needed.

Soon a half-dozen other studios saw how busy they were, heard top acts like Strait, Reba, and the Oak Ridge Boys making music that *sounded* every bit as full and clear as Elton or the Eagles—and they all wanted in. Now there were twenty thirty-two-tracks in town and digital was becoming the standard. Virtually all the rooms on Music Row were competitive with the best pop studios. In July 1989, when I had my own label through MCA, Universal Records, I became the first label president on Music Row to cease production of vinyl LPs in favor of CDs—even before country radio had fully switched to CD 45s. Releasing music on vinyl records, I told *Billboard*, "is like delivering it on sandpaper."

My crusade led to some persistent accusations that I secretly owned pieces of the studios I worked at, thus forcing my artists to work with me and record there, and got kickbacks from the studio owners.

In denying the rumors my position has always been the same: why steal pennies when you can earn millions? I never took a kickback from studio owners, musicians, AFTRA, from singers, from caterers, or from *anyone*. I offered to finance an investigation and challenged people to find one nickel kicked back to me. I didn't *need* nickel kickbacks. I made studios better so that I could make incredible-sounding records and sell them by the ton and earn a couple million dollars in royalties. Most hill-billies in town took their time coming around to my way of do-ing business.

There were other reasons not to own a studio: When the ma-chines break down, do I, as producer, interrupt a session and holler at myself to get it fixed? There was also the risk of obso-lescence. By the time your equipment's paid off, it's out of date. I never saw much upside in owning a studio.

The closest I came to a kickback was when Ron Kerr offered to send me and Ginger to Europe out of gratitude. I asked him what it would cost and he said about $20,000. Now that I knew he had the money, I made a deal. "Don't send us to Europe, but thank you. Instead there's a great piece of electronic gear we could sure use in the front studio that costs about the same."

I usually did little to deny or squelch rumors, figuring it's all bullshit anyway and can't hurt the business. The fact that I was a wheeler-dealer just ruffled people's feathers. But a fellow execu-tive once ruffled mine.

Jim Foglesong made a remark at a meeting of CMA leaders about me owning Sound Stage—and it came back to me. I got steamed. He should have known better and I called him on it.

"I've known you a long time, Jim—and by the way, if the rest of this conversation doesn't go well, I'm gonna sue the hell outta you. If this kind of bullshit goes out at your level, I'm gonna deal with it. I've been lookin' for that one dumb ass stupid enough to say something to get me to go to court and prove all this is crap. I'll bring my tax returns from the day my ass hit this town and open up my books if you'll do yours."

Jim, a real decent guy, apologized, admitted he was way out of line, and that was that.

By the end of the eighties, Nashville acts were being certi-fied gold and platinum more than ever by the Recording Indus-try Association of America. Radio and cable markets were booming. First-rate, experienced musicians from the coasts, burned out and alienated by rock, hard rock, and hip-hop, were drawn to the easier, cheaper, more grown-up lifestyle of Nashville's thriving music scene.

I had once predicted that Nashville would become the most dynamic music center in America by the year 2000. It was a re-mark that led one music magazine to call me the Messiah of Mu-sic Row. My prediction was inaccurate. We were almost a decade ahead of schedule.

●

When I merged Elektra and Warners in 1983, I got rid of most of the Warners people and kept my own staff from Elektra. We had a smooth, tight system worth sticking with. I brought in Jim Ed Norman, who I'd known years earlier when he played in Shiloh, to be my head of A&R. Martha Sharpe, my former assistant at Elektra, moved over to A&R. It was the beginning of two distinguished careers at Warners.

I produced some more hit records and albums that year for the Bellamys, Johnny Lee, Hank Jr., Crystal, and Conway. And I got to work the artist with probably *the* most extraordinary vocal instrument I ever recorded, Gary Morris.

Gary was just short of breaking through. Then we did "The Wind Beneath My Wings," a killer song that got things started for him. I never made music to ride current trends at radio because it's often six months from session to airplay and what's hot is always bound to change. You can't calculate. All you can do is max out the artist and his music at that point in time—and hope it meshes with what's playlisted at radio stations. Country didn't seem ready for "Wind" when we cut it, but we fought hard for Gary. Nick Hunter, my head of promotion, almost gave up on the record three times before it finally took off and reached the Top 5.

Gary was an awesome singer and I enjoyed working with him. I liked golfing with him too. Golf's great for revealing personality—how aggressive or passive, competitive, intense, or honest someone is. If possible, I usually won't close a business deal with someone until I've gone eighteen holes with them.

Gary was proof that God has a weird sense of humor. He gave Gary plenty of muscle power to whack a ball off the tee, but Gary tried to hit four hundred yards and lost half his drives in the rough. God did something similar with Gary's voice. He gave Gary an awesome voice—but it was all over the place and not always hooked up to his brain. Bless his heart, Gary's attitude sometimes got in the way of that amazing gift and he was often his own worst enemy.

Gary was a cocky guy with a healthy ego who would tell fans to keep quiet during his ballads. People stood off from him when he sang and didn't know what to make of him. At a time when country was trapped between pop and New Traditional, Gary crossed over to *opera*. He performed *La Bohème* and *Les Misérables*. What made *him* miserable was hearing someone sing half as well and have a giant country record. Gary, cursed as much as blessed by his powerful voice, had trouble finding his niche.

He also seemed unsure of what image to project: One month he'd have wild shaggy hair and be clean-shaven. Next time he'd have short-cropped hair with a big, heavy beard and you're goin', *Damn, this ol' boy sure can grow some* hair.

To his credit Gary rebelled against the slickness of that era and tried earnestly to stick to his sound. Like me he told people what he thought, as opposed to being political and kissin' butt. I knew you didn't always make friends that way and so did he. Gary's still working today, sounding as great as ever.

A guitarist friend of mine made a wisecrack that attests to the power of Gary's voice. I hadn't seen the player in quite some time and asked him where he'd been hiding. "Been out at the house installin' my new alarm system," he said. "If you touch anything, a Gary Morris record goes off."

Maybe that's the kind of security system we should have had at one of the warehouses the label used to ship records. While running Warners, I learned of a record-piracy scam that pissed me off because it involved records I produced.

WEA's distribution system shipped tens of thousands of newly pressed LPs to warehouses each week. A certain number of boxes were stickered, TO BE PUNCHED. The records inside were to be removed so that a small hole could be punched in a corner of the sleeve with NOT FOR SALE—FOR PROMOTION ONLY on it, or something like that. It then became a "clean," removed from the wholesale-retail chain and used for PR or promotion. This was standard at every label.

I had an inside source who tipped me off to this practice. People were stripping off the TO BE PUNCHED sticker on boxes of Hank Jr. product—and those boxes were then loaded onto a truck and hauled out. The cleans, I assumed, were allegedly being sold by label insiders and put in play on a black market to record dealers—store owners, street dealers, collectors—for a dollar-fifty or two dollars each. These dealers could then resell a new LP by Hank Jr. or any other hot pop or country act for maybe three to five dollars and undercut retail by two or three dollars per unit.

These inside scam artists would then allegedly use that cash—conceivably tens of thousand of dollars—to buy women or drugs, and to influence top deejays or radio programmers by sending them to Vegas—or whatever you do when you buy people off. This underground was screwing Hank, me, the publishers and songwriters, and the *label* out of a lot of money. It was grand-theft country. It was rumored that throughout the record industry this side operation was siphoning off several million dollars a year.

I went to top brass at Warners to have it stopped. "I don't care what goes on in pop," I told a high-ranking executive, "it's stealing." Of course like most whistle-blowers, *I* was then investigated aggressively by Warners for the next year. My informant got severely reprimanded and nearly lost his job. But the practice, as best I knew, never stopped.

Meanwhile Senator Al Gore of Tennessee, before he became Vice President Gore, got wind of this and met with me a couple of times to see if I could help him start a full-scale investigation of payola in pop music. Frankly, I thought what he was after more than anything else was press coverage.

In the fall of 1983 I got a call from Irving Azoff, who was then running MCA Records in L.A. Irving wanted me to leave Warners and fix MCA's sinking Nashville division. He made a remarkable offer: $250,000 in salary, plus $1 million for the catalog of Amos Records and Amos Productions masters. That included Kenny Rogers and the First Edition, and Kim Carnes—but it was mostly a way to get me to come over. It was the highest salary I'd ever been offered and well beyond what division chiefs were earning in Nashville. The offer would lead to a new pay structure for Nashville executives. But I knew that breaking free of Warners could be tricky and could drag on for months.

I decided to use the press to make sure the negotiations remained low-key. I floated a rumor at the *Tennessean* that I was negotiating with Columbia. This kept the heat off the MCA deal. I did this to keep morale and performance high at MCA for when I would take over. I didn't want the staff slacking off for three to six months before I arrived, consumed with concerns about job security under a Bowen regime, which, given my reputation, was hardly unreasonable. Employees get demoralized, dust off their résumés, get frozen. They're not taking care of the music.

Within a month I was rumored to be moving to four different labels. No one was even excited by the speculation anymore.

Except my boss, Mo Ostin. I had some talks with him about Irving's offer, but he didn't get anywhere near it. Then Mo flew in and we met a few times over several days. It came down to a day or two left before I had to make my move.

Aside from the $1.25 million, MCA presented another ideal scenario for rebuilding. It had had a few good years after acquiring ABC Dot's roster in 1979, with Jim Foglesong running the label. But MCA had sunk to fifth among the six majors in town, with a modest market share.

Part of the trouble was a roster top-heavy with aging veterans whose best days were behind them: Barbara Mandrell, Don Williams, the Oak Ridge Boys, Loretta Lynn, Mel Tillis, Jerry Lee Lewis (again), Brenda Lee, Ed Bruce. MCA also had two wonderful artists whose careers had some room to grow: George Strait and that fiery, down-home redhead I had once passed on, Reba McEntire.

Finally, the day before a decision had to be made, Mo came to my home and said he'd match Irving's seven-figure offer. This is several *months*—and a lot of ego games—after my offer from Irving. Why, I wondered, hadn't Mo assessed the situation right off and taken a stab at keeping me? Where were you six months ago, three months ago, *two weeks ago?* The hell with it. The signs were clear: Make the move!

I promised Mo I wouldn't steal my department heads at Warners—*if* he agreed to give them VP titles and decent raises. I was proud of my team there and wanted to leave it in place: Jim Ed Norman moved up to run the label and has done a terrific job throughout the mid-nineties; Martha Sharpe later signed Randy Travis and Faith Hill, among others, and did a wonderful job running A&R until her 1995 retirement. The team I put together was, in my mind, as strong as any in town—and I'd cut a bunch of big hits for both labels. I'd done my job.

Irving threw in some sweeteners. He upped my producer's fee from what I had at Warners and gave me the freedom to continue producing for other labels. He gave me a free hand to fix the label. That, even more than money, was the hook.

EIGHTEEN

I TOOK OVER as president of MCA Records—
Nashville in March 1984, replacing Jim Foglesong. I only kept
two MCA people: Jim's executive assistant, Katie Gillon, who became my head of production; and the sweet old man who delivered the mail and stocked the Coke machine.

Irving was betting a lot of money I could turn the label
around. With stakes higher than ever, my first priority became
putting my houses in order—the one at MCA and the one I went
home to at night.

My first hire, even before I left Warners, was my old friend
and roommate Bruce Hinton, brought in to be VP-GM. Bruce
and I went all the way back to "Everybody Loves Somebody,"
when he ran national promotion for Warners. He had gotten
hooked by country in the seventies and eventually formed a
company with Jim Ed Norman to produce and promote country
records, becoming one of the most tenacious and powerful independent promotion people working Nashville product. Bruce
had integrity, great ears for hits, radio trusted him, labels paid
him. Because I had a tiny in-house promotion budget at Elektra,
our success was in no small part due to Bruce for breaking acts
like Eddie Rabbitt and Hank Jr.

I hired Tony Brown from RCA to be my VP of A&R and run
the department. Tony had signed Alabama and Vince Gill to RCA,
among others, helping them lead the field. That impressed me.

I had seen Alabama back in 1978 at the "New Faces" showcase during Country Radio Seminar week. I liked Randy Owen's

voice, but there was no chance to showcase anything. It was CRS policy that acts played with a house band that had only learned the tunes that day. Which was typical then: radio came first, label second, artist last. Today it's radio first, with artist and label battling for second place. I guess that's progress. But Tony Brown, being a good ol' boy from the North Carolina mountains, heard something down-home and went after them. Starting with "Tennessee River" in mid-1980, they had about a dozen straight No. 1 hits. I started asking around about Tony.

Tony checked out. He was a young, dynamic kid on his way up. It intrigued me that Tony, like me, had been accused of being too hip for Nashville. The people who told me that figured it would turn me off; it only intrigued me more. Tony also had an artist's instincts and background.

He had grown up in Greensboro and played in tent revivals. He toured with the Oaks and spent a couple of years on the road in Elvis's band, right up until the King died in 1977. Tony was always on the leading edge of progressive country. He played with Emmylou Harris's Hot Band, and her protégé, Rodney Crowell, and with Rodney's wife at the time, Rosanne Cash. Tony's instincts were right on again when he signed a sessions singer and guitar picker named Vince Gill. Vince had played with Pure Prairie League, Rodney, and Rosanne and wanted to go solo.

I had to hire Tony my way. I was still locked into my Warners deal when I went after him, so it had to be ultrasecret. I called his office and booked him to play organ on a Hank Jr. session I was producing. Tony was confused and told his assistant at RCA, "I can't play organ, and besides, why would Bowen hire me for this gig?"

She said, "Well, just go anyway and charge him double scale. I hear he's an asshole, so just go. If he doesn't use the track, you'll still pick up five hundred bucks."

Tony thought this over. "That's not a bad idea."

I met Tony at Sound Stage and discreetly told him about my vision to turn MCA into a significant music center. I told him I was leaving Warners and that I'd had my eye on him and wanted him for A&R. Now he looked really confused.

"So," he said, "you *don't* want me to play organ?"

"No."

"Oh." When he got it, he thought it was a "cool" maneuver.

I liked Tony right off. He had confidence in himself and he had vision, he was forward-looking. He didn't focus on where country was but where it was heading. I decided to hire him.

Tony asked his lawyer, Bill Carter, what to do. "As your attorney, I should advise you that if you're lookin' for a sure thing, you should stay at RCA because they love you there and will keep you forever. But as your friend, you've got to go work for Bowen if you want to change your career."

I fueled the rumor mill to keep Music Row confused, and never got back to Tony. This made him crazy. Wherever he went to have lunch, he'd hear different names mentioned as my new A&R guy—if in fact I went to MCA. Tony didn't know what was going on until I knew I was legally cleared to jump ship.

As I was driving my white Fleetwood to a studio, I saw Tony walking down the alley. He must have had a session. I pulled up alongside and lowered my power window. "You still in?" I asked him quietly.

"Yeah," he answered.

"Good," I said as I raised the window and drove off.

Another big piece fell into place at MCA when my old friend Don Lanier came on board. I hired Dirt and gave him the title of a director of A&R, which for me meant he was my in-house "song man." It was the only such position on the Row. I was looking to tap Dirt's extraordinary ears and his network of publishers and writers in order to "cast" the best material for my artists. This is a key part of preproduction, whether you're making records in Nashville, New York, or Los Angeles.

But Dirt almost never made it to Nashville alive. He had parlayed his excellent work as my L.A. contractor in the sixties into a $150,000 a year gig for top West Coast producers. But then he had woman troubles, got messed up on booze, and the work dried up. A mutual friend called me at Elektra in the early eighties and laid it on the line to me: "Bowen, if you don't get Dirt out of here, he's not gonna live six months."

When I got hold of Dirt, I told him, "You'd better come on out to Tennessee. There'll be something here for you. It's wide open, we need good people."

Dirt sobered up enough to manage the four-day drive in his old Lincoln, but he was in real bad shape. He stayed in the guest house on Golf Club Lane, where I still lived with Dixie Two. One night Dirt fell down a metal staircase in the guest unit and broke a couple of ribs, punctured a lung, and lost some front teeth.

He healed his body over the next few months while staying with me, but he was still drinking and keeping his distance from women. One day I said, "Dirt, you know if you get those damned front teeth fixed, there are a couple of women down here that really like you." He looked at me like I was a damn fool and snarled, "I believe that's the point, James."

By the end of 1983, when I knew I was leaving Warners for MCA, I made Dirt a "tough love" deal: "I'll make you my song man at the new place if you check into Betty Ford and get straight. If you don't, I don't ever want to see you again."

Tough love worked. In early 1984, just before I took over at MCA, Dirt came back to town, sober and ready to get to work. Since then he has, I am happy to say, completely turned his life around.

While Dirt was getting his act together, I had an opportunity to finally get my own house in order. I got a call from the principal at my son's private school in Tulsa. Christian was a few months short of ten, going on eighteen.

"I'm really worried about Christian," she said. "I think you need to get him with you. He's hard to discipline and angry around other kids."

I wanted to do the right thing for my son, but if I asked Dixie One to send him to me for a while, it might turn into a big power struggle—and she might not send him.

My decision was made for me later in the day when Christian called. "Pop, send me a ticket, I'm movin' back in with you."

But that was too simple. I called Dixie and told her that Frances Bellamy, Christian's godmother, had not been feeling well and would love to have Christian visit her in Florida. I made up the part about her being sick and calling, not about her loving to see him.

I called Frances. "I need your help," I said, and told her of the ruse I needed to pull.

"Send that boy of yours on down."

After Christian's four-day visit he came back through Nashville—and Ginger and I kept him. We called Dixie and told her he was staying with us.

Dixie handled it well. Christian was a handful for anyone, let alone a single mother. Even double-teaming him, he was rough. He needed discipline—and love.

Christian hated school. He had been diagnosed with ADD, attention deficit disorder, the root of his school problems. His attention span was *seconds*. He lacked focus and discipline. He wasn't connecting with other kids, and talked down to them, pushing them away. He behaved like an adult in their world.

At home he demanded a lot of attention and needed to run the show. Now he was asking Ginger if she had keys and money before she left the house. He drove her nuts at first. This was a woman who had made it clear to me she didn't want to raise kids; now, three months after our idyllic Hawaiian wedding, we had my ten-year-old with us just as I was taking over a major new label.

We got Christian a psychiatrist and had some sessions ourselves with the shrink's partner. All we wanted was for Christian to be a normal, regular kid. I called the guy we were seeing Yoda. He was a short, jolly man who peered out at us from behind a pile of journals and papers and who managed to give us hope. Whatever we laid on him, no problem, he had the solution. It was great for us; like all parents there were times we wanted to put a choke hold on Christian because we were so emotionally involved yet frustrated at our inability to help him.

Things turned around nicely after we put him in Westminster, a school for kids with learning disabilities. I was always fifty-fifty on whether it was the right thing to do since he had no physical impairment. But a conventional school wasn't right either; it was a good move for him and for us.

As he approached his teens, Christian and I began hanging out together on weekends, going to the studios where I was working, talking about everything under the sun. We grew closer than we'd ever been. By the time he was old enough to go to high school, he had improved to the point where we put him in Franklin Road Academy, right up the road from where we were living in Brentwood.

The parallels between his situation and mine as a kid were striking. He saw his mother mostly for Thanksgiving and in summer. He had trouble with school and desperately wanted to be with a father he idolized. And, as Asa and Frances had done for me, Ginger and I provided a secure, two-parent home for him. MCA was my fourth Nashville label, Ginger my fifth wife. I was determined to make both of my new lives work.

Now that I had a crack team in position, my son under the same roof with us, and my lifelong buddy healthy and on hand to help me, I was ready to kick some butt again in the studio.

NINETEEN

PART OF THE EXCITEMENT of rebuilding a label is taking chances on new or unproven artists. Another part is jump-starting artists who you know have talent, but who haven't put out records that the public can like.

I had a chance to do both in four very hectic, successful years at MCA.

I got a call shortly before leaving Warners about John Schneider. John played Bo Duke on the *The Dukes of Hazzard* and thought a country career might play well off Bo's persona. He signed with Scotti Brothers through Columbia, but except for a Top 10 version of "It's Now or Never," he went nowhere. But his manager was a friend, and I agreed to see John as a favor.

John sounded awful on record. He was a tall, handsome, rugged hunk who sang like Leif Erikson. When he came in, I immediately liked his sincere, down-to-earth charm. We chatted and then I cut to the chase: "You talk real low, with a beautiful deep voice. How come you sing so damn high and squeaky?"

John's body stiffened. "Well, to tell you the truth, I never did until I got with those people at my label. They wanted me to appeal to teenage girls."

"Well, that's bullshit and it ain't gonna work in country, first of all. Second of all, I can't stand it. I need to hear you do something low and warm, in your own damn voice. You need to change your image for country. These people have rejected you. You've gotta make 'em want to pull you to their bosom."

Once I saw John could handle my bluntness, we hit it off. He also expressed the usual complaint: he was handed a bunch of songs to learn a week before a session and went in and sang them. No problem. I put my man Dirt on the case and he searched all over town for the right material. They picked their way through some teenybopper junk but finally wound up with a good song list.

In early 1984 I cut John's album as I was leaving Warners. John was in on all the main decisions—songs, keys, arrangements—and he had improved enormously. But Mo Ostin was more than happy to let me take John's LP with me to MCA, since his Nashville staff had no confidence in it.

John threw himself into his new career. He was cooperative, he handled people beautifully, he was a gentleman. He was a perfect case of an artist getting everybody in-house to pull for him. The "give a shit" maxed out for John at MCA.

Bruce Hinton dug the album. John's natural baritone matched to a warm ballad made for a striking first single. We decided to ship it to seventy-five stations as a "white label"—with only a blank MCA logo, the time, and title on it, but no name. This kept radio from prejudging John and added intrigue. Most called to say it was absolutely wonderful. Some guessed it was George Strait.

"It's John Schneider," we told them. "Now, go ahead and play this sucker, because we know you love it."

The song, "I've Been Around Enough to Know," written by Dicky Lee and Bob McDill, was a monster. It hit No. 1 in late 1984 and, more important, gave John a new life in Nashville.

The follow-up, "Country Girls," written by Troy Seals and Eddie Setser, also hit No. 1 and helped make *Too Good to Stop* a gold album. John then scored a couple more big hits in 1986 off *A Memory Like You* album, which we did together. He was rockin'.

Then a funny thing happened: John fell in love with a girl who wanted a rock-and-roll star for a boyfriend. *We* never would have asked John to cross over; she apparently did.

Dirt was laying all kinds of great country tunes on him for an upcoming album, and John tossed them all away. John reinvented himself overnight. All he wanted was to cut rock songs, and it led to an album that was neither fish nor fowl. Radio didn't know what to make of it—and indeed made all too little of it.

John changed his look: now he came roaring out onstage on a motorcycle in ripped jeans, a tank top, leather jacket, and a biker's bandanna around his ankle. He was sporting a beard, and had rock-and-roll hair. It was an amazing piece of acting: his musical persona had gone from Leif Erikson to Jim Reeves to Guns N' Roses.

Back at MCA the phones lit up. Promoters and radio people wanted to know what was up. Crowds were booing John, but the girlfriend was digging every minute of it backstage. John was happy. I called a meeting with him.

"You know, everything you've done so far has been truly exceptional—most notably your recent retirement from country music. It's the most incredible thing! I've never seen a guy get rid of a great career as quickly and efficiently as you have." John dug in, saying, in effect, "This is what I've got to do."

"It's your life." I shrugged. "Whatever you got to do. I'm just telling you, you're through. You've shut this baby down."

That was pretty much the end of it for John. He never charted again after 1987. Then, in 1993, his manager contacted me at Liberty Records. John was ready for a comeback.

"Country music doesn't give a damn anymore," I told her flat-out. He had come into the business during the "urban cowboy" phase, capitalizing on his popularity as a TV star. Then he did a one-eighty, and country people felt it had all been an act. Now the business was changing. "They don't want him back."

Though I was tough on John, I'd come to like him almost as a younger brother. He called himself to say he wanted back in. "Hey," I said, "I told you once, you did a great job of quittin'. I don't think you've got a prayer. It'd be a waste of time."

John produced his own album, for which I made some calls and helped steer him to publishers. But it was awful. I'm not sure he ever got it out. It was dated, and Nashville had moved on.

On the other end of the career spectrum, I worked with acts looking to keep long careers alive. The Oak Ridge Boys had a great run of hits in the seventies and eighties, from "Y'All Come Back Saloon," to "You're the One," and "Elvira." "Elvira" was a monster platinum single and CMA Single of the Year in 1981. The Oaks then had another run of nine or ten No. 1s. But they were mostly a performing group; by the time they asked me to produce them in 1987, their album sales had slipped to only 150,000 to 200,000. The Oaks' gospel-like harmonies sounded old on radio; they had to change.

I had never recorded a quartet and didn't *want* to record one. I prefer solo artists because they don't break up and fight with one another. But when the Oaks came in to see me, they sucked me in with their personalities and humor. I liked Duane Allen's voice, Joe Bonsall's enthusiasm. I thought William Golden was an intriguing, complex character. And they had a wonderful bass singer, Richard Sterban.

They were hilarious guys. Dirt had to do his song meetings with them in hotels because since they smoked so much grass, the entire record company would smell of it.

One problem with keeping a veteran act like the Oaks: longevity can mean big album advances, so you have to sell almost gold to recoup and make money. A new artist whose first record costs $100,000 will earn you a decent profit at 200,000 units. But a stagnating star who sells 200,000 and costs you *$300,000* per album isn't profitable. The Oaks had come to that point.

Worse, there was so much infighting, it was almost impossible to record them together. Bill was an environmentalist with an unusual lifestyle. He had a tepee and a sweat lodge at his house, where he meditated and participated in Native American rituals. He didn't want to be an Oak any longer.

My first album with them was their last with Bill. It was like recording three Arab countries and Israel. There was a lot of unhappiness, tension, and mistrust all around. In the studio the Oaks recorded in "stacks." They'd sing together and then lay another stack of the same vocals on top. And then a third. It sounded like the Oak Ridge Tabernacle Choir. Stacked harmonies vibrated real positively and thickened the vocals to where they cover up an awful lot of pitch problems.

But I told them it sounded dated and hokey. I wanted something *real*, natural-sounding for that time. I *unstacked* them, and cut their parts separately. This was just as well, since they almost couldn't all stand at the mikes together anymore. I did Duane's lead first, then Golden's low harmony, Sterban on bass, and Joe on the high harmony. It was a crazy time and it cost a fortune this way, but we got it right.

The first two singles off *Where the Fast Lane Ends* both made it to No. 1 in 1987. The first was called "It Takes a Little Rain (to Make Love Grow)" and the next was "This Crazy Love."

But even with hits their LP still only did 200,000 or so units.

Years later, when I was leaving MCA-Universal for Capitol, Joe Bonsall came to me and asked if I'd sign them there. It was 1990 and they were leaving MCA. Most fading superstars can't admit the music that made them stars has stopped working. They think the problem must be promotion or marketing. It's safe not to take responsibility for the music. The Oaks didn't seem to really *get* how much the world had changed around them. I, however, was blunt as ever.

"I'd be interested if we could work out the right deal, where, you know, at 150,000 albums we make money."

That didn't exactly fly. Joe called to say they were going to RCA. "We feel [RCA chief] Joe Galante is the best marketing guy in the country and that's where we'll get the biggest push."

I wished Joe and the Oaks luck.

But as luck would have it, Joe Galante marketed himself into a big job in New York and left Nashville right after the Oaks signed. They had a Top 10 record in 1991 and then faded. As I always told anyone who'd listen, hits and stiffs aren't created at the label; they're created in the studio.

Tony Brown was as fine a protégé as I could have had at MCA. He admits he was "new and green" as a producer when we first went in to cut records together, but he was a quick study. Tony cared about and believed in the music, and wanted it to be cutting-edge and worth the money people plunked down. His basic instincts were all right on. By our working together and co-producing I knew he'd find out what he knew—and what he didn't know. Tony was so bright it only took him a few projects and he was on his own. Tony was always gracious in crediting me as a mentor.

Which is not to say I didn't drive him and my staff nuts. I started my days with a round of golf. I called meetings out at my house, making staffers gather up their datebooks and paperwork and pile into cars. I made VPs meet me at recording studios at a moment's notice—day or night. I always pushed myself to be a motivator. If I was notorious for firing employees, I was also damned good at firing them *up*. I harangued Tony endlessly about cutting digital and having DIGITAL on our CD covers before everyone else came around to the same thing.

Tony sensed he was being groomed. He was young and dynamic and had the right feel for Nashville's emerging "progressive" niche. He was out in front on Alabama and Vince Gill; he brought me Lyle Lovett demos and signed Nanci Griffith, Patty Loveless, and Steve Earle to MCA. He's produced Wynonna, Reba, George, Vince, and Marty Stuart among others; since taking over after I left, he's done a tremendous job leading MCA to the top with as much as 24 or 25 percent market share. Tony's just a natural and, like me, a hybrid of artist, producer, and executive.

●

If there was one area where Tony needed to grow, it was in making a commitment to sign an act. He knew I was more blunt than most and sensed that insecure people don't last long around me. I think I pushed Tony to be more decisive, to not be afraid of taking a risk and blowing it.

He had Lyle in his hand, gave me a demo of great songs, including "God Will but I Won't." I told him it was a killer. Tony liked Lyle but didn't know where to put him. "He's not country. Do you think country radio will play it?"

"Shit, probably not, it's too clever and too good. But if you want him, sign him. It's your call."

He didn't sign him, and then a few weeks later Dick White-house, who was Curb Record's A&R guy, was in with Bruce Hinton, my VP–GM, and Bruce called me. We had a joint venture with Curb–MCA Records that included the Bellamy Brothers. "Bowen," he said, "I'm here with Dick Whitehouse and he's played me this guy Lyle Lovett and I think he's incredible and I'd like to bring him in on the Curb-MCA joint venture."

"Hey, if you want to, do it."

"Bowen," he added, "you're gonna love his look."

Because Tony hesitated, we got Lyle through a third-party deal with Curb—and that cost us half the profit we stood to make on Lyle's product.

You want your VPs to have conviction, to move on an act. I'm not putting Tony down. He just needed to get to where he could stand up and say, "I don't give a shit what anybody else thinks. I want this act, I believe in this act."

We went head-on about this one day, when I told him, "You can have anybody you want, but you've gotta have the balls to want 'em. You've gotta put your job on the line." We shared a vision of country that drew me to Tony in the first place; it would have been hypocritical to attack his judgment when he went out on a limb. I never threw a "failure" signing back in Tony's face. You don't want to mess with your best people's confidence.

Tony went out and signed somebody shortly afterward—a clean-cut kid who played piano, guitar, and banjo and worked out at the Opryland and never had a prayer. But what mattered was that Tony did it. He had to learn to make that commitment—and live with the consequences. If you're good, those decisions will work out more often than not. Tony's real good.

While I had mainstream acts like George and Reba, and the Oaks, Tony honed his progressive A&R image. We were a good match: I was the maverick-mentor; he was the upstart pushing the envelope with his "left of center" acts. He often sided with them on creative strategies. He knew I had my eye on the bottom line, but when push came to shove, he did exactly what I hoped he would do: he stood up for his artists.

Tony knew he had my absolute trust, even when his signings backfired. Because of his cool tastes and hip lineage from Elvis through to Emmylou and Rodney, Tony got calls from passé L.A. acts looking to ride in on progressive "country-rock." Which is how he signed Orleans and Nicolette Larsen.

Both stiffed in Nashville, but I never threw any of it back in Tony's face. Came with the territory. Besides, our roster and our wonderful Master Series of great instrumentalists, which Tony spearheaded, still gave MCA the aura of a vanguard along Music Row. The message was, "We're happening, we're contenders, and RCA, CBS, and Warners had better watch out."

Tony says I put him "through hell" over Patty Loveless. Tony signed Patty in 1985 when I thought she was way too raw and piercing to my ears. There was no dehonkin' her. Her sound was almost bluegrass and it didn't turn me on.

But that same voice intrigued Tony. Patty's a down-home Kentucky girl who sang with the Wilburn Brothers in high school. That's the music Tony was raised on, and her voice went right to his heart. It shot straight past my ears, but this was exactly the kind of passion I wanted to see in Tony. I said go for it.

Tony was on a mission when he went in to cut her first album: "Bowen, she's a monster, she's gonna sell platinum."

"Oh, bullshit," I'd say. "She isn't either."

Tony nailed it. It took almost four years, but Patty finally broke through and hit No. 1 for MCA in 1989 with "Timber, I'm Falling in Love."

Actually it was Patty's falling in love with sessions piano player and producer Emory Gordy, Jr., that led to a falling out with me. Tony introduced Patty to Emory, who then coproduced her MCA albums with Tony. Once their romance was known, I warned Tony that pillow talk would be the end of his influence as coproducer. I just knew romance—they got married in February 1989—would interfere. I had Tony tell Emory he wouldn't be coproducing her albums.

Of course the first album Tony produced alone for Patty went gold—not because Emory wasn't there but because Patty *was* there. She was ready. Still, my decision sowed some bitterness between her and the label, between Tony and myself; in Tony's view we never got it all sorted out. Even after I left MCA, Tony believed Patty felt betrayed enough to leave MCA for Epic.

Since she's been there, she and Emory have made some wonderful records and Patty has flourished. To my ears they've cut way back on "the honk factor"; I told Emory how great her records sound when I saw him not long ago.

Another act Tony and I disagreed on but *didn't* sign was the gifted bluegrass fiddler Alison Krauss. She was seventeen when Tony insisted I see her act. "Bowen, this girl's gonna *kill* you."

Alison's as good as it gets in her genre, but she didn't knock me out. I drove off in my Cadillac. I just don't have the roots or the ears for true hillbilly. Alison signed with Rounder and has since won a Grammy and, in 1995, three CMA awards, including Female Vocalist of the Year. One of her CDs has gone double platinum, too.

Signing Steve Earle from Epic was an excellent move. Steve was a strong entertainer and a marvelous poet. He sang rough and angry, but a lot better than, say, Bob Dylan. I liked that Tony was on it. I had a hard time hearing exactly what part of America Steve's music represented. It took a few months once Tony got working with him, but I heard him somewhere between Hank Williams, Jr., and Bruce Springsteen.

Critics dug him, a buzz started, and a cult took hold. He's the next Bruce. John Mellencamp announces in the press that he cranks up Steve drivin' down the highway. The Boss himself loves Steve. Suddenly MCA's "we know better" elite took over in L.A. and brought Steve west to put his records out through the pop-rock division. The old "if it's fixed, break it" syndrome.

They took a terrific songwriter with a distinct, haunting voice and started pumping his head full of "you're the next Springsteen." They got him so worked up and confused between Nashville and L.A. that he wound up musically somewhere around Albuquerque. His *Guitar Town* album was his best, with "Hillbilly Highway" and the title track. That was the real Steve Earle. He came to us pretty much fixed, and they broke him.

Steve had some demons of his own that came between him and his music—drugs and booze. He never seemed like a bad investment until booze changed the way he behaved in public. I'd hear from people working with him that he's a great-looking kid who needs a bath, he's too extreme, really out there. It was such a shame. Just when things were coming together for him, the pressure and hype came down on him and he spun out of control into something of far less value.

•

Tony felt as strongly about Nanci Griffith as he did about Patty and Alison. Nanci had a unique songwriting and singing talent that she called folkabilly. She had cut some records on Philo before Tony signed her, and it was clear her niche was eclectic and hard to pin down. In folk Nanci was a superstar, adored by critics and artists alike. Tony was an artist himself, who communicated his deep respect for—and insights into— what his artists were all about. As Tony put it, he would "buy into" what an artist like Nanci was creating.

What I had to buy into as label chief was that after the two studio albums Tony produced for us, she wasn't getting played on radio or selling any albums. Nanci was a terrific one-of-a-kind talent with that die-hard folk cult behind her. But we just didn't know how to break a "folkabilly" act. Nanci's voice seemed to irritate country radio.

I was so baffled by this that I went so far as to consult an ear, nose, and throat guy named Richard W. Quisling, the first voice doctor in Nashville who specialized in treating hillbilly hoarseness and other throat ailments. I got Dr. Quisling to call in some Japanese acoustic specialists, who flew in from Japan for a meeting.

"Here's the deal," I said to these doctors and scientists. "We have a problem. I got this woman who can sit here and sing to me and it is absolutely gorgeous to listen to. But the minute she goes through a microphone, something happens between two thousand and thirty-five hundred cycles and you lose all her warmth. It turns some people off and scares country radio and that's not what we want. Something in the human ear filters that range out or rejects it."

Microphones were developed for the male speaking voice; I'd rarely heard one that did justice to female singers. I asked the team to develop something to alter her recorded voice and make it warmer, more accessible.

They came up with a synthetic latex membrane similar to the inner ear to place over the mike so that it would soften the voice before it hit the mike and got amplified. Sort of a microphone glove. The first prototype was too thick and it muffled the voice. They were in the process of redesigning a new one when Nanci got impatient and decided the hell with it.

Her attitude was "I am what I am." Tony took this all a little too personally and figured I didn't like her. I was only trying to find a way to harness her vocal gift in a way that would make her more accessible.

A hit record would have been an even better solution. A while later I was off to Hawaii for my summer getaway when Tony gave me a half-dozen projects to listen to. Maui's a great place to hear tapes. No phones, no office. Anyone who wanted to fax or phone me had a five-hour window of opportunity before my noon tee-off. They could call me between seven A.M. and noon, Maui time. When I woke up every morning, my fax had already been spittin' paper for three hours, with all kinds of data and questions to deal with. If they could figure the time zone right and catch me, I was reachable. If they couldn't figure this out, hell, I didn't want 'em working for me.

I also brought Nanci's older stuff to get a feel for where Tony was going with her. I know to this day Tony still cherishes those first albums. But there comes a point when, as far as radio is concerned, you've either got your bullet or you're gone.

I listened to Nanci's new songs and knew the album wasn't going where I wanted it to. I didn't want to keep sending country radio noncountry arrangements so that no matter what you sent them they didn't listen. I got word back to MCA: "Tell Tony if he and Nanci don't cut three singles aimed at radio, it's over. He's not puttin' this album out."

Tony relayed "Bowen's mandate," as he called it, to Nanci.

Nanci had a mandate of her own for me: "I won't cut the record. I want off the label."

"I don't blame you," Tony told her. They both knew she wasn't "country." Tony stood up for his beliefs and sided with her. If he had taken my side, he felt it would have compromised his musical integrity and betrayed his confidence in her.

Tony caught my pregolf window and phoned to share Nanci's reaction with me. "Fine," I said, "let her go."

My boss in L.A. had other notions. "No way," said Irving. He brought Nanci to MCA in Los Angeles—so that the fix-it pop elite could work with her. Tony then put together her *One Fair Summer Evening* live collection as a transition out of Nashville. She stayed with the label's pop division for a couple more albums before moving on to Elektra.

As Tony knows, we affect artists' destinies. But it's a tricky play. Sometimes holding on to an artist can hurt a career—and letting them go can be the best thing you can do for them.

Tony and I had auditioned a wannabe singer-writer together sometime in 1988. It was one of the few times we agreed on a new artist's destiny. I had set up my own independent label, Universal, through a joint venture with MCA. I was legally frozen and unable to sign new acts because I was leaving MCA and looking for a label to buy Universal's roster. Tony was still at MCA.

The artist had been playing the Nashville game—recording demos for songwriter friends, pitching his own demos all over town, doing showcases for talent scouts. Whatever it took.

He came by my house with his comanager, a former RCA label executive Tony and I both knew and respected. He was humble, polite, soft-spoken: "How d'ya do," "Yes, sir," "Sure, ma'am," "Pleased to meet ya." But he also gave off a brooding, reflective aura and stared at us with intense, glaring eyes. He was from Oklahoma, a college jock with a degree; his heroes ranged from George Strait to James Taylor, Billy Joel to Journey.

He was dressed casually, and sat down in my living room with just his acoustic guitar. He did three or four of his songs and I heard some wonderful moments in there. But it didn't strike me as *real* country, though one of his heroes was Merle Haggard. His Top 40 radio influences, like Dan Fogelberg, were apparent. One of his songs was a sweet ballad called "If Tomorrow Never Comes."

There wasn't much exchange, no time afterward for small talk. Tony and I both had other appointments.

We thanked him, walked him out, and said good-bye. Afterward Tony was getting ready to leave. "Boy, he was good," he said. "But he's not very country."

"Yeah, that's right," I said. "Sure as hell isn't."

Earnest and impressive as he was, he was not radically different on first listen from a hundred others who have come to play songs for me. His musical direction didn't seem real focused on what was happening in country. And, besides, I wasn't even free to sign him, so why would I get excited? Tony and I knew we were going to pass on the kid. He wasn't where Nashville was heading.

Tony left and I went back inside. Ginger came around the corner and stopped by the office. "Who was that kid singing?" she asked. "Sounded a lot like Jackson Browne."

Now I had a second opinion. With the exception of fellow Texan Strait, if Ginger responded positively to something, it wasn't country. She's never been wild for country. The fact that she liked this kid told me he was definitely pop.

"His name is Garth Brooks."

TWENTY

ONE OF THE UNSUNG HEROES in MCA's rise from near-worst to first was Don Lanier. Dirt not only made a remarkable personal recovery, he performed minor miracles matching artists to the best material as MCA's song man.

The song is coin of the realm in Nashville. Panning for gold buried in all the melodies and lyrics that flow through Music Row is what drives the place. Dirt hunted through thousands of demos to put a twenty-song list together for an album. His aural memory was astounding. He could reject some ditty for one act but then think of it out of the blue weeks later for another. He'd put a "hold" on a song he liked—an informal option while the artist considered cutting it. A "cut hold" meant we were likely to record it, so the publishers agreed not to pitch it elsewhere.

With one man casting as many as 250 album tracks a year, the best writers' work poured in to Dirt. Then he and the artist would play them for me as producer and we'd whittle that list to ten or twelve. Because it wasn't ultimately Dirt's or my decision, publishers couldn't sway Dirt with a piece of the performance action to get a song on the album. It was the artist's call.

I told my artists, "This isn't rocket science, you don't need two or three years to make forty minutes of great music. If you wait that long, you lose your momentum, the public moves on, you're starting over every time out." But I didn't want songs cluttering their LPs just because they owned them. I wanted a forty-minute performance, paced and sequenced as if they were performing it onstage for ten thousand people: An opener, a closer, and peaks and valleys in between. Entertain, draw people in. And why not make two or three for radio while you're at it, so folks'll drive to the mall and feel good about spending money on your latest CD. Dirt's job was to put that "concert" together—and he did it as well as anyone.

Our system was geared up for preproduction. We booked our sessions four to six months out in front. My A&R manager, Jessie Noble, cast ensembles of compatible musicians the way Dirt cast material. We also had a corps of six first engineers and as many second engineers. Once our roster got up to speed, we had enough projects crankin' for most of them to work sixty to one hundred hours a week. I ran MCA like a guerilla general, working mostly from my home or from satellite offices set up for me at studios. It was my most frenetic and prolific time in Nashville, but my dedicated staff got into it and turned the place around in a hurry.

As Dirt put it, the days of the "trash can" LP were over for us.

I once thought Reba McEntire too country. But she had a few hits for Mercury off a couple of albums shortly before she came to MCA. I took over not long after that, when she seemed about to break out. Yet I thought she still sounded dated.

Reba had a real good instrument but was recording whatever songs they brought her. Same old story. She had never witnessed an overdub or mix-down session. She'd come in, do her takes, get back on the tour bus. She was not in control of her music.

I thought her first MCA album, *Just a Little Love*, was awful—lush, stringy, blah. She had changed producers and gone with Norro Wilson; Reba was stuck on a plateau, and not a very high one: the album barely sold 40,000 units. I didn't feel good about Reba's direction. I called a meeting with Norro, a funny, likable veteran producer-songwriter who'd written a lot of hits through the years.

"You only spent fifty thousand dollars on this album," I told him, "and twenty thousand was your producer's fee. No wonder it doesn't hold up. It sounds like you mixed everything in twenty minutes. Norro, you're a good song man, a terrific guy. But you're Old School. You need someone to bring you to this modern era. Then your experience and song sense will be a great asset for your artists."

I removed Norro from future projects with Reba.

I caught Reba's show and then had a meeting with her when she was back in town. Reba and her first husband, rodeo champ

Charlie Battles, were still living in Oklahoma. I wanted to let her know where I stood.

It was a great first encounter. Dirt's office was on the second floor and mine was on the third. I hated waiting for the elevator, so I went down the stairwell, but the outside door to the floor was locked. I got pissed and started pounding and kicking, yelling for someone to let me in.

A week before, I'd heard a story from a friend about how somebody had cussed and said "f——" in front of Reba and Charlie. Charlie, stout rodeo bull rider that he was, threw the man through a window. You don't cuss around a cowboy's woman.

So as I hollered and kicked, the door swung open from the inside and I tumbled out, angry as hell. As I rounded the first corner, I was still fuming: "Son of a *bitch*, who the *fuck* locked that door?" Which was right when I walked straight into the cute redhead and her burly bull-ridin' husband. Instinct told me to whip around, as if to see where all that ugly cussin' could be coming from. Hmm, nobody there. I held out my hand and introduced myself. We were off to a great start.

"Fifty thousand albums isn't what we're after here," I told Reba. "We want to sell a million. We've got to find you a producer who can cut *your* music and get it on radio. Make me a Reba McEntire album. Quit singin' other people's styles, other people's stuff. Be yourself."

I put Reba with two or three producers and she picked Alabama's acclaimed Harold Shedd. Then Dirt began bringing her to publishers. The problem Reba had was finding pure country songs when many writers were still thinking crossover. No one knew it, but Reba was on the cutting edge of the New Traditional movement.

She did find some great tunes, such as Harlan Howard's "Somebody Should Leave." She and Shedd then went in and recorded the tracks for *My Kind of Country*. Reba definitely got into it. She put steel guitar here, a fiddle track there, an electric-guitar solo right *there*. She had a very specific sense of where she wanted this record to go. But she and Harold hadn't seen eye to eye on everything. He wanted to use a costly string section and take her into bland Adult Contemporary. Reba just wanted to come home to her musical roots.

She thought she was on her way until she got back to town from the road and listened to the tracks. Harold had taken off a lot of her stuff and resweetened it with his. This pissed that red-head off; she was good and livid when she heard those tracks. This wasn't her kind of country at all.

Reba stormed in to see me at the office on West End Avenue. She was mad as a yard dog. "Bowen" she said, "don't you think he could have at least talked to me before he did that? He has no respect for me and for what I want. I had it the way I wanted it and he erased it. This ain't gonna work."

Here I had just begun to make Reba understand that it's *her* music, *her* life, *her* money. "Hold it right there," I said, trying to calm her down. "It's real simple. He works for you. You want to fire him, I'll fire him for you. That's my job."

Then Reba leaned forward and fixed a look of intense deter-mination in her bright blue eyes. "I want *you* to produce me," she said. "Nobody else. You can make it happen."

I was reluctant. "Woman," I said, "I can get you the right band, I can make you sound wonderful. But you're gonna have to tell them what to play. Then it'll be your music. I'll put you to-gether with my song man. But if you don't know what a woman should say to cause another woman to drive to a mall, go into a record store, go back under 'Country' and hunt for Reba, it's not gonna work anyway."

She sat up straight, gave me one of her earnest frowns, and said, "Bowen, I can do that. I love a challenge. But why don't *you* help me with this album?"

Finally I did agree to help her straighten out *My Kind of Country*—but left her to decide whether we'd work together in the future.

I gave Reba a quick course in engineering. I brought her to Ronnie Milsap's studio and sat her right behind me at the mixing board as I took apart Harold's tracks and remixed the album. We brought her fiddle, steel, and guitar players back in and recut their tracks, the ones Harold had replaced. We put on the vocal harmonies the way Reba wanted. If Harold took it off, we put it back. I talked her through the entire mix-down at the computer-ized digital board—faders, EQ, overdubs—so she'd know how to re-create her sound. If the musicians had a question, they asked her, not me. It was her call.

She had never been so in charge—and she was up to the chal-lenge. Her voice has the power and range to blow away all oth-ers. Now she knew how to get it to sound its best, and she had a kick-butt attitude to drive her career.

Having seen her show, I knew Reba had a great jazzy way of

getting to pitch—she'd overshoot and come back down, or ride under it and bend it back up. While dubbing a vocal I was surprised now by how plain her voice sounded. I switched the talkback mike on and, looking at her through the glass, asked, "Reba, where are all those jazzy, curlicue licks, bends, and cracks you do onstage? Your voice on records is kinda bland and flattened out. Why sing one way live and another in the studio?"

"They told me at Mercury never to do that in the studio."

"Well," I said, "how well are they doin' today?"

"Not real good, I guess."

"Well, listen to me instead of them. *I'm* doin' real good."

It scared some record people to hear how country Reba really was. I'd passed on her myself, but now tastes were swinging back. "See, what they were doing with you was bullshit," I said. "Just be yourself. Sing the song the way you feel it. And you'll be the class of country."

In her memoir Reba generously called me "a very patient teacher—or maybe I should say 'preacher.'"

If so, I was soon preaching to the converted. Reba had two No. 1 hits off the album—"How Blue" and "Somebody Should Leave"—and now felt thoroughly *involved* with her music. Still, despite a half-dozen No. 1s, she was only selling 150,000 LPs. What she needed to be a superstar was a killer career record.

Because *My Kind* was rooted in honky-tonk tunes, Dirt held off pushing her to include a song called "Whoever's in New England." He had put a hold on it and then assured the publisher, "If y'all stick it under a rock and hold it till next album, I'll run it in there."

It was a poignant ballad written by Kendal Franceschi and Quentin Powers. The song was about a southern wife who's beginning to wonder if her husband's mixing pleasure with his frequent business trips to Boston. I felt Reba was concerned that the melody and lyrics were too pop—or that the cheating theme was off-limits. The song was a departure, and they were both right to hold off before. But Dirt couldn't keep his hold on it forever. "James," he insisted, "this here's a career record."

Reba was at a turning point. Her reticence was about not wanting to make a career mistake. The pressure artists feel in choosing singles is about more than heavy rotation on radio, bullets, and tonnage. If *we're* wrong about a couple of singles, we can turn to ten other acts and move on with our lives. The artist is stuck with those stiffs with nowhere to go until next album. If a song clicks, they have to sing it the rest of their lives.

"New England" made the last cut on our song list as we got to ten. Our feeling was, Cut it, and if it doesn't work, we don't have to release it to radio. Reba kept putting off a decision, but finally decided to cut it last. She was weary but determined to make it work—not unlike the wife in the song.

I knew Reba was a fighter. She reached back and gave me a great live vocal we knew immediately was a killer. I'm sure she didn't even know how good it was at the time. With her headphones on, it would be hard for the singer to judge.

"That was wonderful, Reba," I said. "Now, just give me three more vocals and don't worry about being tired."

Reba wrapped and hit the road. I put together the vocal comp most of the night and crashed just before dawn. There were no computers then, so you worked for hours throwing faders up and back to get the volume balanced just right.

The moment I heard it again in the morning, I knew Dirt was right: a career record. "New England" became the title track and first single off the album. Reba also shot a video that helped push the single to No. 1 by the end of May 1986. "Little Rock," a bouncy little ditty about an ignored, fed-up wife who removes the "little rock" from her finger to strike out on her own, also went No. 1 four months later. The album became Reba's first gold record. That fall she won her third CMA award for Best Female Vocalist and Entertainer of the Year. In February 1987 "New England" earned Reba her first Grammy, for Best Country Vocal Performance, Female.

Good thing Dirt stayed on us to get her to sing it.

You couldn't help but admire Reba's drive, and her businesslike focus. Even while she and Battles were divorcing, she was never less than absolutely professional in our song meetings and recording sessions. If we shipped her demos to consider while she was on the road, she always found time to listen and make up her song lists. In the studio no matter what else was going on in her career or personal life, she could, without fail, nail me one killer take out of the four I needed for my comp vocal.

After the divorce I watched Reba's transformation into a take-charge, independent, self-assured woman. She married her former pedal-steel player and road manager, Narvel Blackstock, who now oversees her sprawling Starstruck businesses. Reba managed to seize total control of her career without becoming a control freak. She is tough, secure, and driven. But she never overlorded, never allowed *my* need to improve or fix her tracks to threaten her self-confidence. I could set her down and say,

"These two vocals aren't up to par. We gotta fix 'em." She didn't need to hear sugar-coated yesses all day long. She'd go and do 'em, no questions asked. She just wanted to be the best Reba possible. There was total respect and trust between us.

Reba's fierce, grounded work ethic was tied to her having grown up in a rough and rugged cattle-ranching family from Oklahoma. Whatever it took, Reba rolled up her sleeves and got down to it. Even with her TV specials, awards shows, touring, movies, and businesses, the music always got done.

When Reba and I were doing our last album together, I told her I heard a slight rattle and distortion at the top end of her voice. She went to see Dr. Quisling, the voice doctor. He went down in there with a laser beam and took something out. It hurt her like the dickens. But damn if she didn't come back to Emerald Studios that same afternoon. She had a stern look on her face, and it felt like daggers shooting through me. But she went right out into the studio and started singing as if nothing had happened. Sure, she was mad as hell at me, but when she came in and heard the first playback, the top end of her voice was crystal clear.

She turned and smiled and said, "Bowen, he nearly killed me, but, hey, it's okay, he fixed the problem."

George Strait needed some fixing, too, when we started working together in 1984, but it was clear he was going to be a giant. I still saw plenty of room for growth. Nine of the ten singles he had released since his wonderful "Unwound" in 1981 had been Top 10. George didn't need direction; he knew his strengths. Like Reba, all he needed was to make his music his own.

George grew up, like Reba, in a cattle-ranching family. When he signed with MCA in early 1981, he was still working as a ranch foreman down in San Marcos, Texas, where he grew up. He had already performed in Texas dancehalls with his Ace in the Hole Band and cut a few tracks with them for a small local label.

George was a real Texas roper and rancher doing pure, old-time Texas swing. He had tried and failed to get a record gig in Nashville and gone home, nearly quitting music for a ranching job in Texas. No one took him seriously; country was too busy with urban cowboys.

It wasn't just George who had this experience. Ricky Skaggs, a Kentucky mandolin and guitar picker who'd played with Emmylou's Hot Band, had a similar problem when he first went solo around the same time, in 1980. His bluegrass roots were as pure Kentucky as George's were pure Texas. But both were "too country."

George's *Strait Country* in 1981, with "Unwound," was a solid debut album produced by Blake Mevis. He and Blake did another LP together, but by 1983 they parted ways. Blake was moving George from his Texas roots toward a slicker pop sound. Eight tracks for a third album went unreleased. MCA, under Jim Foglesong, was eager to get an album out. *Straight From the Heart* had already been mined for four singles, and MCA didn't want to lose George's momentum.

Producer Ray Baker spent a couple of intense days helping George finish the album. At the very end of the sessions they added "Right or Wrong," an old Bob Wills tune George played live. It became the title track—and George's third straight No. 1 hit just as I took over MCA. George was driving women fans crazy on the road and was one of the hottest acts in country.

Skaggs meanwhile had broken through by then as well, running up eight or nine No. 1s between 1982 and 1984 and winning CMA's Best Male Vocalist in 1982. Times were changing.

Three months before I took over MCA, knowing I was headed there, I had called Erv Woolsey, the label's VP for promotion, and set up a meeting. Erv had worked hard to sign George to MCA in 1980, when virtually no one else believed in him, including label president Jim Foglesong and the head of A&R, Ron Chancey. Knowing my reputation for taking over and cleaning house, Erv pretty much knew what was coming down. I told him he should go pack his things and leave MCA. But Erv had his next move mapped out: he became George's manager. "Well, then, I guess we need to have a real good working relationship," I said. And we did.

One of my first duties at MCA was to meet with George and Erv and get the lay of the land. George's album sales were stuck in the 200,000 to 250,000 range—solid but not killer. There was no reason you couldn't hit gold or platinum with two or three hits off every album.

George told me he had put test vocals on an album's worth of material with Ray Baker for his next album, but didn't like any of them. "I've got ten tracks done and I'm never going to put my voice on 'em—and I'm never workin' with Ray again."

George had Reba's problem: music was being imposed on him. "They're not my tracks. I didn't participate in any of 'em," he said. "They give me the song to learn and then I had to set on the couch in the studio and have a beer with Johnny Rodriguez while the producer and the band got the track ready. Then they said, 'Ready, George,' and I went out and sang the lyrics."

George had to take control, but I felt he also needed a more modern set of studio musicians. His sound was already getting complacent, a powerful engine stopped dead in its tracks. The situation was a mess.

"You've got the look, the sound, the voice, but it's gonna be your own," I said. "Not mine." I told him we would coproduce, but he would pick his songs and decide how they should sound. "We'll sell platinum," I said. "I'll put together a band doing George Strait music that'll knock your hat in the dirt, pal. Trust me."

George, a shy but direct man of few words, said, "That is what I want to do."

Dirt put the word out on the Row that we were on a crash hunt. "Strait's comin' in in two weeks, find us a hit."

As I'd done with Haggard and Hank, I saw George live and got a tape of his show. The idea, again, was to capture George's distinct and evocative Texas swing sound, but liven things up with great session pickers. If George had a weakness, it was that his albums were a couple of radio hits and the rest was filler. His heart often wasn't in recording, and as forty-minute performances, his LPs lacked variety and pacing.

I booked Reggie Young and Larry Byron on electric guitar; Eddie Bayers on drums; Randy Scruggs on acoustic guitar; John Hobbs for piano; Hank DeVito on steel; David Hungate on bass; and Curtis Young on harmony vocals. For fiddle, George suggested Johnny Gimble, Wills's wonderfully fluid, lyrical fiddler. He was perfect and we ended up using him a lot with Strait.

We put together some terrific songs that fit George's style. Four of them were written by Whitey Shafer, Sonny Throckmorton, and Wayne Kemp. One of them, "Does Fort Worth Ever Cross Your Mind?," struck me as the first single—and title track. Reba had almost cut it earlier, but passed on it—supposedly because of a reference to beer.

Barely a month after I took over MCA, I went into the small Back Stage studio at the rear of Sound Stage and played the live tape for my musicians. "Okay," I said. "Now you guys are the Ace in the Hole Band for the next three days."

George is real slow and relaxed. It takes forever to get him into high gear. When we got around to doing the first track, some of the players asked me some questions about the arrangement. "How do I know? It's not my record. Ask George."

George took charge, perked up, telling these pickers what he wanted and where. This took the focus off me and turned it right on George. You could feel the energy kick up on both sides of the glass. The players loved cutting those tracks.

George would then come in for the playback and come alive when he heard it all falling into place. And that in turn caused him to sing better. The fewer takes, the better to get a mood flowing and the adrenaline kickin' in. There wasn't time to get stale. The emotions of the songs were fresh and intense.

These great players got it down quick and never needed more than two or three takes. We cut ten songs with George in three days. This was much faster than I liked to work, but George had already squandered a lot of time and energy on the Baker tracks. I didn't want to lose our momentum—or good faith.

We made a real good team. "Fort Worth" became the career record George needed to help him soar into superstardom. While the song was climbing to No. 1 in January 1985, George's *Right or Wrong* album, which was at 220,000 units when I got to MCA, went gold. *Fort Worth* then went gold and platinum, as did most of the albums we did together into the early nineties—*Beyond the Blue Neon, Livin' It Up, Chill of an Early Fall, Holding My Own.*

Fort Worth played its part in ushering in the New Traditional era. Both the CMA and the Academy of Country Music named it their album of the year on their nationally televised awards shows and named George as Male Vocalist of the Year.

George hated having to record and hang out in Nashville. One reason was that he'd been dismissed early on. Though women always thought he was gorgeous, music people never imagined he'd be a platinum superstar. But after that first meeting when he told me about the Ray Baker tracks, I understood the presence and charisma behind the Strait phenomenon.

Another reason he hated Nashville: he'd get pitched mercilessly by wannabe songwriters, who'd ambush him anywhere he went. Soon Dirt couldn't take George around with him on song hunts. Wherever they'd go, a crush of autograph-hungry fans ambushed them. They walked into Welk Publishing once and sixty girls were crammed downstairs. "You coulda cut the hair spray in there with a knife," Dirt said.

Dirt and George had to create their song lists by swapping

demos through the mail months before the sessions. To find ten songs, Dirt might consider twelve hundred to fifteen hundred and listen closely to one hundred. George would then come into town the Sunday before going in. We'd meet at Woolsey's office on Eighteenth Avenue South and spend three or four hours as Dirt and George played the songs to cut the list down from twenty to ten or twelve. I'd sit with a score sheet and rate them. Anything under seven we tossed. I never tried to talk George into a song, only asked him to reconsider it.

Then I'd give the demos to an assistant and he'd put together lyric sheets with chord notations for each song. We'd record Monday, Tuesday, Wednesday, and *bam!* Just like that, we figured out a way to make it work.

Once George was gone, the first engineer and I would get the vocal comping done to arrive at the master vocal. All we needed to do was overdub the background vocals. I'd send George a rough mix on the road and he literally phoned it in: he'd sit with a lyric sheet identical to mine and tell me just where in the tracks he wanted harmonies dubbed and whether he heard two- or three-part harmony.

George and I got on one helluva roll. In a three-year period between 1986 and 1989, eleven straight singles George and I co-produced went to No. 1.

Even after I left MCA in 1988, I produced George and Reba for a while longer. Thank goodness I was also able to teach them to have the guts to tell me when it was over for us.

Knowing when to quit is crucial. You never want to go one record too long. I knew when the magic was gone with Hank Jr. The last album felt stale. I was bored and had lost the ability to help Hank when he needed a change. It wasn't turning me on anymore. The incentive to carry on after it's over with a superstar is strong: a platinum record was worth between $200,000 and $300,000 in royalties in the CD economy. But more important than that is the obligation, the relationship you form. You hate to back away and quit. And as label chief you don't want to jerk the components out of a platinum-selling team. Sometimes getting out's the best thing you can do. But it can be as hard as getting off a drug.

Reba and George made it easy: each personally made the call to fire me.

I felt I had gone one album too long when I was mastering George's *Holding My Own*. I think we worked so fast and efficiently together, it hadn't yet hit me. But I wasn't totally surprised when George called and left his number on the road.

When I reached him, we exchanged chit-chat and then the two Texans got down to it. "Look, Bowen, this is the hardest phone call of my life," he said, and I knew.

"I understand that, George."

"You know, they want me to do something fresh."

"Hey, I understand absolutely, and you need it. It'll be good for you."

"Well, I knew you'd understand. I just had to call you myself." I thanked him for that.

Click. He hung up and that was it.

Reba had been listening to demos in 1989 for what would become her *Rumor Has It* album the following year. Reba was also pregnant with her son, Shelby, and she was on the road. I had been sort of ignoring the redhead because I had come to feel it just wasn't working anymore. Our last two LPs, *Sweet Sixteen* and *Live* had gone gold—but I felt our act was getting old. Plus I had just gone over to Capitol Records's Nashville division to turn that label around, though I was still free to produce anyone I desired.

Reba had sent me some songs she was thinking of cutting while I was in Hawaii for the holidays. I sent them back indicating I only liked one of the fifteen or so she sent.

Reba meanwhile was booked to record with me in mid-January. Shelby was due in February 1990. But she had been having a difficult pregnancy. After a road trip she was hospitalized twice and confined to her bed at home. She had been doing some serious thinking through it all. Something was bugging her, a gut feeling she called the whisper of God.

Reba is a sensitive, beautiful, warm, loving, loyal human being. I know she agonized over this decision. A meeting was set up by Narvel for us to talk at her condo on Hillsboro Road when I got back to town. Reba was hugely pregnant and we joked about her size and talked of the excitement of her first baby.

There wasn't going to be any smooth segues, so she got to the point: "Like you always said, Bowen, there comes a time when you've got to change. I feel we've worked together long enough. It's time I got someone different to produce me."

"Yep. I think you're one hundred percent right, Reba."

And that was about it. She didn't have to look too far or long to find my replacement—Tony Brown.

Reba, George, and I had a lot to show when it was over: more than forty Top 5 hits and some twenty albums (including collections), almost all of them eventually going gold, platinum, or double platinum. But beyond the numbers, the most lasting, enriching payoff for me was helping to shape the careers of two of the finest, most decent artists Nashville has ever known.

The MCA years were my favorite, most prolific, and successful in Nashville. Everything I had been working for fell into place and meshed smoothly: artists in control, digital recording quality, smart song selection and efficient preproduction, in-house teamwork, tonnage. During my tenure revenues soared nearly 400 percent to $50 million a year, while market share jumped past—and stayed above—20 percent. MCA passed RCA for the first time ever as the new powerhouse on Music Row, and was *Billboard*'s top overall album and singles label for 1987.

There was an excitement on Music Row again. Album sales were up, radio became aggressive in courting a younger audience, country cable expanded rapidly, and all the labels fought for a piece of the "New Traditional" action. RCA had Alabama and the Judds. Epic had Ricky Skaggs. We had Reba and George. And Randy Travis had his watershed *Storms of Life* album in 1985 for Warners.

Because country was still recorded mostly "live" with everyone together for basic tracks, we were seeing more and more musicians drawn to Nashville for the immediacy and spontaneity of the studio ambience, an easygoing lifestyle, and a sense of community. I had pop players tell me they cut albums in L.A. without even knowing who played on them until they opened up the CD and read the liner notes.

Demographics were in our favor too. Baby boomers raised on rock and roll had grown alienated by (and too old for) hard rock or rap. The first boomers turned forty in 1986. They were settling down, mellowing out. Just as I had discovered the adult appeal of country before I came to Nashville, many of them were drawn to country's real-life stories from the heartland, lyrics they could understand and melodies they could sing—or line-dance—to. The music and musicianship sounded fuller, you could *hear* the voices and drums, there was an edge on the electric guitar. Country music, no longer rural, blue-collar, and southern, had been digitally "dehonked" and brought into the mainstream.

I knew my days at MCA were numbered when Irving hired Al Teller from Columbia as president of MCA Records in Los Ange-

les. There was talk that Irving, who was now head of MCA Music
Entertainment Group, Inc., was told by his boss, Sid Sheinberg,
to hire Al. I knew this would be trouble. Teller had been at
United Artists when I was at MGM and we shared the same distribution system. As is usually the case with a non-musical business guy, Al figured to be a natural enemy to anyone like myself
who lived in studios and made records. At times he also seemed
to be on a bigger ego trip than any artist. The kind who loves the
power trip of it all, wants you to kiss the ring. But Sid had this
thing that if you were a record person at CBS Records, you had
to be great.

When Al came to MCA, I sensed trouble. After ten minutes on
the phone I knew I couldn't stand the man I would now be reporting to. I wasn't going to kiss his ring—or his butt. I immediately wanted out. I later told a trade-paper reporter, "I get along
with Teller about as well as I do with my first four wives—except
that they write occasionally and he doesn't."

Besides, after four high-intensity years at MCA, I wanted a
better deal for myself. I was ready for some kind of change. I
briefly considered retiring to Hawaii, but I wasn't ready yet. I
had a battle or two left in me. One would be over money, so I told
Irving, "I'm not getting properly compensated." Another issue:
MCA had grown to some thirty acts, stretching our A&R and
promotion departments.

"I want to make you happy," Azoff said. "Let's do a joint venture." After some wrangling I wound up with an extraordinary
opportunity—to head and co-own a subsidiary label with MCA,
which financed the operation.

On December 5, three hundred people showed up for a press
conference to launch Universal Records. We had our own in-
house producers and A&R people and a roster featuring Lacy J.
Dalton, Larry Gatlin and the Gatlin Brothers, Eddie Rabbitt,
Gary Morris, John Anderson, Carl Perkins, and the Nitty Gritty
Dirt Band. Some acts were signed to me, others to MCA. I also
made a $2 million deal to get the Judds from RCA upon expira-
tion of their contract two years down the road. I knew Wynonna
would be an enormous superstar on her own someday.

The deal also included setting up my own publishing company, Great Cumberland Music, with a Texas-based partner
named Bill Hamm, better known for managing ZZ Top and Clint
Black, and James Stroud, my VP of A&R.

One major success that year was the Dirt Band's *Will the Circle Be Unbroken II*, which won Album of the Year at the CMA
awards—a double CD that sold 700,000 units. We were also the

first label in town to make a switch to all-CDs official. There were some holdouts, like Jim Foglesong, who was quoted as saying, "The fact that Universal is doing it, I don't think, will cause a snowball effect."

Of course not! I'd only been saying for a *decade* that it was only a matter of time. Vinyl didn't have a snowball's chance in hell of surviving: after all, the switch to CDs saved the entire music industry by nearly doubling the price of records, leading music lovers to update their vinyl collections to digital.

Some time later Azoff, as executive VP of MCA, Inc., and Teller came back to me and discussed my running MCA-Nashville—again—as chairman. Tony Brown would be label president, and Bruce Hinton the president of Universal. But Tony, having been groomed as the future for MCA-Nashville, wouldn't go for it. He wanted to be out from under me.

Ginger and I spent a month on Maui in the summer of 1989 as I mulled over retiring—again. But by the fourth week of golfing with my retired friends, it got boring. I got restless. As I later told writer Bob Allen, "I thought I might as well ride the wave as long as I can because it does knock you off at some point."

I put the word out to my longtime friend Joe Smith, then president of EMI–North America in L.A., that I might be interested in making a deal to sell Universal and bring over some of its acts as a way of getting me to come fix a label that needed it. Thus began four months of negotiations through the fall of 1989, during which time Ginger and I essentially camped out at the Westwood Marquis Hotel in L.A. and I got to play golf with all my old L.A. golfing buddies. Finally I decided the best place was Capitol-Nashville, where I took over in December 1989.

I would soon have my hands full. The label's hottest new act had a song off his debut album just hitting No. 1 as I took over. The artist was that soft-spoken, but fiercely determined kid Tony and I had auditioned—and passed on—a year or so earlier in my living room. The hit record sounded familiar to me. It was titled "If Tomorrow Never Comes." The artist was Garth Brooks.

For Capitol—and for Nashville—tomorrow had just arrived.

TWENTY-ONE

WITH THE MOVE to Capitol-Nashville, my career had come full circle in a sense.

The man who hired me to fix his failing division was Joe Smith, head of Capitol/EMI. Joe and I went all the way back to the late fifties, when I was a Rhythm Orchid and he worked in radio. Then we worked together at Warner Brothers in the sixties.

Now, thirty years later, Joe was paying me megabucks to acquire some of the artists I had signed at Universal and a solid six-figure base salary to rebuild Capitol. "This is good, overall, for everybody," I told the local paper my first day on the job. "In six or seven months Capitol will be looked at as a major label."

In six or seven months Capitol would have a monster bigger than anything anyone had ever seen on Music Row.

Joe and I barely needed an hour to reach a basic agreement when we met at his L.A. home. I told him I could turn the label into a $50- to $60-million-a-year business within five years, with a 10 to 15 percent bottom-line profit. Capitol would pay in the millions for Universal, with my split in the seven-figure range.

I demanded complete autonomy in creating a label, not a division. I wanted control over budgets, and our own sales and marketing and A&R departments. I couldn't be hamstrung by corporate bean counters on the coasts. Joe agreed.

The roster doubled in size to fifty-eight acts, Nashville's largest—if not its best. We had a lot of midlevel and aging artists selling in the 150,000 range. I had to drop three dozen acts, and decided to ease them out over a couple of years to avoid a blood-bath. I was letting some record-label people go for the second and third times. It was déjà vu for Jim Foglesong, who I was re-placing again, having done it at MCA. Jim was gracious, telling the press, "It's a sad day. These things always are. I don't think there's anything personal between me and Jimmy. It's just the way things worked out."

I wanted a staff with a proud, kick-butt attitude. There's a negativity that comes with being a perennial loser. Too many em-ployees on Music Row never believed their divisions could be prominent and have impact. They bought the L.A. and New York rap—that they were poor distant cousins for whom the big-city majors didn't give a damn. That can crush morale. It wasn't the kind of energy I needed around me.

One of my tougher firings was Lynn Shults, the A&R man who saw Garth sing at the Bluebird Cafe and signed him. Lynn had finally struck the mother lode. But when I looked at him next to James Stroud, a sessions drummer, up-and-coming pro-ducer, and my head A&R man at Universal, there was no ques-tion, and I hired Stroud. (James has gone on to run Geffen's Giant Records and produce a half-dozen superstars, including Tracy Lawrence, Tim McGraw, and John Anderson.)

Still, I paid a price. The downside wasn't about hiring Stroud; it was about dumping the hero who had landed Garth. It was an unpopular move that made me enemies all over town—starting with Garth. But early on in Nashville I asked myself a big ques-tion: Which do you want to be—successful or popular? Build a winner or be a good ol' boy everyone on the Row loves? I decided I'd rather win at the bottom-line than on the popularity polls.

But I felt Lynn, a smart man, understood. Still, the label never did anything for him—and he didn't have any points for artist signings. So, in Garth's second year I offered Lynn, then working at *Billboard*, a forty-thousand-dollar-a-year deal as an independent talent scout. I didn't owe him a reward for Garth, but the label did.

For reasons never made known to me Lynn turned it down.

The roster had some wonderful artists who sold terribly. We had Anne Murray, a former franchise artist who hadn't had a Top 10 hit in four years and whose album sales had dropped to around 150,000 units; Barbara Mandrell, who I'd let go from MCA, was holding on at 50,000. Dan Seals, a wonderful songwriter, had had nine or ten No. 1s but didn't sell more than 200,000 albums. We had a talented, eclectic singer named Suzy Bogguss, who was being recorded all wrong. Only one single had made Top 20; radio was all but ignoring her.

And somewhere on that list of fifty-eight acts was a keeper named Garth Brooks.

I discovered something interesting about Garth's breakout: four times more money had been spent getting Anne Murray's current album to 200,000 than on Garth Brooks's 200,000. By the end of 1989 the label's funds for marketing and co-op advertising—the money that buys you choice in-store "real estate"— were depleted until the next fiscal year began, on April 1, 1990.

It was clear Garth was the best investment I could make.

I had an early talk with his producer, Allen Reynolds, who wanted to play me Garth's entire album and talk over singles. I had a great digital playback system in the back of my car, so I rode around with Allen between a couple of meetings.

Garth's next single was "Not Counting You," due for release in late January. When Allen played me "The Dance," I turned to him and said, "Promotion'll hate that one. It's a slow ballad and it's not very country."

"Trust me," he said. "It's a monster. It's a career record. This kid is just incredible. Just go see him, please."

Garth was on a bill with the Statler Brothers and Suzy Bogguss in some small town in Tennessee. I felt young again among all the elderly "blue hairs" who'd come to see the Statlers.

Suzy opened and sang some real bad material with her real good voice. I felt confident she had a future. Then Garth came out. Onstage Garth's eyes got so wide and fiery, you could tell what color they were from twenty rows back. He looks out over four hundred people in one area of the crowd, and every person thinks he's making eye contact with him or her. He performed magic out there.

Garth was backed by Stillwater, the campus band from his days at Oklahoma State University. In a half hour he took that godawful gym full of senior citizens and wrapped them around his finger. Garth jumped off the low stage, grabbed a baby out of its mother's arms, and cradled it while singing "If Tomorrow Never Comes." There wasn't a dry eye in the hall. I turned to Ginger: "He is going to be the biggest ever."

Incredibly the old-timers got up out of their folding chairs and gave Garth a standing ovation—from the center of the hall to the back and front. When the record company puts people in front and *they* stand up to hype the act, everyone else has to rise just to see the stage, so it *becomes* a standing ovation. But this started from the middle and swept to the back. It was for real.

I went backstage and congratulated Garth on a terrific show and told him to get in touch with me the next day. I walked over to Garth's managers, Bob Doyle and Pam Lewis, and said, "You lucky bastards. The kid will be a monster."

The next morning I called in my VPs and department heads and announced, "We've got the franchise. Garth Brooks. From now on, eighty percent of every dollar, fifty minutes of every hour I want spent on, devoted to, Garth Brooks until I tell you differently."

Any record chief who'd gone and seen Elvis or the Beatles would have done the same. Garth's power over his audience was mesmerizing.

Garth never liked me from the start. We were like two stallions in a pen. He didn't like that, because once he got going, he had yes-people everywhere else in his life and absolute control over everything. He was always polite, cordial—but I felt it was phony. We just got off to a rocky start.

I had passed on him, for one thing, which caused resentment and bitterness that never went away. Garth has tremendous pride and drive, and he could get surly and bristly around me because of that lingering hurt.

Firing Lynn Shults didn't help. Lynn *believed in* Garth from the moment he heard him showcase at the Bluebird in May 1988, and fought long and hard to sign him. There was also the issue of independent promotion. Garth had hired outside promotion to work his first singles and was adamant about keeping them on. But that irritates the label's promotion department. They feel a loss of control and worry that it sends a message down the roster that the promotion team's no good.

It can also be chaotic. If you need twelve stations added to keep your single's bullet on the charts, and the indies work the wrong stations, you could lose your bullet. It drove my VP crazy to have to deal with indies he couldn't control. They often do more harm than good.

I held a meeting at my house about promotion with Garth; his wife, Sandy; Bob and Pam; and my VP of promotion, Bill Catino. At one point Bob Doyle hinted that we hadn't spent enough on promotion and marketing. "Bob," I said, "we've already spent a million, we're doin' it." And Garth, sitting opposite me at a long table, snapped, "Yeah, but you're *makin'* a lot of money, too, aren't you?" It was never good between us.

When we discussed using indies, Garth got up, circled the table silently, getting real intense. "Trust is on a bus," he said, "down the road a few hundred miles, but it ain't got here yet." Garth didn't trust me to look after *his* needs: "They're part of my team, my team's working and they're staying in place."

Garth had also bought into a rumor that I had tried to have Bob and Pam fired, which wasn't true. And I felt it irked Garth that I passed on a close friend of his, Trisha Yearwood, when Pam and Bob brought me tapes of what later became her debut album. They might have figured it would be easier to get her signed to Garth's label, given his new clout.

Garth Fundis had produced Trisha's first record and she had sung some nice harmonies on Garth's second album. Being almost Capitol "family," Pam and Bob wanted me to sign her. I liked what I heard, and it was clear Trisha could sing. But the timing was off.

I had just had a series of talks with Suzy Bogguss about switching producers, becoming less eclectic, zeroing in on the country marketplace. Suzy then fired her band, got a new producer, made a whole lifestyle change, and went in to record a new album, *Moment of Truth*. It was a huge commitment she and I had made to each other to break her wide open. I believed she had superstar potential. And our roster was already enormous.

I passed on Trisha. It's in the nature of our business that label heads pass on artists who go on to sell millions of records elsewhere. Record people passed on the Beatles, film studios passed on *E.T.* But the Garth Brooks camp took my pass as an insult: *How could he not sign someone Garth believes in?*

I didn't regret passing on Trisha. I'm delighted she's gone on to sell platinum for Tony at MCA. If you lived your life full of regrets, you'd be too afraid to drop anyone or sign anyone. Every move's a gamble. Some people take it too personally.

Pam and Bob should have been glad Trisha wound up at MCA, probably a better choice for her. But the more cynical story making the rounds was that it was Trisha who passed on Capitol because, for one thing, she didn't want her deal to look like a favor to Garth and, second, that, as one author of a book about Trisha put it, she was afraid that if I signed her, I'd then "pressure her" to record with me. Not true.

From day one there was more wariness than warmth between Garth and me. I wasn't among the faithful who had believed in him from the beginning. Our egos started buttin' up against each other. I was the hotshot label chief–producer who mouthed off, shook things up, sold millions of records, and made enemies. He was the new kid climbing to the top of the heap, gunning to be bigger than everyone—and looking to knock me down a notch or two.

I called a meeting with Garth and decided to be real straight with him. "I've listened to your album," I said, "and I frankly don't feel it's up to the standards, technically, of your competition. Allen is a good man, and when it works with him, he is a terrific producer. But he owns his own studio and cuts a certain old-fashioned way, which worked with Crystal Gayle and others. But it's not gonna work with you. More money has to be spent, and your tracks have to be mixed for the modern world." Garth, as always, listened politely, intently. "The other thing," I went on. "I've seen you in person. Onstage you're this vibrant, electrifying presence, and that's not in the album." I had told Allen Reynolds the same things.

"That's on purpose," he said. "I feel the album and the show have to be two different things."

"No, no, no. If *you* knock me out in person and then I go spend fifteen dollars and that CD doesn't, then the hell with you, I ain't buyin' any more of your records, ya dig? Be consistent. Knock 'em out in person, make an album that'll let 'em relive that experience."

He nodded earnestly. It was the only serious advice I offered at the outset. Back then Garth was still open to hearing the truth. Five years of adulation, success, money, and yessing later and he couldn't handle it the same way.

There were rumors for years all over Music Row that I'd tried to split Garth and Allen and take over producing Garth. Not true. Why break up a winning combination? I absolutely wanted Garth to max out, and, true, I'd like to be sitting on Allen's $15 million to $20 million in royalties today. Who wouldn't? But it might not have worked as well with me anyway.

Garth's album and all Capitol-Nashville product was selling for a dollar less than pop product. The previous regime didn't believe that country was worth the same price as pop and must have figured that with no more ad dollars to spend, sales had peaked. But the Franchise was killin' 'em on the road. It would be a disaster to lose that momentum because there was no product in the racks. That's what happens when a record label is deteriorating. I had to go after that record.

Knowing I had no more advertising money coming in until April, I raised Garth's cassette and CD prices one dollar to match the market. I also needed to buy aggressive pricing and position from retailers. We went to our rack-jobbers—our wholesale distributors—and spelled it out: "This kid's gonna be *such* a monster and I believe in this record so much that I'll give you a 15 percent discount, with a 10 percent advertising budget, and I want you to take twenty thousand for your Tower chain." To Handleman, the biggest rack-jobber: "I want you to take 100,000 and spread them across this country in your KMarts, Wal-Marts, whatever."

It worked. By giving wholesalers a discount and a wider profit margin, and retailers an extra dollar, both were more willing to lay the LP out to the public.

The adrenaline was pumping. With this high-stakes campaign taking shape, I hired Joe Mansfield to be my VP for sales and marketing in the spring of 1990. New budgets were nearly in place, so I was ready to put some money behind our marketing muscle.

Joe came from EMI's CEMA Distribution unit in L.A. CEMA developed marketing strategies, manufacturing, and distribution and had a dozen U.S. sales offices for all the labels. Joe was the right guy at the right time, the one the labels funneled all their co-op ad dollars through. No other label in town had an in-house top-level business guy like Mansfield who could make deals himself, but instead had third-tier types who had to go to L.A. or New York to get a green light on a deal.

I told Joe, "I've just heard half of Garth's next album, *No Fences*, and it's incredible." Actually I'd heard two cuts, but I didn't care. "It's platinum or double platinum. I want you to buy me every piece of shelf space that you can for this fall. If retail wants the money now, give it to 'em. I want that space."

More than committing money to Garth, I knew Joe's effort would create a buzz in the industry, at ratio and retail. It wasn't so much hype as a mood of intense anticipation. When a major label explodes with a new act, it's expected. When a perennial loser does, it's dramatic, it's news—and you run with it.

I called Garth and his management team to be there when I hired L.A.'s savvy Brokaw Company—the brothers Sandy and David—to help spin the label's new image. I wanted Garth on national television and I made sure Garth knew he was the label's top priority. "I want people to see those eyes," I told the Brokaws, "and discover how incredible this kid is."

The Brokaws got Garth on *Night of 1000 Stars* at Radio City

Music Hall in New York. They got him on some telethons. Garth played the West Coast, did fairs with Reba McEntire, joined the A-list roster at Willie Nelson's Farm Aid IV in April. I got press. The label got local press. Things started rolling.

Garth's next single, "Not Counting You," was a light, up-tempo number that I felt sounded better live than on radio, but it got to No. 2 on *Billboard*'s country singles chart and kept the momentum going. By then I'd decided that "The Dance" would be the fourth single. My promotion people resisted, fearing radio would never play it. My reaction was "That's your problem. I don't give a shit. Ballads touch people and become the career records. Get it played." Allen was right. It would be a monster.

A sideshow to the Garth buzz was fierce competition shaping up with RCA's Clint Black. Their debut LPs charted the same week in the spring of 1989, but Clint got the big jump with an incredible four straight No. 1s—including "Better Man" and "Killin' Time."

I thought Clint's *Killin' Time* LP was terrific. He was a good-looking singer-songwriter who had been playing around Houston and who sounded like a young Haggard. Their battle of the "hat acts" was great for Nashville—especially after both Garth and Clint were nominated head-to-head for a few categories at the upcoming Academy of Country Music Awards in late April.

It was evident that no one marketed Garth better than Garth himself. One key performance that helped break Garth was at the annual Country Radio Seminar, a big week-long schmooze for radio people and artists. Garth and Clint were too established for the New Faces showcase during CRS, but Pam Lewis and Bob Doyle prevailed upon ASCAP executive Merlin Littlefield to let Garth play one number at ASCAP's luncheon, a key CRS event each year. Garth had gotten in to see Littlefield on his first visit to Nashville in 1985—a year after graduating Oklahoma State. He was still living in Stillwater, where he had been playing campus hangouts and working as a bouncer. (He met his future wife, Sandy Mahl, when he broke up a catfight in the ladies room and offered to escort her home.)

While Littlefield told Garth all about Nashville's legendary starving songwriters, one of them showed up and told Merlin he couldn't pay off a $500 loan. Garth was stunned and told Littlefield, "Geez, I make that back home."

To which Littlefield answered, "Well, if that's true, then you're better off goin' home." Garth lasted less than twenty-four hours that time around. He wasn't ready for Nashville.

Nashville was ready for him now. Garth did "The Dance" and "Friends in Low Places," from his upcoming LP. He killed the radio people. It was as good as having 150 stations locked up for both singles before we even shipped to radio.

We were all disappointed when the ACMs didn't go Garth's way—though I honestly never paid much attention to awards and reviews unless it was good news. Up for three awards, he went home empty-handed and, worse, lost out to Clint in two categories. Clint definitely walked off the winner: his four awards were the most ever for a newcomer.

I explained to Garth that to be—and to remain—a superstar he needed more than trophies; he needed one LP each fall. That was how he'd keep the excitement rolling, not by waiting two years for a follow-up, which is what Clint did.

In May we released "The Dance" and got Garth's video all over TNN and CMT to push the record. In June he caused a mob scene at Fan Fair, where he performed a couple of songs before I presented him with a gold record for *Garth Brooks*. In July "The Dance" went to No. 1 and stayed there three weeks. By then Clint's album was way out ahead of Garth's—about 1.6 million to 800,000. But Garth was gaining fast—and Clint didn't have another album ready.

A month later we shipped "Friends in Low Places" to radio, and *No Fences* to retail. It was a fabulous album—a big jump beyond the first one in capturing the intense emotion, heart, and soul of Garth's concert. He kicked ass on "Friends" and the up-tempo numbers and he had some beautiful, soulful ballads.

Garth had accomplished much of our promotion goals by performing "Friends" at CRS. Joe Mansfield had locked up price, position, and shelf space at retail. Records started flying out of stores with startling velocity.

"Friends" was a killer record in every way, a national anthem for underdogs. Kids clear down to grade school were singing it. He showcased it for a network TV audience during the CMA Awards, an awful piece of staging despite a special stage set for a saloon and cocktail party and live actors milling about onstage as Garth sang in his tux. I felt the actors distracted viewers from Garth. Part of the problem was that the show's producer, Irving Waugh, in my opinion was a control freak with dated ideas. Still, "Friends" became one of the giant career records of all time. It reached No. 1 and stayed there for four weeks. Garth then won the CMA's Horizon Award and Best Video for "The Dance."

We were seeing sales spikes on our printouts that made us gasp. It was *unreal*. It once took an artist months, even years, to go gold. Platinum might be a career's worth of records. *Garth Brooks* had just gone platinum. Now *No Fences* went from gold to platinum almost instantaneously—a little more than a month after being shipped. We had projected sales of 500,000 by Christmas—and were already at *2 million*.

In the spring of 1991 Mansfield walked into my office holding some sales reports and announced, "We're at four million on *Fences*. It's unbelievable. It's gonna hit ten million."

"Sit down," I said. "From your lips to God's ears, now, *what* was that you said—and why?"

"That's right. Ten million." Joe had analyzed the flow-throughs and sell-throughs and saw that the album was still gaining speed. "Well," I said, "we'll just ride this baby as long and as hard as we can. We got us a gusher here."

TWENTY-TWO

AT THE END OF 1990, seeing that Garth's first two albums were both headed to multiplatinum status, I initiated discussions to give him a new contract to replace his "beginning artist" Capitol deal that gave him a 10 or 11 percent participation "all in." An "all in" deal includes the producer's percentage, so if Allen had 3 percent and Garth had 7 or 8, our total payout would be 10 or 11 percent. That was simply too low, unfair, and no longer fit where his sales were.

The new deal bumped him to a more respectable 15 percent range (all in)—with some escalations beyond that based on sales.

It was a realistic deal that made Garth happy. He took out a full-page ad in *Billboard* in December that showed him bug-eyed with his jaw dropping as he read the contract. The ad read, "Whoa . . . !!! What a contract! Capitol-Nashville, you are an answered prayer. I love you." ("Unanswered Prayers" was a No. 1 hit off *No Fences*.)

Garth was still gaining momentum. In April 1991 he swept the Academy of Country Music Awards, winning for Best Single, Album, Video, Song, Entertainer, and Male Vocalist. A few days later we stumbled upon a new marketing ploy that would send album sales into the stratosphere: controversy.

Garth's video for "The Thunder Rolls" had some people at the label worried. They anticipated trouble. It was a dark, dramatic (and, at $100,000, expensive) clip about domestic violence that ends when a wife shoots her abusive husband in front of their daughter on a stormy night. Garth wore a beard and played the evil husband. He wanted to push some buttons.

First time I watched it, I never imagined it would make heavy rotation on country cable. Second time, a light went off in my head: This is *perfect*. If it gets banned, the son of a bitch'll be a household name across America within three weeks.

Country Music Television aired the video as its pick of the week, but its board of directors decided to pull it. Instead of risking charges of blatant censorship, they cited a so-called deluge of call-ins and letters from outraged viewers. I happened to *know*, however, from one of our insiders who worked there, that they did not have one call or letter. CMT then claimed it would air the video only if Garth tacked on a disclaimer saying that violence is not a solution. Garth taped it—then agonized over adding it. His instincts were to refuse. He asked my opinion.

"It's a great piece of work," I said. "Why would you do a disclaimer?" When Garth refused, both cable channels formally banned it and all hell broke loose. "Thunder" became a major national news story about censorship and it fueled the public debate about domestic violence. I hired extra press people to spin the controversy in our favor. I told them to pitch TV news and print pieces on the issue of censorship; I told them to contact women's groups in every city with more than 50,000 people and relate the video to domestic-violence issues. Local and network stations aired excerpts with every story. Major magazines ran pieces. Radio stations wanted to play the song and draw attention to the video. Tower Records in Nashville played the video for hours on end after the ban. VH-1 aired the video on their country show. The ban was a hot topic on talk radio. The National Organization for Women and other women's and domestic-abuse groups voiced support. At least one NOW branch, while not condoning murder, used the video as a training film to get the message out that abused women could fight back.

It had played perfectly and got us a massive windfall of exposure. The record exploded off radio, album sales shot up, and "Thunder" became *Fences*'s fourth straight No. 1 hit.

It wasn't until *Billboard* went over to the computerized SoundScan system to measure real point-of-sale numbers that America and the record business in L.A. and New York knew just *how* huge Garth was. Ranking records had gone from reading tea leaves to bar-code scanners. There was no more guesswork—and no more discrimination against hillbilly records, which we knew were flying out of the stores.

The immediate effect was that major country acts' records

jumped upward on the Top 200 pop album charts. *No Fences* went from No. 16 to No. 4 in one week. SoundScan proved what we already knew in Nashville: Country had arrived.

The numbers were startling: While only sixteen country albums went gold in 1985, more than thirty-five had gone platinum in 1991. In the same time frame TNN had exploded from 7 million subscribers to more than 50 million and the number of country radio stations had shot to some 2,500.

This wasn't about crossing over, but rather bringing sound (and video) quality and mass merchandising to modern country. And letting the music take care of the rest. This was the crusade I'd been on for years.

By end of summer the timing was perfect for us to come with Garth's third album, *Ropin' the Wind.* I decided to raise the price of the product one dollar. Advance orders were up to an astounding 1 million units; it was the first country album in history to *enter Billboard's* Top 200 at No. 1, selling hundreds of thousands of copies a week through the fall, pushed by the radio hits "Rodeo" and "Shameless."

Garth's amazing two-year rise culminated in his winning four major CMA awards in October 1991, including Entertainer of the Year and—naturally—Best Video, for "Thunder Rolls." By the end of the month *No Fences* had become the first country album ever to reach 5 million sales. According to one report, Garth was accounting for 85 percent of our label's albums that year—and more than a quarter of all country albums.

I was feeling uneasy about the way Garth was handling it all. A year after his "Whoa . . . !!! What a contract!" valentine, Garth decided to push me for another new contract. The prior deal had doubled his back-end points, but now he felt the numbers on *No Fences* and *Ropin'* warranted a new deal.

Garth and his team came to my office at the label. (I had changed the name from Capitol to Liberty to emphasize our autonomy.) We were leasing the eleventh floor of a modern building on West End Avenue a few miles from Music Row. Garth's people had begun to refer to 3322 West End Avenue as "The House That Garth Built," even though some church owned the building and we only leased space there for about $250,000 a year. It was just another way of stirring him up.

My first response was to laugh. "The last deal isn't even cold yet," I said. But they came back with "We're selling so many records, we feel we oughta be getting a bigger piece."

I told Joe Smith, my boss, that I was prepared to give him another deal that started at 21 percent and went to 25 percent. (Allen's producer's fee of, say, 4 percent, would be deducted from that.) This deal would probably have put him several points or so ahead of superstars like Reba and Strait.

As I figured it, a royalty point was worth $.08 per unit sold. A platinum record would be worth $80,000 per point. A superstar with a 20 percent deal (and 4 percent producer's fee) would generate $1.6 million on a million sales—$1.28 million for the artist, $320,000 for the producer.

Now, with Garth selling 5 million to 10 million albums, that deal could be worth well over $10 million. I was prepared to offer up to 25 percent royalty—an awfully rich deal for him.

But Garth wasn't interested in bettering just the top artists in country. His sights were set much higher: "I want the Michael Jackson deal," Garth said, referring to Jackson's then-recent multimedia joint venture with Sony with a supposed 30 percent royalty participation potentially worth hundreds of millions to Jackson.

Garth didn't want huge cash advances per album. He was after something even more precious to major pop stars: absolute, total creative control. He wanted equity, he wanted to own his own masters, an extremely rare situation very few artists ever enjoy, and he wanted to be able to release an album when he felt like it rather than be tied to one a year.

This was ironic: I had busted my butt for years to get Nashville artists to sell more albums and be more in charge of their music. Now I had the most commercial country act in history demanding an unprecedented degree of control. And I was telling him, "You're not Michael Jackson, the Beatles, or Elvis."

I explained how Jackson had been a worldwide superstar for twenty years. That's staying power. And he had one album, *Thriller,* sell 40 million units. Elvis and the Beatles profoundly changed the culture and the times they were in. "You don't deserve a Michael Jackson deal. When you do, if I'm still here, I'll give it to you. I'll give you a new deal, but not a joint venture."

This reality check turned Garth stone cold. He was seething. Fortunately he was at the office, so he couldn't explode. I didn't care. I had a company to run. I wasn't about to surrender ownership and control of the label's music. Labels only have two things of real value: their catalog, through ownership of their masters; and their contracts with artists. Everything else can be replaced. If they don't own the masters, they're doing distribution. Directors don't usually *own* their movies; the film studios do. Tom

Hanks doesn't own *Forrest Gump*. Similarly record labels never relinquish ownership of their masters.

EMI should have simply stonewalled Garth and sent him back to me. We still had him for another four or five albums; I'd have told him no again.

The catch of a joint venture was that Garth would get half the profits but bear none of the costs. A chunk of my profits were allocated to EMI's distribution and manufacturing units, separate profit centers. There was the expense of co-op advertising to retailers and discounts to wholesalers. If you don't pay for that retail real estate, some other label will. Therefore Garth would actually be getting the equivalent of between 55 and 58 percent of the Liberty pie after these label expenses against my upside.

It gets more intricate. To arrive at this so-called joint venture and, say, a 31 percent royalty figure, they used an *average* for advertising, marketing, and discounts that had derived from the huge numbers on *Fences* and *Ropin'* at a time when Garth's sales were maxing out. I still needed that money of course, but the *percentage* they came up with was way too low. As anyone in retail knows, the more you sell of something, your fixed dollar amount for marketing and advertising will drop as a *percentage*—simply because you're generating so much volume. And that figure starts looking *real* low when sales of new product start to dip.

Another sticky issue is that record labels are held hostage not just by radio but by retail. Rack-jobbers such as Handleman, which services K Mart and some Wal-Marts, have some 8,000 retail accounts. They're so powerful, they can beat you up for discounts and co-op advertising, which they have to do for their bottom line. I would also have to deduct any record returns, so I'd have been working off net rather than gross in figuring his back-end royalties.

If the deal is too strong for Garth, then where's the money going to come from to market him—especially if sales start to flatten out? Neither Garth nor EMI was thinking about that—but I damn sure was. With this kind of deal it would be hard to even make a profit. I wouldn't have the money to spend on marketing Garth's catalog properly, let alone develop my other artists.

And what if Garth stops *selling* 10 million every time out?

The eight-hundred-pound gorilla got mad, I got mad, and communication shut down. Everything I knew about the music business told me with absolute conviction this would be a bad deal. I wouldn't talk to Garth's handlers—Rusty Jones, a lawyer, and Kerry O'Neil, a CPA and sometime manager who managed

John Anderson when I signed John to MCA and then to Universal. Kerry was real abrasive and aggressive by Nashville's standards. Several of my VPs told me they'd rather see us drop Anderson than have to deal with Kerry. I found him to be a manipulative player who helped influence Garth's dark view of me and the label. I even felt at times that it was Kerry who was the power behind Garth.

My stance was clear: I don't need to negotiate, we have a deal in place from a year ago. Kerry's stance to Garth was: Bowen's your problem. Garth seemed at that unfortunate point in a superstar's career where he wanted to just kill any messenger with bad news instead of seeing if he could learn anything from it.

In early 1992 I made a move of my own. I put the word out that I'd consider leaving to run one more label. In my heart I knew it would be my last deal before retiring. I was in my mid-fifties, and if the thrill wasn't *gone*, it was starting a quick fadeout.

I was in my final year of my three-year contract. It was as good a time for me to be in play as it was for Garth. Garth's success had allowed me to steer Liberty through an astounding comeback. Most labels operate on a 5 to 8 percent return on sales. My first year we gave corporate a 14 percent return on their money; the next year it nearly doubled to more than 25 percent, with *No Fences* and *Ropin'* counting for some 60 percent of our album revenue. But we also enjoyed solid sales from promising artists like Suzy Bogguss, Billy Dean, the Pirates of the Mississippi, and our label catalog.

And that was with a staff that more than doubled from twenty-nine to sixty-three employees to handle "the GB situation." Suddenly Liberty was the hot label in town. To keep my rivals from stealing the key people at the label who were part of the most explosive commercial success in Nashville history, I gave some high-level executives expensive three-year deals to lock them down.

With gross sales soaring from $48 million my first year to $90-plus million in 1991, and then $130 million or so, we absorbed the heavier overhead and still sent plenty of profit to corporate.

The downside was that it soon became difficult to break *other* acts when all anyone wanted was Garth. I had so little sway over Garth that I couldn't trade access to Garth for press on, say, Billy Dean or Suzy. Working Garth was equal to six platinum acts at the same time. And again, what if Garth's sales started to drop?

To stir things up, I floated a rumor on the street that I was in secret negotiations with PolyGram—and damn if they didn't call me to make sure that I was. One reason to consider leaving was that my own bargaining stance was strengthened by Garth's numbers; another was simply to get out from under the gorilla. I had also been producing Suzy Bogguss and got a breakthrough hit with "Someday Soon," followed by her first Top 10s, "Southbound Plane," "Aces," and John Hiatt's "Drive South" in 1992. But I was fairly burned out in the studio with all the focus on Garth. I asked Joe Smith to make me an offer to stay at Liberty and he said EMI's best offer would be $500,000 a year for three years.

It seemed that PolyGram was the obvious place to move to. I heard from their VP for acquisitions in North America, Eric Kronfeld, whom I'd known for years and who had once been my lawyer. He made it clear he wanted me; I told him I was listening if he could make it attractive. My Capitol salary had bumped to about $300,000 by then—plus a 50 percent bonus—but I could still expect millions more in royalties from my big album sellers. This wasn't about salary per se; it was about making a strong deal and fixing one more label.

Kronfeld made me a compelling offer: a $500,000 salary, another $500,000 if I made my numbers, and my own half-stake in a PolyGram publishing company.

One key in the mix was my long-range vision for the emerging Contemporary Christian market. I wanted to get in on that action and create a new Christian division. There seemed to be a huge upside in the Christian market if it was marketed right. I didn't get the impression at my lunch meeting in New York with Eric and his boss, Alain Levy, head of PolyGram-Worldwide's office in France, that these two Jewish businessmen were hooked by my pitch on trends in "white gospel," or Christian music.

I decided to turn PolyGram down. But then my lawyer, John Mason, urged me to demand $750,000—plus some sweeteners— to see how serious they were. He told me he'd get back to me— and I went off to play some golf.

John called the cell phone in my golf cart. "I've been thinking it over and you don't need seven-fifty. You need to have a million." I laughed. "Hold on. I'm making a putt." I didn't want to blow a putt for par over a million bucks. Then I got back on. "Okay, see what you can get, whatever." It was wild: $1 million to run a hillbilly division. Times sure had changed.

PolyGram didn't flinch: $1 million in salary with a guaranteed $500,000 bonus (or 10 percent of net profit, whichever was higher); a $250,000 signing bonus; 50 percent of a joint-venture publishing company; a low-interest $1.5 million loan; and a 25 percent stake as CEO of a new PolyGram Christian label. By this time Jim Fifield knew I was talking to PolyGram, so Mason started negotiating with both labels.

It was true PolyGram's offer took my breath away. But there was a more sobering explanation for why I was in fact having trouble breathing. I learned that I had polyps in my sinuses and needed surgery.

In early April, as I was about to leave for Hawaii to recover from surgery at the Mayo Clinic, Fifield called. "Hey, I'm not gonna lose you," he said.

"Well, you *can* make me stay the year," I answered.

"I don't believe that," he said. "You aren't leaving me. What do I have to do to keep you from leaving?"

"Well, then, it's real simple. Call my lawyer and match or beat that other offer."

I spent a month recuperating in Hawaii. Mercury Records, PolyGram's Nashville label, had released Billy Ray Cyrus's "Achy Breaky Heart." Pretty soon that little ditty was going to make Mercury *the* hot label in town.

Mason, a bulldog of a lawyer, wrangled my deal out of EMI. While I was in Maui, Fifield pulled out all the big guns. He had Charles Koppelman call me to express his desire that I stay on. Charles was then president of SBK Records, a joint venture with EMI, and had enjoyed great, if fleeting, success with Vanilla Ice and Wilson Phillips. EMI had purchased Charles's publishing company for something like $300 million, and he was rumored to be heir apparent to my boss, Joe Smith. Jim also had Sir Colin Southgate, the head of England's Thorn Industries, call me at six A.M. in Hawaii and say, "I hope I haven't woke you. We just want you to know we want you to stay."

There were some negatives about staying. One was Garth. I saw where he was headed emotionally and didn't like it. One close friend of mine said Garth was turning into the Antichrist and that before long, people would be tossing rose petals before him as he walked by. But I looked at Mercury and saw another negative: Billy Ray Cyrus—a Roman candle that would likely flare and burn out after his one giant CD.

And there was Koppelman, the man I'd be reporting to once Joe Smith retired a few months down the road. Fifield was a music junkie, but he didn't know much about it. He was a hardball numbers-and-business guy. He was fascinated by Koppelman's elegance, wealth, the way he schmoozed artists and flew private jets. But Koppelman's a publisher; I'm a record guy. Sheep and cattle. Again, natural enemies. And New Yorkers all look down on Nashville and think, *Hee-haw.*

I decided to stay at Liberty. They offered me a five-year deal that would run out at the end of 1997—right at my sixtieth birthday. Mason had put together an extraordinary package that guaranteed me not only millions in salary, bonuses, music-publishing interests, and other perks, but also a Christian-music deal potentially worth tens of millions of dollars through the life of the contract.

As I told Mason, "This is an incredible deal!"

And he structured it so that he didn't have to collect his fees from me.

The clincher was the Christian deal. Fifield's brother is a deacon in an important Baptist church in Houston. When Fifield came to see me at my house, his brother joined us to hear my pitch on Contemporary Christian. I did ten minutes for Jim, his brother did thirty, and that sold Fifield for me. So Jim bought the gospel according to Bowen—and I stayed with Liberty.

My positive feeling about Fifield was a key in staying. I didn't like the PolyGram chief in my one meeting. One company was owned by the Dutch, the other by the Brits. At the end of the day it's all the same corporate number-crunching shit on a whole other continent. It comes down to this: one guy'll stick the knife in a little; the other guy'll try to go clear to the bone. But I could relate to Jim better—and knew that his word was good.

This was the first deal I had ever made based more on money than on music, and I sensed from the day I put my name on it that I would regret it. Creatively I knew it was time to get out. If building turned me on, maintaining was boring. Massaging numbers so that the accountants can make the stockholders happy was boring. But they romanced me and made the deal so big I had to stay.

When Garth went to the NARM convention in spring, Joe Smith was there and got to wrap his arm around Garth and pose for a bunch of trade-paper photo ops. Joe liked that. So did Garth. That's when Garth made his move: he went over my head and told Joe, the head of EMI–North America, "I can't make a deal with Bowen. Bowen's not taking care of me properly."

Joe's reply was a big mistake: "Try to work it out with Bowen, but if you can't, give me a call and we'll sit down and see if we can make you happy." I never felt Joe was out to betray or undermine me, just trying to make everything come out cool.

But it wasn't cool: once an artist can go over your head, you're powerless from that day forward.

Garth made sure he met with Fifield, Joe Smith's boss, because he was smart enough to know it was Fifield, not Joe, who could really say yes or no to the deal Garth wanted. After a meeting with Garth, Fifield called to tell me, "I worked it out with the kid." He felt good about it.

Garth had by now become such a control freak, he spent much of 1992 negotiating his own deal. While he was in negotiations, Garth came in to see me. Despite everything, we still shared an unusual connection: Garth could still talk things out with me, and with so much insulation and rumor around him, it still mattered to the kid that I get things firsthand from him. And he still appreciated my views and advice—despite the deepening antagonism between him and the label that was being fueled by his handlers. He had had a bad reaction to the New York corporate lawyer Fifield had sent down to negotiate with Garth, who by now was running all his business meetings himself. The lawyer had pissed him off royally, he said. That didn't surprise me. Folks in Nashville generally assumed New York lawyers were coming down there to screw them somehow. I figured this lawyer had played typical hardball games, which you can play with other lawyers but not with an artist like Garth.

"I know what Fifield's up to," he said angrily. "He agreed to a joint venture, but now they're trying to take it all back. I'm gonna stick it to him."

I sensed that, unlike Elvis or the Beatles, who both went to drugs, Garth's "drug" was power, which can be worse. Garth is real bright, but he was beginning to slip into the bubble, being fed only the information he wanted to hear.

As power plays go, Garth's worked as well as any ever has. He stuck it to them—big time. It ended months of distracting negotiations for Garth; for EMI, the fiscal year-end was approaching and they needed the billings with his new deal. Something for everyone!

It was an incredible play that gave Garth absolute "final cut" control of the product. He pays for it himself—cover, sessions, everything. No advance, no recoupment. Garth hands it over for release is all. Garth was also free not to record for as long as he liked. He could take five years to release a record. He gets control of his masters twenty years down the road—when he could sell or lease them to anyone he wanted.

It was a deal I would have never given Garth.

No matter what else was going on, I could always be straight with Garth as an artist. He still valued—and trusted—my perspective. I told him at one point I thought the deal would prove as bad for him as for us. Bright as he was, he didn't seem to grasp the big picture—how profits from Capitol superstars like the Beatles, Glen Campbell, Steve Miller, Bob Seger, and Anne Murray got Garth Brooks's career off the ground. Money doesn't drop from the sky. This year's profits go into next year's A&R; that's what grows and sustains a roster. It was all part of one great food chain.

My remarks only seemed to irritate him. The welfare and future of Liberty was not a subject he was eager to grasp. With his new deal, Garth would have the size and muscle to disturb the label's ecology. Like a giant bear in the woods, wherever he'd step, something underfoot would die.

I didn't want it to be my label. But I could already feel tremors in the House That Garth Built. It was obvious that the people who gave him his big new deal didn't know any more about the business than he did.

TWENTY-THREE

Y THE TIME *The Chase* came out in late summer 1993, Joe Mansfield's contract as my VP for sales and marketing had come up for renewal. We met to iron out some problems.

I'd hired Joe in the spring of 1990. In his first year he did one very smart thing for himself: he shrewdly positioned himself as Garth's Mr. Inside—the in-house genius behind Garth's takeoff.

Joe was an old pro. He knew the game as well as anyone. He worked the phones constantly, pumped the GB camp with numbers, projections, and hype. But in maneuvering himself between Garth and my other VPs, he was causing dissension among my staff.

Joe was without question an overall asset. But the truth was Joe didn't spend one dollar without my approval—and I found myself giving him direction half the time on things he did. Joe also needed to be more of a team player. He'd come to meetings late, he was aloof and did as he pleased. And he had a way of taking credit for our success without citing the contributions and hard work of other key executives. At one meeting I held up a *Billboard* where he had made some self-serving claims. "You ain't the only one here," I said. "You're making people not like you. This isn't a Garth Brooks company. It's got to be a real company."

I offered Joe a one-year renewal with a two-year option with a nominal bump in salary—provided he get his act together. He came in the next day and told me, "I can't accept your offer."

"Well, fine, good luck, you've done a fine job." I replaced Joe with Bob Freese from Minneapolis, a good, solid hardworking kid.

The Chase and Garth's *Beyond the Season* Christmas album were set for a late-September release. Garth insisted on leading off with the single "We Shall Be Free." Garth had gone out to L.A. after the riots and given a benefit concert that raised $1 million for an inner-city rebuilding project. His fine humanitarian effort inspired him to write the song, a life-affirming work very close to his heart.

But there was one problem with the song as a single: to radio it wasn't country. Stations played it for six or eight weeks and dumped it. They expected Garth to remain loyal to his roots; going pop felt like a betrayal to radio. "Free" also showed Garth had evolved from having friends in low places to preaching on how to save the world. For Garth a No. 12 record is a stiff—the only Garth A-side single out of fifteen that hadn't made Top 10. To me it sounded like warmed-over protest music from the late sixties and early seventies.

People tried to make him understand it wasn't the time in the world to be putting out a "We Shall Be Free." It might have been too liberal for country's demographics, or too simplistic and idealistic for America after the social and racial upheaval of the riots. As a song it didn't hold up against his best work.

By the time "Free" faded, I had already shipped 3 million *Chase* units and had 2 million reorders. Once I heard the entire album, I started backing sales down as much as I could. It makes great trade copy when you "ship triple platinum"; you don't hear about the double-platinum returns. I backed off from giving 600,000 more to Wal-Mart and K Mart alone.

The impact of Garth's new deal was immediately felt at Liberty. With a normal superstar deal there would have been funds to develop the roster, operate the label properly, and still return 10 percent profit on corporate's money. But this so-called joint venture caused no fewer than ten acts to be dropped. Yet Garth was on a mission to change the way business was done, change the way artists get treated.

Also midrange acts like Billy Dean, Suzy, Tanya Tucker, and Chris Ledoux—acts that were almost there or, in Tanya's case, coming back big—suffered to an extent. With corporate understandably looking for a return on their money—and it had worked until then—Garth's extraordinary new deal didn't leave me enough cash to bring along all my other artists. There just wasn't enough to go around.

My payroll had doubled in three years and we still had all our contractual obligations from the large combined roster of 1989. As a result new acts weren't signed that should have been. Or they didn't want to sign with us and disappear in Garth's shadow. Others left before we could bring them along. Certainly no hat act would figure to have a prayer on Liberty. There were several acts we could not sign simply because we did not have the dollars—and I watched a couple of them become instant stars with No. 1 records. We had a shot at signing Clay Walker and didn't— and he had two No. 1s right away for Giant Records. Same with John Michael Montgomery, and he's become a superstar with Atlantic.

I would also have had more to spend on selling Garth's catalog while floating through the weak single and getting on to the next—making things look better.

EMI had its headaches. Capitol was having a terrible year in pop and rock, waiting for the Savior to bail 'em out. It's all about the billing game. The U.K. closes its half-year books on September 30th. That's when they report to their stockholders. So the word had gone out: Ship those records, we need the $30-some-odd million in billings to get on the books.

Though *The Chase* did take over No. 1 from *Some Gave All*, Billy Ray Cyrus's monster album, its sales flattened from the weak first single. I was soon twisting out there with a million-plus too many records.

Bob Freese did everything Joe Mansfield had done—co-op ads, price, position—to work *The Chase*. He was out to prove he could be a winner. I had that record in *gas stations*, had the whole damn country covered.

But reviews were uneven. The record was inconsistent and simply not as strong as the two previous ones. And there was another factor going against Garth at radio: he was not only competing against a tougher field that included Clint Black, Vince Gill, Wynonna, Trisha Yearwood, Alan Jackson, Brooks and Dunn, Mary-Chapin Carpenter, Travis Tritt, and Tim McGraw; he was going up against Garth Brooks. If radio didn't like his new one, they played "The Dance" or "Friends in Low Places." Classics don't stimulate sales of a new album.

I wasn't surprised that *The Chase* was less of a record. Garth had spent much of the year on renegotiating his record deal, a film deal with Disney, other business deals. One of my first comments back in 1989 was "Focus on the music, spend more time, more money, make great music." When he and Allen did that, the music they created made history.

In the fall we came back with a great ballad, "Somewhere Other Than the Night," which went to No. 1 early in 1993. But *The Chase* album was still lying out there real heavy.

Garth's image had suffered, I felt, when he and Sandy discussed his infidelity in a national magazine; when his eyes teared up on TV and he threatened to quit music; when he'd talk about all the pressure of his fame and wealth. No one was going to feel real sorry for Garth.

He really did a number on himself when he appeared on a *Barbara Walters Special* at the end of March 1993. I felt the interview backfired and further damaged his image. Walters interviewed Garth where it all started for him—the Bluebird Cafe on Hillsboro Road in the Green Hills section of town. Again Garth spoke of his "retirement" plans, his marital crisis with Sandy. To his credit he had tried to turn it into a positive, had vowed to "stay clean, stay straight."

But when Walters asked if the lyrics of "We Shall Be Free" was an endorsement of gay love, Garth obliged Barbara and said yes. Then he added, "It's a known fact from the tabloids that my sister is homosexual. I love my sister to death, and I'm sorry, I just can't condemn somebody for being happy and loving someone else. I'm sorry if [people] think loving somebody is a crime."

No, but a bunch of Garth fans probably felt outing your own sister *was*. Betsy Smittle had been Garth's bass player on the road for a couple of years. She had not come out on her own, and Garth had not cleared his remarks with her. He handled it poorly and showed his real colors in so doing. Their own family did not know. Her partner's family did not know. But now all of America did know.

Garth also made an unfortunate remark to Walters that was just as offensive. He told of having "more money than my grandchildren's grandchildren can spend." He was trying to say how his commitment to music wasn't about playing it safe and getting rich. Fair enough, but it came off like an arrogant boast that pissed off a good number of hardworking folks whose paychecks had helped him build that financial empire. Once true believers, some felt betrayed by what they saw as Garth's greed.

Walters had courted Garth for two years. There was some feeling in his own camp that he wasn't emotionally ready to handle a big TV interview. I was against it and told Pam Lewis, as Garth's publicist and comanager, to keep him off TV: "Don't let him do any more of these things where he says things that expose him, and hurt his sales and his career. Colonel Parker never had Elvis on prime-time interviews. He knew better."

Garth was determined, I later heard, to do something incredible on TV. Clinton had just been elected, and Garth had suggested using the interview to demand Clinton reopen the JFK assassination case. He had finally seen the Oliver Stone movie and was suddenly fascinated by the conspiracy thing. He was talked out of it because it would have come off all wrong.

By the time of the Walters interview he was stronger, in better shape emotionally, rested from the road, his baby daughter had come along. But Garth, on a program that also featured Denzel Washington and Sharon Stone, showed up looking like a lumberjack, with flannel shirt, mud-caked boots, jeans, and a couple days' beard.

The fallout from *Walters* was painful. Rednecks were sending back tapes and CDs with nasty letters saying, "We burned the rest of 'em, but we sent you this one so you'd know we're serious. Screw Garth Brooks! He's a phony. He lied to us. Now the true Garth comes out."

I was told Betsy was deeply hurt in the aftermath of his remark. She later quit his band to pursue a solo career. I honestly don't believe Garth meant to hurt Betsy; he just talked too much.

If TV had the potential to cause Garth image problems, he had clearly regained his touch at radio. After "Somewhere" he hit No. 2 with another ballad, "Learning to Live Again," and No. 1 with "That Summer" after its spring 1993 release. But it was still too late to save the album. The preachy tone of "Free" had failed to fire up critics and deejays and it just didn't fit country radio. Moreover the songs on that album simply weren't as strong as those of the previous albums. With a million-five CDs and cassettes coming back by spring, *The Chase* was projecting out at a drop in sales of more than 50 percent from the two before it. Of course any country artist would kill to sell 4 or 5 million records. But to Garth a steep drop from so high up smarts. So when he and his handlers looked to assign blame, they had only to look at the arrogant old bastard who ran the label and played golf every morning. I called Garth in to talk things over before it got out of control.

I assured him that all of us had done everything possible to sell the record, from midnight store openings to his appearance on *The Tonight Show*. No one had done a better job than Garth himself. He had even sung the national anthem at the Super Bowl in January 1993. Part of his agreement with NBC was that the network would premiere a video of "We Shall Be Free," which NBC had asked him to create.

Garth didn't think much of videos after "Thunder," but his new song's message was so important that he agreed—even though it had already stiffed. He edited the "Free" clip around the clock to make his game-day deadline. It all worked out, but not before Garth threatened to leave the stadium and refuse to sing the national anthem when NBC said it had not gotten the video in time to air it. Everything, it seemed, was becoming high drama around Garth.

Bottom-line, I told him, it just wasn't there. The album had but one killer single. "You did a great job sellin' your record," I said. "Everybody knows it's out there. But you can't spend money that will *make* people buy something. The music has to do that."

Garth's comeback: If Joe Mansfield were still on the team, Garth would have had another 10-million seller. He accused me of not buying enough TV, not working the music in promotion. To an artist, promotion only works the hits, never the stiffs.

"Garth," I explained, "we bought air time during *Fences* and *Ropin'* because we had tremendous surplus profits and we were making you a household name. Our own research told us it didn't sell any records, but people saw you all over the place, all the time, it bought you recognition." I told him we spent more money to market *The Chase* than the first three records. They just happened to be much better.

You can't buy success, I said. What happens in the studio determines 90 percent of whether music sells or not. There's no marketing genius behind this horseshit, I told him. If there were, why did the business have so many stiffs?

To prove me wrong, Garth spent a half-million of his own dollars in January to advertise *The Chase*. He made his own commercial, but all it did was boast how he'd sold more records than anyone else. It made him sound like a carny barker. Our market research showed that the ad cost $70 per album sold while it ran. *What was he thinking?*

We still had our million-plus returns fixin' to come home like bad relatives. But if EMI–North America was to make the right kind of profit for Worldwide and its stockholders, we'd have to stall the returns past the fiscal year-end. One way to do that, sometimes, is TV. So Bob Freese and I sat down with Garth and explained, "You put up half a million, we'll put up half a million. We'll do a million dollars of TV, which you think will work if done right. We'll buy it better this time."

Garth went with the same Dallas firm that did the first awful ad. This time the research showed we spent $7 for each album bought, a nice improvement but nowhere near cost-effective. I never believed TV ads can pick an album up once it quits selling. But our million-dollar buy *did* stall my customers just enough so that they didn't return *The Chase* in March. This shell game allowed me to close out my year on March 31st showing bigger profits for corporate—knowing of course that by April and May a million of those babies were comin' home.

Garth and his people were inside their tiny yessir cocoon, focusing on me as the root of Garth's problems: I had passed on him; then passed on his friend Trisha; fired the man who discovered him; suggested he improve his music; refused to give him a joint venture; told him he wasn't Elvis, Jackson, or Lennon and McCartney; *and* forced out the marketing-sales genius who'd "made" Garth. It hardly helped that there had also been rumors on the street that I had told Garth to get rid of his managers and his producer—though Bob, Pam, and Allen all knew face-to-face from me that the rumors were absolutely not true.

By this time Joe Smith had retired and was replaced by Koppelman, the ex-publishing tycoon in New York. Koppelman's SBK Records broke huge superstars Vanilla Ice and Wilson Phillips—but still lost money. You just never heard about the acts they signed and couldn't break.

Koppelman didn't have a feel for country or Nashville and he hadn't hired me. I knew that once he saw that Liberty was having a bad year, it wouldn't be long before he'd want my ass gone and my big salary off his books. His executive vice president of EMI–North America was a woman named Terri Santisi, who was under tremendous pressure herself because the numbers weren't coming in from anywhere. I sensed some friction between her and Koppelman. It was her job to go up in Carnegie Towers and tell Jim Fifield the big numbers weren't flowing from the House That Garth Built.

Santisi was tough. She once told my sales VP Bob Freese, "You wouldn't be doing so badly if you weren't paying your president so much money!" That was the New York way: you get your butt reamed, so you immediately find a way to pass it on. There was no love lost between us. My reaction was, before you go shooting off your mouth, what about that multimillion-dollar lease on the corporate jet, the one being refurbished for hundreds of thousands of dollars? I knew shit they had *no idea* I knew. I had my informants.

Garth's fifth album, *In Pieces*, came out in September 1993, and it was unquestionably better than *The Chase*, with some fun, kick-ass radio records. Instead of changing the world, Garth had tried to change his music and draw people to it.

It seemed to be working. Radio was all over Garth again, as the first two singles—"Ain't Going Down (Till the Sun Comes Up)" and "American Honky-Tonk Bar Association"—both went to No. 1. Yet by the end of the year *In Pieces* showed signs of plateauing. For one thing a lot of fans who first came to Garth on *The Chase* were disappointed and held off on *In Pieces*. Plus *Pieces*, like *The Chase*, did have weak spots. A lot of others already had all the Garth they needed in the house. Even for a superstar, after a point people have about had enough. He was no longer the hip thing to run out and get—after having been that twice already. The singles, though they might hit the top of the charts, aren't always an artist's best work, and these two weren't necessarily the kind of hits to make people rush out and buy the next Garth Brooks album. He had already, by his actions and statements, turned off a large number of people who wouldn't buy his music.

I had learned not to overship after eating 2 million of *The Chase. Pieces* looked to be a 4-million seller and we only had 7 or 8 percent returns—300,000 or so units. Because EMI now had Janet Jackson exploding on Virgin, no one was pressuring me to ship an extra million units just to get the orders on the books for the CPAs.

Garth came to see me alone at my house for another of our candid ninety-minute reality checks. We got into all of it—again. He listened and nodded politely, taking it all in. I wasn't the label, I emphasized. There were a half-dozen factors behind the slide from 10 million to 5 to 4. One, simply, was that no one sustains the heat of 10 million units every album. Can't be done. I mentioned reviews, his focus, pissing people off with dumb statements on TV.

"If you want to get back up to ten million, don't shoot the

messenger," I said. "Go fix the damn music." I had a plan that would work: "You should do a hits album for fall '94, throw in a new song or two, and make it a wonderful, elaborate package— an event. You'll own Christmas again, which is when half of all records are sold in this country. That'll generate dollars I can use—including for TV ads—to get your catalog up front and visible. Then, next fall, give me an album of new tracks and we'll be off and rockin'."

As Garth left, I was absolutely certain I had gotten through. He drove from my house to his managers' office and met with Bob Doyle and Kerry O'Neil. An hour and a half later, while I was in a meeting, he called me and said, "I gotta talk to you."

When Garth rolled up in his pickup, I excused myself from my meeting and met him out on my front porch. "I was hearin' you earlier," he said, "but I went to my people and they all said they don't buy any of it. They want me to go to war with the label. When I say 'my people,' Bowen, that means me, too."

"If a song publisher and an accountant know more about the record business than I do, Garth, then listen to them. These are the choices you have to make in life. But I'd be very careful about taking advice from people that want you to go to war when they have nothing to lose and *you* do."

"Yessir, that's a good thought," he said, eyes blazing with intensity. "But I gotta tell ya, I think I agree with them."

In early 1994 I attended EMI–North America's "Key Issues and Strategy" meeting in Turnberry Isle, Florida. One issue that began to sink in was the shortage of "real estate" in retail and the narrow playlisting going on in the trendy new "hot country" and "young country" formats. Sometime around then Charles Koppelman came up with an interesting way around retail and radio: a promotional Garth Brooks CD and cassette distributed through McDonald's. I honestly don't know if this was Charlie's idea or if it came from one of his own people or an ad agency guy. But he seemed to want to take credit for it, as he did with most things that worked. This worked. Garth was looking for a new charity after working with Feed the Children, and a smart, talented guy from McDonald's' ad agency, DDB Needham, helped get Garth behind it. At Garth's insistence, one dollar per sale, whether from Garth's or from another artist's album, would be earmarked for the Ronald McDonald House charities.

While Koppelman and Garth put their heads together for what became *The Garth Brooks Collection: My Favorites*, Ginger and I went off to Maui for my summer break. I had been feeling sluggish and stressed out by "the GB situation." The McGarth project would consist of two songs picked by Garth from each of his five albums; it would sell at McDonald's for $3.99 and $5.99, cassettes and CD. It was a greatest-hits collection of nonhits.

Koppelman flew into Nashville to meet with Garth. It was at that meeting that Garth declared, "I'm not delivering a new album as long as Bowen's running Liberty."

Koppelman had the right answer: "We can't let you or any artist dictate how we run our business. Let's talk about positives, let's talk about the future." Garth had hit a wall.

After Maui we all met at my house. The deal *was* a real positive for the charities and good exposure for Garth. But the meeting brought to the surface some edge between Garth and Koppelman, a tough former publisher, when they wrangled over how much publishers should be paid for the *Collection* songs.

Garth was determined to gouge the label for full-freight in his crusade to protect "my kids" who cowrote or published those songs. (Garth was the writer on most of them, and his manager was his publisher anyway, so he stood to gain more than anyone.) It's ridiculous to get paid full royalty when you're selling for a third of the usual price. And it was found money. But his mission was to squeeze every penny he could out of the deal.

Koppelman was thinking more along the lines of half rates for any EMI song because of the bargain prices. Since such discount projects almost always call for *half-rate* publishing, I knew Koppelman was in for a difficult negotiation with Garth. But Charles was confident. After all, he believed he could get Garth to deliver us an album when we couldn't. Garth, bright, ballsy kid that he is, eventually got his way on many of his demands. What Charles didn't realize perhaps was that one of Garth's favorite cowriters had allegedly had trouble collecting payments in a timely fashion from EMI's publishing unit, which was run by Koppelman's SBK partner, Marty Bandier. Garth called Charles on that one and nailed him during a big meeting with some top label executives in my house. Koppelman, perhaps caught off guard, assured his superstar, "I'm glad to know that, we will correct that." But he eventually conceded on most of Garth's demands.

I wasn't surprised by that outcome. After all, Koppelman described the meeting in which Garth refused to turn in any new music as "the single worst meeting I've ever had with an artist in my entire career. I didn't get anywhere with him. I thought I had him in a corner—with logic—but no dice. Didn't work."

The project raised close to $5 million for the charities. But there was a downside for Liberty. The deal pissed off all our major retail customers. They buy Garth Brooks CDs for $10.30 and sell them for $14.00 or $15.00. Now you could go to McDonald's and for a hamburger and $5.99 walk out with a Garth CD. And Garth had never let us lower any of his stuff to $7.99, let alone $5.99. He wanted the price to stay up as high as possible.

Anytime you sell 3 million units anywhere but retail, retail gets scared; then retail gets even. Blockbuster canceled a $1 million order with our low-end special-markets stuff—old repackaged $4.98 albums—to show their disgust. They'd gladly take Sony's low-end products instead. We lost between $3 million and $4 million in "we'll get even" deals.

Retailers of course come back for the big hits. Where they hurt you is when they don't buy your catalog, don't buy as much of your midline roster or budget line. You lose real estate.

Koppelman's deal made sense, but it was handled wrong. We should have gone to retail in front and told them that after the three-week promotion, we'd give them what they'd been after for four years—Garth bargains. We'd do a few million units that way, I figured. But Garth wouldn't let us sell that low.

To appease our major retailers, who were angry at EMI for going outside the normal distribution channel, EMI decided to discount Garth's entire catalogue. The hope was that this would stimulate catalog orders during McDonald's' $15 million TV campaign. The problem was that we already *had* a full supply of Garth catalog lying out there. I always made sure I had plenty—not too much, just the right amount—in retail. We were also taking some returns on *Pieces* and *The Chase* from retailers who had overbought, reshrinking them (as in shrink-wrapping them again) if they weren't damaged, and redirecting them to understocked retailers who could sell them.

Another problem was that DDB Needham's ads were designed to sell Big Macs and McNuggets, not catalog. As a result we only sold another 400,000 discounted units. So while Koppelman may have foreseen some $10 million in EMI profit with all that free advertising (other EMI acts were in on the promotion), the deal in the end really didn't help Liberty or our bottom line.

The McDonald's deal not only got retail in an uproar with me; because of the size of Garth's EMI deal, it cut sharply into Liberty's profit on catalog sales. Again I was caught in a crossfire between Garth and New York.

Garth had made it clear he wanted my ass gone. I had become a liability to Koppelman and Santisi because I had no sway over Garth. I didn't even have any new music from him. In the end, the McDonald's deal squeezed my profit margin, but EMI sold more than 4 million Garth CDs.

I came close several times to telling them all to stick it. I made a remark about taking a golden parachute and flying way to Lahaina and a life of golfing and sunsets. I was trying hard to chill out, kick back, not panic or overreact to the provocations and paranoia at the label. But emotions, pride, arrogance came into play. It would have truly angered me to be run off after forty years in music, after $1 billion of hit records on Music Row. I wasn't going to let anyone have the satisfaction. I wanted the last pass I threw in this game to go for a touchdown, not a damn interception.

The McDonald's deal did underscore two interesting trends: that retail's exclusive hold on digital CD was over, and that Garth's hold on his public was showing signs of weakening.

The CD had saved retail. But someday soon people will be ordering music by digitally downloading it onto a blank CD linked to their home computers. There will always be purists who will drive to a record store to hold a CD, look at the cover art, and read the label. But millions of others will bypass retail by cruising the information superhighway.

Retail does not want to get shut out. Such electronic and, in Garth's case, marketing alternatives make them nervous. McDonald's has 10,000 outlets. That's a *lot* of real estate. When retail sees history's biggest country act selling millions of CDs with burgers and shakes, they panic. They know they'll have to adapt to survive.

And so, it seems, will Garth. We commissioned Needham to conduct an eighty-thousand-dollar market research study during the promotion. It showed that nearly 80 percent of those who bought the *Collection* already owned three or more Garth albums. In other words they *already had* most of those tracks. Garth, then, had a core of about 3.5 million people who'd buy virtually anything he put out.

Given that his two latest albums had sold only slightly higher than 3.5 million, the implication was disturbing: fewer than a million buyers were first- or second-timers, meaning the number of people *discovering* Garth was flattening out. If he were still on the rise, especially at those rock-bottom prices, we should have picked up 3 or 4 million people who had *none* of those cuts at home.

Ironically the Needham study helped Garth see it was time for a real greatest hits CD. Bob Doyle had resisted it because he felt it would cannibalize Garth's catalog. By putting out a *non-hits* collection, he hoped to boost catalog, but it didn't. Most country superstars have shown that Hits CDs do sell catalog.

My opportunity to coax a collection out of him came during what seemed a momentary cease-fire in Garth's war. My VP for International called from Australia to tell me of a talk she'd had with Garth and Bob Doyle. After failing to get Koppelman behind the campaign to fire me, she said, they were tired and frustrated at the way their year had gone. She sensed they were in a more conciliatory mood. She suggested a summit meeting.

People close to Garth who felt the label had in fact done a great job were baffled by his negativity. Maybe it had run its course. I told them I always felt his dark edge was in part due to the efforts of his scheming inner circle to poison the air around him.

Even Joe Mansfield had become an asset. I had been paying Joe ten thousand dollars a month to do independent marketing on Garth's product. Joe had also told Garth about the negative impact at retail of the McDonald's project, and Garth had heard him.

I set up a meeting out at Garth's big brick house on a vast rolling spread out in the lush Tennessee woods. The house was like driving up into a giant fireplace. There was a warm and casual feeling inside the home. The second baby girl was in a little basket in the kitchen, Taylor was running all over the place, and Sandy was being the mom. They were living a pretty simple, contented down-home lifestyle, and you had to give Garth plenty of credit for that—for keeping his private life normal and on track after all he had accomplished and weathered.

Still, part of me wanted to tell Garth to shove it. But EMI wasn't paying me all that money to do that. Instead I used the meeting to coax Garth into giving us a hits package for Christmas. We all knew the time had come. Garth knew it.

The *Hits* project nearly turned into a nightmare. Garth pushed everyone to the last second and squeezed every concession he could out of EMI—eighteen songs, not twelve or fifteen; a twenty-four-page booklet; an expensive folding J-card for the cassette; a gimmicky "CD zooming disk" you send away for that samples twenty or thirty seconds of the tracks.

As always Garth played the drama to the hilt, held the gun to EMI's head, and got exactly what he wanted. We agreed to a $2 million TV ad campaign to launch *The Hits*. Once again the deal would knock out most of Liberty's profits.

There was no time to waste. If we crash-released it before Christmas, it would bail out EMI's numbers for the fiscal year ending March 31, 1995. I could see them all up there in New York going, "Five million times nine dollars wholesale, forty-five million dollars! Holy Shit! This'll make our year."

And of course all the big shots would get their bonuses and look like saviors. *The Hits* came out just in time, once again, for Garth to own Christmas.

I was deeply hurt when Garth's people had made me a scapegoat and tried to get me fired. I decided to take measures to protect myself if I ever had to fight back in a legal tangle.

I wasn't going to let some CPA jeopardize my gig. Nashville's a small town. I'd made my enemies, but I'd also helped a lot of people and had plenty of friends. I'd gotten a fair number of women off the phones at the receptionist's desk and given them meaningful jobs. Young, idealistic people in town saw me as a guy who didn't like the way things were and who made a difference.

It has always been easy to stay wired and to know what was going on at rival labels. I had a private network of gossips with whom I often traded information. I was sure I knew pretty much what was going on inside Garth's camp, if not his house. If he continued to push me far enough in his drive to get me fired, I'd have produced a damn good bit of ammunition against him personally.

If I sued someone for destroying my career, I'd need data. I had preliminary discussions with some people in that business to make sure I could get it: Who said what to whom, when they said it. Get it documented, taped, witnessed, whatever. Counterespionage. Everybody gathering data on everybody. I was fully prepared to do it to protect my livelihood and my family life.

I was hoping it would never come to that.

It had been an emotionally charged year that left me utterly drained. December is usually quiet on Music Row. All the seasonal product has been shipped and worked, many artists come in off the road and go home, and label people take off between Christmas and New Year's. I've always gone to Hawaii. With Garth in the pipeline again, I was still running the label. It was a good time for a break.

I knew something was wrong. I was not in good health. I was run-down. My sinuses were plugging up. My feet and back hurt. I couldn't breathe and was feeling miserable. Even when producing a couple of albums—by John Berry and Willie Nelson—I didn't feel all there.

"Before we go to Maui," I told Ginger, "something tells me it'd be a good time to go on up to the Mayo Clinic, check those polyps in my sinuses, and see what this is all about."

I've followed some hunches in my career that made me loads of money and others that left me broke.

This one just might have saved my life.

TWENTY-FOUR

I'VE ALWAYS KNOWN how to read the signs around me, known when to make my next move. The door cracks, go through it. Act. Don't freeze in the headlights. It's about having the intelligence, the nerve—sometimes the *craziness*—to let go of one thing and grab on to the next. Sitting still has never been an option.

As road signs go, cancer's a hard one to miss. It's one sharp slap in the face, a wake-up call to kick off the next chapter of life.

After Dr. David Sherris of the Mayo Clinic set up my surgery date, he sent Ginger and me over to another specialist who talked us through thyroid cancer and gave us some literature. We learned that thyroid cancer has only a 5 percent mortality rate at twenty years if treated properly, if the cancer is encapsulated. Not our usual dinner conversation, but nothing else seemed to matter now.

I never consciously feared dying, though Ginger says I was scared out of my mind. I was only trying to be a tough Texas boy. It was easier for me to be the one with the disease. If it had been Ginger, I'd have panicked. Seeing that she was stunned, I tried to hang tough and get on with it.

Still, I dreaded radiation and chemotherapy, having heard so many horror stories about their side effects. And I had already lost a fair amount of hair to age, so I wanted to hold on to what little I had left. I blocked out what I could, and focused briefly on the hair loss for comic relief.

But soon there I was, lying on a gurney, about to be rolled

into an operating room with my head hanging off the table and my throat stretched taut. I wasn't thinking of Garth's zoom disk or a 7 percent return. The 5 percent mortality rate at twenty years *was* a figure, however, that stuck in my mind.

Ginger had a tough time coping that day. She had been on an emotional roller coaster since Thanksgiving, when we learned that her beloved Airedale, Josh, had cancer that was spreading throughout his body. Ginger was devastated. Josh had been like a child to her for thirteen years.

But then we had gotten some good news in Rochester. When my driver Mike Jones took Josh for a follow-up exam after his tumor was removed, the vet didn't find any cancer. "In all my experience," he told Ginger by phone, "I've never seen anything like this." Of course, Ginger's relief only lasted until Dr. Sherris sucked some of those "abnormal cells" from my thyroid and ordered surgery. A bizarre twist to the story was that Josh's tumor had been almost exactly where mine was.

I went in about 11:30 A.M. for a 1 P.M. operation. Dr. Kerry Olsen would perform the surgery to remove the tumor along with the thyroid gland itself. Ginger read a book in a crowded waiting room, but by the end of the afternoon, she found herself all alone. The nurses would tell her only that I was still in surgery, which just freaked her out. Finally Dr. Olsen came out in his scrubs, dropped his mask, and announced, "Well it *was* cancer. In the thyroid it's called Hürthle-cell carcinoma—but we got it all. We removed the entire thyroid."

Her immediate thought was, *Oh my God, this is it, he's dying.* Ginger tried to hang on to everything Dr. Olsen was saying, but it went by pretty fast. He told her the surgery had lasted four hours so that he could save three of the four parathyroid glands and attach one of them to an adjacent neck muscle. Parathyroids are critical, he said, because they secrete a hormone that controls the body's calcium-phosphorous. "It was such a large tumor," he went on, "that we brought in a photographer so we could use pictures of it." (That was one photo op I could have done without.) Then Dr. Olsen walked off, leaving Ginger to cry alone in the waiting room.

When I finally got to my room a couple of hours later, Ginger says I was making wisecracks. My friends always did say I was pretty amusing when loaded. My neck hurt real bad and I had severe headaches from having my head stretched back.

A cute young nurse-trainee would ask me to rate my pain from 1 to 10 so they'd know how much morphine I needed.

Every time I mumbled, "Ohhh, I'm about a two," Ginger corrected me and told her I *meant* eight or nine, meaning major pain. I must have been thinking about a Top 10 record chart, with No. 1 being the peak, the most. I had the scale all upside down. Pain-wise, I was about No. 9 with a bullet.

Late that night, one of the surgery residents came in with some tissue-test results. I was still a little groggy, but Ginger cut to the chase: "What's the deal here? Is he going to die?"

"No, no, no," she said reassuringly. "This is a great kind of cancer to have. It was completely encapsulated." Somehow, I wasn't so reassured. I was still too fogged in to really get what was happening. I'd heard about the "mass," the "tumor," and the "abnormal cells," but they'd all talked around the c-word. When my head cleared enough, I was barely able to whisper. The first question out of my mouth was, "Is it cancer?"

"Well, yes," she said. Being out of it on dope made it seem unreal. Still, Ginger says a look of horror came over me. "But it's okay," the resident said. "They got it all."

"Do I have to do chemo?" I whispered. She shook her head. No chemo, no radiation. And no further hair loss. I was relieved on all fronts.

A hospital room after surgery is about as level a playing field as there is in life. Titles, toys, and net worth don't mean a thing; everyone gets the same chance to heal, to redefine their values, and make life-saving resolutions. It's a place to seek the clarity we're blind to while our lives are caught up in the grind.

It seemed apparent that the turmoil at Liberty had contributed significantly to my developing cancer. But I never showed my stress or pressure; I concealed them behind a veneer of cool and control, and that, Ginger believed, must have had something to do with it.

Ginger had probably heard me threaten to "retire" three or four times, so she'd just roll her eyes when I mentioned it now. She knew I'd been working way too long to walk away from the action. You get hooked, you can't let go. Even with the Garth madness, I had never really considered hanging it up, except for one half-assed bluff about taking a golden parachute. But a diagnosis of cancer and immediate surgery to cure it can sure shake up your priorities in a hurry.

Jim Fifield sent the company plane to fly Ginger and me back to Nashville on December 12. I didn't work and only took a few calls. A couple of days later, he sent the plane to take us back to

Maui for our Christmas break. It was agreed in New York that I'd take an extra six weeks to heal and "de-stress," as one Mayo doctor put it in no uncertain terms. I would return to work on February 4, 1995.

When I was told to de-stress, the doctor was, of course, prescribing retirement. How was I supposed to reduce stress *and* keep that job? Once on the island of Maui, it was a no-brainer. The successful surgery had given me a chance to start my life over, to enjoy all the things I'd never taken the time to experience. The door had flown open and there was no way I wasn't going through it.

Up to now, my downtime in Hawaii was never everyone's idea of taking it slow: I'd listen to demos, call artists who needed an immediate answer from me, rip off and read ten or twelve feet of faxes during my pre-golf breakfast. I'd list phone calls to make based on priority and time zone, and check in with the office daily. If three stations dropped a new single, promotion needed to know how I wanted to handle it. A&R would have some new act that had to be signed *today*. An obsessive extremist like myself never traveled light. I packed a lot of Nashville with me, and Ginger hated that.

This time, though, I was healing and that made everything different. I discovered that I loved not working. I was never bored; in fact, I felt more alive and content than I had in years. That month at Christmas was my first real vacation after forty years solid without a break. No wonder I had been playing golf every day. Those three hours were the closest I ever got to peace of mind. Still, like most CEO's, I had always kept my cell phone right there in the cart. You never *really* unplug.

One evening in early January 1995, after my eighteen holes, Ginger and I were sitting on the lanai at sunset, sipping Cristal champagne. Our house then was on the fifth hole of the Kaanapali golf course, barely a quarter of a mile from the Pacific. The rolling fairway sat on a hillside sloping gently toward the ocean. We couldn't hear or see the road between the fairways and the beach, but from the lanai we had a breathtaking vista of blue sky, waves, and whales. And then it hit me.

"That's it," I said, just like that. "I'm not going back, not messin' with Garth Brooks anymore. Or Koppelman, or any of them."

"Doesn't the word retirement scare you?" Ginger asked.

I shook my head. "Wouldn't it be exciting," I said, "to just let go and see what the next chapter of my life's gonna be? I ain't diggin' that world anymore. But I'm sure liking *this*."

Ginger knew I had an addictive personality that makes it impossible to give up control. What's in your head keeps working wherever you go. But I wasn't just out of the loop; I didn't even *miss* the loop. My head was clearing. I was taking almost no calls and feeling a wonderful absence of pressure. Nobody was singing me songs on my message tape. I could rip all my faxes, squeeze them into one big worthless ball, and toss them, yelling, "Who cares?" I felt terrific. What was there to fear?

Running the label was all numbers and corporate hassles. It had nothing to do with what got me into it in the first place—and what kept me going at such a furious pace all those years: the music. I had especially enjoyed being in the studio and coproducing two young artists I had signed to Liberty, John Berry, whose first album had just gone gold that fall, and the wonderful Deana Carter. But it was getting harder every day to focus on making music and breaking new acts.

I had come to feel strongly that Deana could make it big. She was a real positive person with the talent and intelligence to be a star. Plus, she knew what she wanted with her music. She was no puppet act. It was clear she had a music to do. And it was in her blood. Deana had been born a couple blocks from Music Row at Baptist Hospital and raised in Goodlettsville, a half-hour outside Nashville. Her dad, Fred Carter, Jr., was a great sessions guitarist and songwriter in town.

Deana was just twenty-six when my A&R director, Herky Williams, brought her to my home for an audition in early 1992. She sat there in her jeans and sweater, pulled out her acoustic guitar, and sang. She just had something that drew you in when she performed. She was so quiet and nervous with this little-girl voice that I could barely hear her. I leaned forward, listened hard, and felt there was something unique about her voice and material.

But what I told her was, "You sure sang awful quiet and shy," which she likely mistook as a lack of enthusiasm. Then Deana told me she had been named for Dean Martin because her dad had written a song that Dean recorded right around the time she was born in 1966. I recalled that I had, in fact, *produced* those sessions for Dean, but Deana was way ahead of me on all this. She got up the nerve to tell me how I had supposedly decided against Fred Carter's song, "It Just Happened That Way," as the single and instead worked the B-side, "Nobody's Baby Again" (which didn't get past No. 60 on the charts in the fall of 1966). But here we were, twenty-five years later, with Deana feeling it was my destiny, or karma, as she put it, to work with her and get it right this time. You might say it just happened that way. I couldn't help but be drawn to Deana's super spirit and determination.

She was much less nervous when she came by for a second audition, and she just knocked me out. When Herky played me Deana's work tape of some songs just before my Christmas 1992 break in Hawaii, he urged me to move on her and bring her to the label. He said she'd paid her dues, surviving on janitorial, preschool teaching, and waitressing jobs while working on her songs. By early 1993, we had signed Deana to Liberty.

Still, I told Deana she needed more time to develop, to exploit her distinct gifts before I'd go into the studio with her. So for the next eighteen months, she and Herky worked real hard and put together acoustic demos of more than forty songs, most of them written by Deana or cowritten by her with Nashville's top writers.

In August 1994, I began coproducing Deana's album at Emerald with John Guess, making sure Deana understood this was *her* record, *her* music. I loved what I heard; I also knew that "Did I Shave My Legs for This?" *had* to be the title track. That fall had been a busy time for me in the studio. I had just finished John Berry's next album, as well as a Willie Nelson project of classic songs that he and other great songwriters had written. Those tracks were recorded in L.A. with a big orchestra. It turned out to be the perfect way to complete the circle for me musically.

Nashville had been a wonderful place before the number crunchers took over. Sure, I wanted to do tonnage, wanted mass merchandising, state-of-the-art digital hardware, and great music to run through it. What I didn't want was music created and marketed to make stockholders happy. Music was never meant to be an assembly-line product sold like lighting fixtures.

Now, the business was driving the music. I couldn't blame Garth for any of that. He is just one reason country became a big-money game. As for his dark side, it was probably there beforehand. It's just been magnified by the power he's been given— and the adulation he has rightly earned. If not him, it would have been someone else. A Garth Brooks was inevitable.

I hadn't gone to Nashville in 1976 to run labels for global industrial giants, but to help artists create music. Almost two decades later it had all been turned upside down. Eighty-five percent of what I dealt with was office nonsense: insecure people needing answers, needing to be propped up, having to hear directly from the general, not a lieutenant. I didn't want to be the general anymore. I was loving the beauty of Maui more than ever. I was loving golf more than ever—the gambling, the pace, the shots, the scenery. I could *see* the game better. I was loving life with Ginger more than ever.

Ginger was amazed at how fast everything was changing in me, but I knew she was still a little skeptical. She had heard my "I'll slow down" rap a hundred times before. "Okay, Bowen," she said, "what about the Christian-music stuff? You don't want God mad at you after where you just came from." That was Ginger's humor and cut-to-the-core pragmatism working together.

I laughed. "Funny, but I actually did think about that," I told her. The music was business, though, not religion. Truth was, I didn't know one Christian record from another. My role was to bring EMI a vision—not of Jesus, but of nineties synergy. To help them see they had the muscle to bring this powerful music to the secular world.

I had three years left on the EMI deal, so Ginger was just making sure I had thought all this through. "I'll settle out now," I said. "It'll save EMI money if I do it now and not in three or five years."

The day after telling Ginger I was ready to quit, I called my lawyer, John Mason, and told him to negotiate a strong severance package with New York and end it all. I figured this would please Koppelman; he could then install his own label chief. But if I didn't get a decent, equitable settlement, I was also prepared to take EMI to court and fight for ten times what a settlement would get me. I didn't care if it cost me a half a million dollars and three or four years to do it. I figured we had a case and mapped it out with John. They were smart enough to know that I had the resources—and that I was not afraid of a fight.

Things heated up quickly. When John called Fifield, he mentioned that I would be returning to work, as agreed, on February 4, 1995, following my six-week recovery. Fifield got a little worked up and snapped back to John something to the effect that there was no way New York wanted me back at Liberty.

This was news to us. It gave John an excuse to fire off a letter to EMI's lawyers saying, in effect, that I'd been fired that morning. We gave them a deadline to settle. I felt I had a strong bargaining position, because I had, after all, made EMI tens of millions of dollars in profits over my four years. I would link

278 JIMMY BOWEN *and* JIM JEROME

Garth's war with the label to the prolonged stress and weakened immune system that heightened my susceptibility to cancer.

Meanwhile, Ginger flew into Nashville to fold up the tent. (Sadly, she had to put Josh to sleep when his cancer reappeared.) I joined her there in late January on my way to Mayo in Rochester for a series of follow-up tests. I stayed in Nashville just long enough to help her put our big brick house on Franklin Road on the market, say a few goodbyes, and get our finances and paperwork in order. I've never been given to nesting, to sentimental attachments. I wasn't nearly as wrapped up in our house and all the stuff inside it as Ginger was. None of that mattered to me. I suppose that's a defense against the hurt I felt as a kid from a broken home who got shuffled around plenty among relatives. A lot of folks wanted some closure after being in our lives for so long. Mostly, I used my illness to avoid all that emotion. When it was finally time to split, I couldn't get away fast enough. There's a part of me that's been a nomad all my life.

EMI and I settled rather quickly and painlessly. I was quite satisfied with my buyout package; I imagine they felt it was worth it to get me out of the way. After some hardball on one or two issues, it was over. Fifield came through in the end and I was pleased by his show of integrity and decency. Jim's a good guy who lived up to his word. I felt great relief that my own hardball days on Music Row were behind me.

Predictably, there were rumors trailing me all the way to Maui, ranging from my being terminally ill to the cancer being an elaborate hoax to save face after being deposed in the EMI coup led by Garth. The most persistent gossip had me actually coming back to take over another major label. As always, though, I let the rumors run. After surgery, I frankly didn't give a damn. It was a fitting way to go out—in a flurry of speculation. But this time, I wasn't there to control the rumors, or deny that I might have even *started* them myself.

Ginger told me the press release announcing my retirement due to "health problems" and effective March 31, 1995, was about as lively as an obituary. Which was how a bunch of folks on Music Row probably read it. I never did expect to hear from Garth personally—and I didn't. But he was quoted in a trade paper as saying, "Right now, all I care about is [Bowen] feeling good and being healthy."

In fact I was in excellent shape, though I have had to go back to Mayo several times since the surgery to check for errant cancer cells from the thyroid. I go off Cytomel, a synthetic thyroid hormone, for two weeks before the week of tests. My hormones and metabolism go awry. My nerves are shattered. I once shanked a wedge shot during one of these periods and next thing I knew my wedge was whirring like a helicopter rotor through the air, the first time I'd ever lost control and hurled a club—at least since the sixties. I eat anything I can get my hands on, get headaches, the bladder and bowel don't work real good, I bloat up fifteen, twenty pounds, and feel crabby and listless all the time with ugly bags under my eyes. It's industrial-strength PMS is what it is. Which has made me extremely empathetic to what women go through. The thyroid's an important piece of business in the human body.

The test is like something out of sci-fi. I go into a tiny room with a stainless-steel floor and a special floor covering to stand on. A lab technician in a white astronaut mask, hat, and rubber gloves hands me a glass of tasteless radioactive iodine, fitted inside a stainless-steel container. The temptation to shout, "HEY!" and pretend I'm about to toss this nuclear cocktail at the guy is enormous, just to watch him jump.

When you've gone off Cytomel, any remaining thyroid cells in the body will be pinpointed and bonded to by the iodine because thyroid cells crave iodine. This is a magic bullet compared to chemo and radiation, which destroy tissue around the target area. It's why they'll tell you thyroid is *the* cancer to get.

To avoid contamination, no one can go near me or touch me for five days after I come out. I can't touch, kiss, hug, or sleep with Ginger; she'd glow in the dark if I did. Anything I touch has to be washed separately, including clothes. When I go to the bathroom I flush several times. Our housekeepers have to wear rubber gloves to touch anything I've had contact with. Any silverware or dishes or glasses I use have to be washed separately. Forty hours after drinking the iodine, the thyroid area gets scanned by a handheld ultrasound device that precisely tracks any thyroid cells. Then I get a full-body scan.

There were some scares. My first time, I tested positive in the neck. So I got a much bigger dose of radioactive iodine to zap the cells, the strongest dose that doesn't require hospitalization. What's unnerving is that if the tests miss any microscopic malignant remnants—and the doctors say you never get them all— they can metastasize two or three years later and nail you.

The second time I tested positive again—same area, but less than half the prior amount. Again, they were confident a second big dose would wipe out the thyroid cells for good—and they did. Now, I just need annual checkups, and my prognosis remains excellent.

The same can be said for the last new artist I produced in Nashville. Deana Carter's career has exploded. But it wasn't easy. She very nearly became a casualty of the new regime. Feeling Deana had some potential internationally, we had decided to release her album first in Europe, where she toured quite successfully as an opening act in the early months of 1995. By the time she came back to prepare for her U.S. debut, however, I was gone. My successor, Scott Hendricks, who took over in May 1995, shelved Deana's album the week before she was to go to radio with her first U.S. single. Scott might well have dropped her altogether had she not done so well for EMI in Europe.

He simply didn't hear any hits on our album. I can understand that. Everyone's got different opinions. I once dumped sixteen tracks by Suzy Bogguss and recut an album. Did the same once for George Strait. So the album John and I had coproduced for Deana was basically scrapped and Scott brought in guitarist/producer Chris Farren to revamp it. A bunch of songs were dumped and replaced by new ones. Some were retained. Deana fought to keep "Did I Shave My Legs for This?" (cowritten with Rhonda Hart) as the title track, but it was rerecorded.

You can't fault anyone for making changes when you wind up with a monster. *Did I Shave My Legs for This?* was finally released in September 1996. "Strawberry Wine," written by Matraca Berg and Gary Harrison, reached No. 1 in November 1996 and earned Deana a Grammy nomination in the Best Female Country Vocal Performance category. By early 1997, "We Danced Anyway," written by Matraca and Randy Scruggs, also hit No. 1, while the album had shot past the 2 million, double-platinum mark. And there were still probably two more singles, including the wonderful title track, waiting to go to radio.

At the end of the day, the truth was this: The GB Situation hadn't done me in—and neither had the big C. So whatever anyone else wanted to think back in Nashville, I left knowing that I had achieved all the goals I had set for myself.

I, too, had gone there with a music to do—and I had done it.

EPILOGUE

UNLIKE ALMOST EVERYWHERE else I've gone in my life, Maui was one place my lifelong buddy Don Lanier never seemed keen on visiting. But when I sent him a ticket for his birthday a few years ago, he flew in for a long weekend of golf.

"Just tell me how windy it gets down there, James," he asked before leaving. I knew why he needed to know. Dirt hits a real high ball off the tee. A strong breeze can wreck his long game. "Gentle trade winds," I reassured him.

The day Dirt flew in, the island was buffeted by fierce fifty-mile-an-hour gusts. His small plane almost couldn't land. When he stepped onto the tarmac, his baseball hat blew off his head and chunks of tin flew by. Dirt immediately started cussin' me.

Next day wasn't much better. After five holes poor Dirt had lost four new balls and wanted to strangle someone. The wind was carrying his tee shots clear out into the surrounding pineapple fields. Dirt's got about as dry a sense of humor as anyone I've ever known. When we came off the eighteenth green, he squinted hard with a look of disgust I've known all my life, and said, "James, what you've got down here, basically, is Amarillo with shrubs."

It's been a long, wild ride from the Texas Panhandle to Paradise. Maui may not be Dirt's idea of heaven on earth, but it sure has been mine.

Like many retired couples, Ginger and I have reduced our overhead for retirement. We left an eight-thousand-square-foot home for one a third as big. The seventy-five-year-old place was costing us a half-million dollars a year for staff, taxes, three heating systems, landscaping, pool, my driver, and his guest bungalow. You could have run a small hotel on our utility bills.

Less, it turns out, is more. You can't help but be transformed by Maui. Life is simpler, slower; my energies are more focused and in the moment. The weather and beauty of the island are magnificent. Ginger and I love to sit out on our lanai—protected from those gentle trade winds—and watch sunrises and sunsets. I've maybe looked at two *Billboards*.

It blew Ginger's mind the first time I wadded up a scroll of faxes and tossed them. She knows my addictive personality better than anyone: when I quit, I quit 110 percent. One of our close friends on the island said to Ginger, "Jeez, you know he's not *Bowen* anymore. He's turned into a Jimmy."

I'm secure with the contribution I made to the world of music—and with my decision to leave it. Like an athlete who retires before he makes mistakes that could hurt—or embarrass—him, I knew it was time to go. The ego isn't gone, but it's changed. I now bitch and moan mostly to our housekeepers instead of to VPs.

The fun had gone out of it for me. With music now under the magnifying glass of the bean counters, the timing was perfect. The industry's being run from the top down, not the bottom up. In a small community like Music Row, you need fresh innovative music to filter up from the street and change the industry creatively; instead CPAs send their profit projections down from corporate—and that determines the music that'll make their bottom line.

The music today suffers from a disturbing conformity. You listen to country radio for a couple of hours and you can't tell whose records you've heard. So much of it sounds the same. The *sound* is technically wonderful, more in tune, and musicianship is better. Instead of ten great players doing all the sessions, Nashville has lured a new crop of superb players from all over America, making it, finally, the most vibrant, dynamic music center in America.

But the songs, the guitar licks, the drums all sound interchangeable. I produced Strait for years. I should know if it's him on radio, but I don't. Aspiring country acts once copied Hank, Haggard, Lefty Frizzell, George Jones. Now their big influence is whoever was No. 1 last year. The music is standing still. A lot of it sounds like ear candy.

Videos are no less clichéd: just about every barn door, bale of hay, and dirt road in the state of Tennessee's been shot for one damn video or another.

The enormous growth of radio hasn't improved the music either. When I started out, radio was run by colorful, quirky music junkies who'd fly to another city and sit in hotel rooms twisting clock-radio dials to check out what was on the air. Or they'd drive around in rented cars punching stations. Now you have investment groups who buy a station for, say, $5 million. They warn the GM that if their five-point market share drops a half point, he's fired, goes up a half point he gets a bonus.

The GM hires a program director and then has to report to lawyers, investors, and board members who know much more about the Standard & Poors' 500 than they do about the *Billboard* Top 200. To these money people, music is still just what fills gaps between cash-generating commercials. They could care less what it sounds like. Whatever format—country, hard rock, "classic rock"—delivers the most listeners and best demographics for the station's sponsors, *that's* what's hot.

The pressure is on, so the nervous program director hires a consultant to tell him what people want to hear. The name of the game is, don't take chances and lose market turf. The investors sell after three or five years, take their profit, and move on. That doesn't make for a lot of excitement and novelty on the airwaves. When the consultants got the power in country radio, I could no longer sustain my passion to go into the studio. Country has finally become a victim of its own extraordinary success.

It seems fitting, maybe *fated*, that my final battles in Nashville would pit me against a Garth Brooks—a clash of intense, strong personalities and wills. The irony was that as label chief I'd prayed for a Garth Brooks to come along and blow the roof off sales. Then when I had him selling 10 million records, I'd have been better off selling the same 10 million but by seven different artists each doing a million-four. That would have been a whole other situation.

In a sense Garth embodied my vision for Nashville when I arrived: his first songs were fresh and exciting; he brilliantly redefined live performance in country; he was passionate about controlling his music and directing his destiny; and he had a gift for working TV, radio, Fan Fair, the CMA, *whatever it took*, to sell records.

Like me, Garth was everything the old hillbillies were not.

Maybe each of us got what we deserved. He got the label chief who'd shaken the place up and done more business than anyone else; I got the one artist, out of all who had come to Music Row, who was destined to sell 60 million albums faster than anyone ever.

Having cut myself loose from all that, it seems far away and unimportant now. Ginger assures me I've made a smooth back-to-basics transition into civilian life: laundry, ironing, cooking, exercising, feeding the birds in our yard. Because Ginger still has so much going on in Nashville, I've been on my own more in Hawaii than ever before. But I've been digging that too.

I did my first load of wash at age fifty-eight. I've had to learn not to mix darks and whites. I figured out you don't dry the golf shirts, but take them out after five minutes and hang them up. Ginger's showed me how to iron my Hawaiian shirts, but not before I scorched a hole in one of them.

I learned never to go to the grocery store when you're hungry. Go after you've eaten. I've gone hungry and come home with $200 worth of stuff in the cart. Ginger taught me to do curried chicken, pastas, and my low-fat amaranth burgers. I get a real giggle out of watching myself doing these things.

After Ginger started feeding the local bird population, I've loved sunrises on the lanai, when sixty of them swoop down for a feeding. If Ginger's back in Nashville, then I have to feed them before golf or they raise hell, fighting and pecking and screwing with each other if there's no food. It's amazing. I never had—or never *took*—the time to just sit quietly and watch birds. I don't imagine my friends on Music Row would recognize the new Bowen.

The almost meditative simplicity and serenity of life's simplest pleasures have helped my body heal. Basic tasks—which I used to pay other people to do—are now part of this new adventure of living. Those moments allow my mind to empty and recharge itself after forty years of battle in the music business.

I've never felt physically better. I have time for my half hour of back stretches. I play golf every day. I get to see my incredible healer Gene Clark three times a week at dawn. He comes over at six-thirty and starts beating up on me in a good way. Gene's half Hawaiian and he does reflexology and *lomi-lomi* massage. He rubs in this weird oil he made up that's so stinky, you can smell him coming around the corner. Makes you feel incredible.

I found Gene years ago when Ginger and I vacationed on

Maui. I was having kidney and colon trouble, smoking way too much pot, and wondering if I had neurological problems because I had fallen down twice. Gene made everything work perfectly again.

He gets on you and mashes down and pops everything loose until you hurt real good and feel better than ever. It must be all about leverage and position. He's a little sixty-year-old fellow with soft hands and a gentle handshake. But he could snap your neck with his crushing strength.

He doesn't make much money. The local folks who bring their babies to him to get them to stop crying often pay him with tomatoes or beer. I used to fly Gene into Nashville and pay him $500 a day for two weeks of tuneups. It was money awfully well spent.

Gene makes amazing diagnoses. One day during a week-long series of treatments in Nashville, he rubbed some new fiery-hot oil on my thighs and said, "Haven't been having much sex?"

He was right. "Haven't felt like it," I said.

"You will." He was right again. I liked *that* oil—until he accidentally spilled some on my crotch and it felt like it had caught fire.

Gene agreed to see a woman friend of ours. When he first met her, he shook her hand and said, "Oooh, mercury poisoning."

She gasped. "You're right." She had had extensive reconstructive dental work after a serious car accident and had all kinds of metal in her mouth.

When Gene does reflexology, you don't tell *him* what's wrong; he tells *you*. He works the bottom of your feet and crushes your toes. As you're screaming, he'll say, "Sinuses, bad sinuses." Gene's kept me disease-free and limber. He's been a godsend, a true miracle worker.

Aside from my daily golf game and my physical well-being, the most important project in my new life has been my relationship with my wife. I think by now Ginger and I have found out something pretty amazing: we damn near like each other. We're both hybrids—artistic souls crossed with heads for business. I'm thrilled that she's been painting and getting her stuff shown in galleries around Maui. She's also on top of that 401(k) pension stuff, which is in much better hands with her. Ginger's been back and forth to Nashville much more than I have because she's still real attached to friends there. Christian's living there too, making his way in the world of management and marketing.

The best thing for our marriage is having the time to just sit and talk and get to know each other again, explore our thoughts, take the time for intimate communication. We've needed to adjust to being around each other so much more all day, but that's led to a pleasant discovery: we seem to really dig being together. It's like starting over. When we're together, we're truly alone and present with each other, and that's a new one for me.

One thing has not changed: I don't enjoy sitting at home alone in total quiet. With my massage, golf, gym, shopping, and housework routines, I'm almost never alone more than three hours at a time, usually at the end of the day. And when I am, I always have either the TV or radio going. Even when Ginger's home, I'll be in another room with the TV on low, or some Hawaiian music on the radio in the background. In the car I don't listen to tapes now, but I punch Hawaiian-music stations on the radio.

Ginger has tried to break my CNN habit and get me on an all-music format around the house. She thinks I need to go on a news fast. I don't listen to much music. She tried for years to get me into contemporary Hawaiian music, which is a growing market, but I resisted. But when she was away for a few weeks once, I listened to a station that plays it and got into it, especially the unusual sound of Hawaiian slack-key guitar music. I do seem to need to hear something playing in the background. I've spent most of my life making or selling music that brought people pleasure and gave me a wonderful life in the record industry. I have never been one for silence.

Life after Liberty has proven what I've always believed: No one is irreplaceable. If you take a tooth out, it's not long before you quit missing it. I imagine that's what happened at the label. Garth's *Hits* has sold 9 million, half the people were fired, and the new people in charge have shrunk the label back to a boutique operation until they can break some new artists. The label can't be run off Garth Brooks anymore. And my successors changed the label name back from Liberty to Capitol-Nashville and planned to return to Music Row. I had tried to break the sanctity of Music Row—by demonstrating that it doesn't matter where the *office* is, it's where the *music* is that counts. And Garth's *Fresh Horses* CD barely edged past sales of 4 million— well below his previous weakest release to date. Because of his deal, he would have had to sell twice that, 8 million, for it to really help the label.

I never did listen to the record because I had all the Garth

Brooks I needed. But I did read in the Honolulu *Advertiser* that Garth had apparently searched all over Nashville and listened to thousands of songs and didn't think any were good enough. So he wound up cowriting most of them. What does that sound like? Meanwhile hundreds of hits were coming out of the same Nashville songwriters during that same time. Then he was quoted as saying that if his fans really didn't want his music any longer, he probably just wouldn't make any more.

Whining once again. No one can say I hadn't seen it coming.

Garth will always sell out concerts because onstage he gives people what they want. But on record, it seems, he's had his day. Then again 4 million ain't bad. But he's dropped out of the stratosphere and back down to earth and will sell what a normal artist will sell based on the quality of the songs.

I sometimes wonder if the once wide-open "frontier" of country has closed, if the era of a "maverick" producer-executive coming in and shaking things up is over. My sense is that, just as I'd come to Nashville at the end of one era, I left at the end of another. In between, country grew up, matured, and brought itself into the modern world. But in the process it has become just another high-yield asset controlled by global media giants based on far-off continents. Perhaps that, too, is just the way of the world—another good reason to get out. A Nashville friend sent me a thoughtful note recently in which she wrote, "Music Row's definitely not as interesting since you left. It's real boring. Come on back."

I actually had my chance not long ago. A label offered me $25,000 a month to come to Nashville as a "consultant" for three days every four or five weeks. I considered it, then turned it down—but only after Ginger and our CPA assured me we didn't need the money. One reason I said no was that I'd really have had to be there *five* days a week for a *year* to fix the label and make it right. The other reason was that I had absolutely no desire to run a record company and deal with that world anymore. I had played that song already.

Besides, my life, like my body, has finally been popped loose, cleaned out, realigned, and healed since I left Music City.

And I've never been one to look back.

INDEX